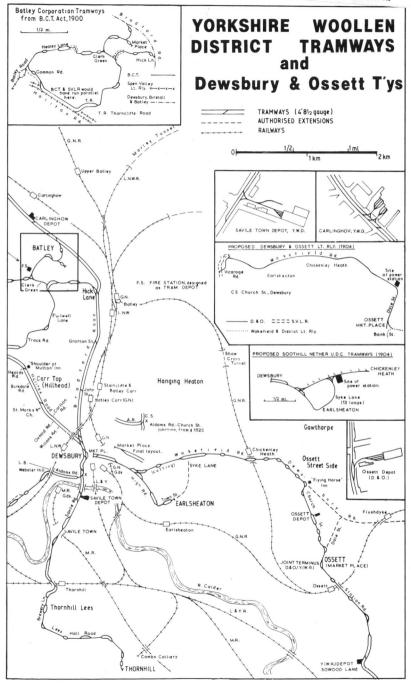

THE

TRAMWAYS

OF

DEWSBURY

AND

WAKEFIELD

In 1903, Batley Corporation almost achieved its ambition of becoming a tramway operator. Negotiations with the Yorkshire (Woollen District) Electric Tramways Ltd. had broken down, and Batley Council, who already had tracks, operating powers, and a generating station, ordered eight tramcars from Westinghouse, started to build a depot, and were all set to begin operating that autumn. Then the deadlock was broken, and the tracks and cars were leased to the Yorkshire Woollen District. The proposed depot became a fire station, and from 1905 the Batley trams were kept in the former steam tram depot at Carlinghow, still in their Batley green livery but with Yorkshire (Woollen District) fleet numbers and B.E.T. coat-of-arms. This 1905 picture shows six of the Batley trams, with the staff and Mr. E. A. Paris, the Y.W.D. managing director.   (Yorkshire Woollen District Transport Co. Ltd.

The Tramways of Dewsbury and Wakefield

By
W. PICKLES

Published in London by

THE LIGHT RAIL TRANSIT ASSOCIATION
13A The Precinct, Broxbourne, Herts EN10 7HY

1980

———

Printed by W. J. Ray & Co. Ltd., Warewell Street,
Walsall, West Midlands WS1 2HQ.

ISBN: 0 900433 73 6

CONTENTS

MAPS

INTRODUCTION

The manufacturing towns of Dewsbury and Wakefield lie six miles from each other and some eight miles south of Leeds. Until the early 1930's this area, noted for its woollen and mining industries, boasted three connecting tramway systems and an isolated branch which would have been part of the network if one of the authorised extensions had been constructed.

The Yorkshire Woollen District together with the mining district of Castleford and Pontefract comprises a region about 22 miles from east to west and 10 miles from north to south at its greatest dimensions. This area at the time when the tramways were being laid had a population of about 850,000. The western part of the district lies in the foothills of the eastern Pennines, which have deep valleys separating the ridges. In the bottoms of these valleys lie the towns of Dewsbury, Batley, Birstall, Heckmondwike and Cleckheaton, whose principal industries were coalmining and the manufacture of textiles, with mills straggling along the banks of the River Calder.

The hills of the region top the 500 foot contour, and the bottom of the Calder Valley at Thornhill Lees is around the 120 foot mark. With such differences in altitude it is no wonder that when the tramways were being constructed, the Board of Trade inspectors were worried about the gradients. The eastern portion of the Woollen District (Wakefield, Ossett, Castleford, Normanton and Pontefract) is much flatter, ranging from around the 250 foot contour at South Ossett to about 38 feet above sea level at Castleford. The broad, wide valleys of the rivers Aire and Calder converge at Castleford and the road gradients are not so steep as in the western part of the area. This area has coalmining (which was to play havoc with the tramways), textiles and glassworks, and chemicals at Castleford. Pontefract was the only town in the region where the liquorice plant grew, and the juice from this plant led to the establishment of the manufacture of sweetmeats (liquorice allsorts, Pomfret Cakes). This industry is still flourishing, even though the plant has ceased to be grown there.

At the turn of the century, an extensive network of tramways was envisaged linking Knottingley with Dewsbury and Dewsbury with the Huddersfield and Bradford systems. Unfortunately much of this network remained only as Board of Trade Orders and many projects got no further than the drawing board, but maps and plans exist to show us what parts of this network would have been like had they materialised. Much of this unmade network of tramways created more enthusiasm, talking, discussing and planning than the parts which were actually constructed. To name but one, the Dewsbury Corporation Tramways to Westborough and Shaw Cross engaged the minds of the local inhabitants and the local council for almost twenty years before the idea was abandoned. Similarly the extensions proposed by the Wakefield and District Light Railway to Alverthorpe and Tingley occupied the Y.W.R. Tramways for nigh on twenty years. Other extensions were abandoned when the lines already built failed to bring the hoped-for returns, especially in the case of West Riding.

Instead of this vast network, the lengths of actual line laid down and worked were but a fraction of those envisaged. The Yorkshire Woollen District system consisted of the Spen Valley lines and the route of the former Dewsbury, Batley and Birstal Tramway, part of which was subsequently sold to Batley Corporation and leased by them to B.E.T., owners of the Spen Valley lines. A subsidiary of the

National Electric Construction Company operated a link line between the Woollen District system and that of the Yorkshire West Riding Tramways at Wakefield. This latter system, which also connected with the Leeds City Tramways, was independent of the large financial groups and was ultimately replaced by the West Riding buses.

Altogether there was a total of just over 50 miles of tramways in the Dewsbury and Wakefield area. The detached portion of the Yorkshire (W.R.) Electric Tramways at Pontefract—Castleford—Normanton was twice as big as the Dewsbury and Ossett system.

All these electric tramway systems had their origins in Board of Trade Orders and Parliamentary Bills and Acts at the turn of the century, and in a period of time of about thirty years they were constructed, operated, maintained and finally scrapped. So much of our town streets had been under upheaval for something which was, from an historical point of view, of very short duration; in the case of the Castleford section for only nineteen years. Granted, the steam and the horse tramways at Dewsbury, Batley and Birstall gave a longer period of tramway life, but by 1934 all the tramways in the area had ceased to exist and had given place to the bus services operated by the two bigger companies.

This history deals in turn with the Dewsbury, Batley and Birstal Tramway Company, the Spen Valley lines, the operation of all the Dewsbury-based lines by Yorkshire W.D. Tramways, the Dewsbury & Ossett lines, and the West Riding system. Statistical and mileage tables will be found at the end of the relevant chapters and rolling stock details have been arranged at the end of each section.

A 1924 guide book to Dewsbury states that the town "owes its pre-eminence as a market town largely to its excellent tramway facilities". A similar statement, could, of course, be applied to Wakefield and the other smaller towns in the Woollen District. Extensions of the tramways were envisaged, but these became financially impracticable and bus services were run from the tram termini to villages further afield. These eventually became a network of bus routes, which was expanded between 1932 and 1934 to replace the tramways. The bus routes as we know them to-day are the direct successors of the tramways of the first three decades of this century. An example is that the one way routing of buses in the town centre at Castleford is a direct consequence of the one-way routing of the trams in that town.

Two anniversaries connected with the tramways have taken place recently. On 4 June, 1978 the Yorkshire Woollen District Transport Company celebrated the 75th anniversary of the opening of the Yorkshire (Woollen District) Electric Tramways in 1903, and in September, 1979 the West Riding Automobile Co. Ltd., celebrated the 75th anniversary of the opening of the Wakefield and District Light Railway in 1904. Both bus operators are now part of the National Bus Company with a common headquarters at Belle Isle, Wakefield, formerly the headquarters of the Wakefield & District Light Railway, and Yorkshire Woollen District buses also cover the route of the third tramway undertaking, from Dewsbury to Ossett. It is therefore appropriate that the histories of the three formerly independent tramways should be brought together in this one book.

ACKNOWLEDGMENTS

No work of this kind can be undertaken without a great deal of help from other people, and I wish to thank very sincerely everyone who has helped me in any way whatsoever.

Most of the initial research for this book was carried out in the public reference libraries and municipal offices in its area, and I must first thank the Town Clerks of Dewsbury, Batley, Morley, Ossett, Spenborough, Wakefield, Leeds, Castleford and Pontefract, and the Clerks of the urban districts of Stanley, Rothwell, Garforth, Heckmondwike and Normanton who freely gave me their consent for me to study and abstract relevant matter from the council minutes in their charge, including those councils now absorbed by others but which were separate entities when the tramways were being laid down. Similar help was given by the borough librarians of Dewsbury, Wakefield, Castleford, Ossett and Batley, the librarians of the urban districts of Rothwell and Normanton, and the chief librarians of Bradford and Huddersfield, with a special mention of the great assistance given by the Dewsbury librarian, Mr. F. Smith. Others in the district who have helped are the borough engineers of Dewsbury, Ossett, Castleford and Pontefract, the Yorkshire Electricity Board, the Archives Department of the former West Riding of Yorkshire County Council at Wakefield, the Dewsbury Club and Institute, and the editors of the *Ossett Observer,* the *Dewsbury Reporter,* the *Dewsbury District News, The Spenborough Guardian, The Wakefield Express,* and *The Pontefract and Castleford Express.*

Although this is not to be considered an official history of the undertakings concerned, I was afforded considerable help by the former and present general managers of the Yorkshire (Woollen District) Transport Company Ltd. and the West Riding Automobile Company Ltd. (successors to the tramway companies). Mr. F. E. Darke gave permission for me to see and take abstracts from the Board minutes of the Yorkshire (Woollen District) Electric Tramways Co. Ltd., and the Yorkshire (West Riding) Electric Tramways Co. Ltd., and Mr. K. A. R. Davis of the West Riding company kindly supplied historical material and photographs. The general manager of Leeds City Transport provided information on through running of company tramcars into the city, and many former tramwaymen have shared with me their memories of the tramways. The late Mr. R. Ede England, son of Harry England (managing director of the West Riding tramways), gave me a great deal of help some years ago, and the B.E.T. Federation kindly allowed access to their file of the privately-circulated *B.E.T. Gazette.*

Some of the research for this book was carried out in London, and I must record my thanks to Mrs. F. Manley for providing a temporary home for me in London during that period, and to the staff of the House of Lords Record Office, Public Record Office, the Companies Registry, the Science Museum, the British Museum Map Room, the British Museum Newspaper Library, the British Railways Board Archivist's Department, and the Ministry of Transport Library for their assistance. Their titles are here given in the form used at the date of my visit, but subsequent reorganisation has brought much of the material into the present-day care of the British Library and the new Public Record Office at Kew. I am grateful to the Controller of HM Stationery Office for permission to reproduce the car drawings on pages 74 and 83, and to Merryweather & Sons Ltd. for much original material on the Dewsbury, Batley and Birstal steam tramway used in the first chapter. The lending branch of the British Library at Boston Spa in Yorkshire helped me with some of the less readily available source material.

Those who have supplied information as individuals for this book are so numerous that an alphabetical list must need suffice, to include also those who have read portions of the manuscripts and given me their comments: F. Armitage, A. Bacon, G. E. Baddeley, G. M. Baxter, the late W. H. Bett, J. Breeze Bentley, H. Brearley, R. Brook, A. W. Brotchie, J. Bushell, W. Castle, G. B. Claydon, P. Dowd, the late Mrs. F. M. Driver, R. Elliott, G. R. Forrester, D. E. Gledhill, F. P.

Groves, C. C. Hall, F. Hartley D. K. Hepworth, the late C. T. Humpidge, J. S. King, F. Marton C. Moorhouse, M. J. O'Connor, A. D. Packer, the late R. B. Parr H. B. Priestley, J. H. Price, W. N. Sagar, J. Soper, the late H. Tolson, J. G. D. Whitaker and C. Wood. Of these, Roy Brook and Frank Hartley also gave me access to the tables of car dimensions compiled by the late Walter Gratwicke, and C. C. Hall, H. B. Priestley and C. Wood have loaned precious documents and tickets for reproduction.

The illustrations are acknowledged individually on each page, but special mention must be made of the late Dr. Hugh Nicol, who in October 1967 granted me permission to use in this book the splendid series of tramway photographs taken by him in the Dewsbury and Wakefield area in 1932. Similar thanks are due to Mrs. Edith Holt, for permission to use the excellent Wakefield & District photographs taken in 1904-6 by her late husband Lewis Holt, and I must record my particular debt to the late R. B. Parr, who gave me permission to use in this book the fine photographs of tramways in and around Dewsbury of which he had purchased the glass plate negatives and copyrights from Fred Hartley & Son of Glover Works, Dewsbury (photographers, printers and publishers); these plates are now in the expert care of Robert F. Mack. Permission to use other photographs from the R. B. Parr collection has been given by the Board of the Tramway Museum Society. Thanks for help in tracing other illustrations are due to G. E. Baddeley, R. Brook, J. H. Price and R. J. S. Wiseman. It is hoped that we have given full acknowledgement to the correct source of each illustration, but we offer our apologies to anyone whose name we may have inadvertently omitted. Apologies are also offered to those who supplied photographs which have not been used, for a problem in illustrating this book has been to know what to leave out! Seldom can so many high-quality photographs have been offered for use in illustrating the history of tramways of which the last ceased operation nearly half a century ago.

A list of the books and periodicals consulted appears on page 182, and we offer our acknowledgement to all those authors whose works are quoted, whether or not an individual mention is given in the text. For help in arranging and typing the manuscript I must thank Miss D. Ramsden, Miss M. Driver, Mrs. M. Parker and Mrs. S. Mallorie, with a special word of thanks for deciphering my notes. R. A. Platt and J. H. Price edited the manuscript, G. E. Baddeley drew the cover artwork, and Brian Connelly the maps, for which R. A. Platt carried out research at the Ordnance Survey, Southampton. J. H. Price and J. A. Cadisch of the LRTL Publications Committee deserve especial thanks for their encouragement during the several years the book has been in preparation, and for their very hard work in completing the finished product. Lastly, but far from least, to my wife, whose help and encouragement and whose hours of "tramway widowhood" have enabled this work to come to full fruition.

To any, not named, who have helped in any way whatever, I say "Thank you".

Garforth, Summer 1979   W. Pickles

9

Horse traction on the Dewsbury, Batley & Birstal Tramway is commemmorated by this model displayed in the Dewsbury Museum in Crow Nest Park, Dewsbury. The small cars of 1874 were withdrawn after steam traction was adopted in 1879-81.

(Courtesy Dewsbury Libraries Committee

CHAPTER ONE

THE DEWSBURY, BATLEY & BIRSTAL TRAMWAY COMPANY

The Heavy Woollen District of Yorkshire, particularly the Dewsbury and Batley area, was very quick to take advantage of the Tramways Act of 1870. Here a group of public-spirited gentlemen, with Mr. Joseph Sheard of Sunny Bank, Batley, as chairman, formed the Dewsbury & Batley Tramways Company, with Registered Offices at 31, Park Square, Leeds. Incorporated under the Companies Act of 1862 on 13 November 1872 the nominal capital of the Company was £50,000 divided into 5,000 shares of £10 each. Other directors were J. E. Greaves, Tom Gomersal, John Hirst, John Walker, J. F. Middlebrook and George Sheard, with J. S. Muir as Secretary; Muir was succeeded by George Truswell, secretary and manager. The name of the Company was changed to the Dewsbury, Batley & Birstal Tramway Company on 16 April 1873. For some reason, the already obsolescent spelling of Birstall was used in the title. The current form was already in common use in 1874 and will be used throughout this book except when using the formal company title.

The tramway of the Dewsbury, Batley & Birstal Company was one of the first twenty in the country. Only fourteen companies and corporations applied for Bills before 1873 and there were five other undertakings who applied in that year, besides the Dewsbury, Batley & Birstal Company.

The 123 shareholders were local men and ranged from wealthy manufacturers and hotel keepers to loom tuners, coal miners and tradespeople, several of whom held five £10 shares; few individual shareholdings exceeded £200. Of the well-known families, three names are in the list of subscribers, Chaley Fox, Walter Walker and Mr. Stubley. The company's issued capital amounted to £33,120 in 1879, £47,320 in 1884 and £43,088 in 1899.

Construction of the line

The Dewsbury, Batley & Birstal Tramways Order Confirmation Act, 1873, authorised the company to lay down and operate horse trams between Dewsbury and Birstall and passing through Batley, a distance of about three miles. The tramway was constructed during 1874 and 1875, and the engineers were successively Mr. M. Paters and Mr. Gomersal. It was laid on Kincaid's system according to the first patent of 1872. The length of the tramway was 3.325 miles and it was opened for traffic from Dewsbury to Batley (1.325 miles) on 25 July 1874, from Batley to Carlinghow (one mile) on 25 March 1875 and from Carlinghow to Birstall (one mile) on 23 June 1875. The line was on an easy gradient of 1 in 200, falling all the way from Birstall to Dewsbury with slight exceptions.

The track was single throughout, with eight 66-yard passing loops and two of 55 yards. The first loop was at the Dewsbury terminus in Northgate (at Halifax Road), the next was beneath the L&NWR railway arch, with others at about 750-yd. intervals to the terminus at Birstall Smithies, and an extra loop at the depot. At the Birstall terminus the tramway ended in a short length of double line, but when the tramway was converted to steam traction, this piece of double line was extended and formed a passing place.

The cost of construction of the first two miles from Dewsbury to Carlinghow in a paved road was £4,600 per mile, whilst the last mile from Carlinghow to Birstall in a macadamised road was constructed complete with paving for £4,000. Details of the complete costs to 30 June 1876 are given in "Tramways: their Construction and Working" by D. Kinnear Clark (1st Edition 1878, page 253):

	Total	Per Mile
Preliminary expenses, legal and Parliamentary	1,622	487.8
Construction of the way	17,327	5,211.0
Construction of stables	2,507	754.0
Office furniture	50	15.0
Saddlery	100	30.1
40 horses	1,705	512.8
7 cars	1,273	382.9
Omnibus	123	37.2
Plant: steam engine, corn mill, hay chopper etc.	413	124.2
Actual cost	25,120	7,555.0
Auditor	10	3.0
Total cost	25,130	7,558.0

In addition, £646 was paid to the local authorities.

The first section, from Dewsbury to Batley, was ready for opening in July 1874, and on Saturday 25 July the Board of Trade inspected the system. It would seem that the five cars ordered by the Dewsbury Batley & Birstal Company were not available at the date of the inspection, for the Leeds Tramways Company sent two of its cars for the occasion. No-one appears to have worried about the fact that someone else's car was being used. The inspection was followed by a dinner at the Royal Hotel in Dewsbury. According to the report issued after the inspection, the car ran very smoothly and the quicker the horses were driven the smoother was the ride. Public service began on the same day; the two Leeds cars were retained to start the service and were subsequently purchased. The next mile, from Batley to Carlinghow, was inspected and opened on 25 March 1875, and the remaining mile from Carlinghow to Birstall Smithies on 23 June 1875.

The number of miles run by the trams in the first year amounted to 106,500 miles in 313 days. This works out at 340½ car miles per day, or 67 miles per day per car on regular duty, and 22½ miles per day per pair of horses.

By the Dewsbury, Batley & Birstal Tramways (Extension) Order Confirmation Act 1879 (42 and 43 Victoria. ch. CCXCIII) a further addition to the tramway was made from Birstall Smithies to Moor Lane at Gomersal. This remained the terminus of the system until the line was electrified. At the time of the construction in 1880-1, this last mile was quite sparsely populated although there were some collieries near the terminus which may well have been a reason for the extension. It was single line throughout except for passing places and these were laid symmetrically on the centre line of the tramway, unlike the passing places on the original part of the line between Dewsbury and Birstall which were mostly constructed on the east side of the line. The precise date of opening in 1881 has not been traced, but the "Dewsbury Reporter" for 6 August 1881 said that the delay in opening was due to delay in the delivery of engines and cars, and that the line was expected to open in a fortnight. It was definitely operating in October.

On the original line, the rails were of wrought iron and weighed 41 lb. per yard. They were 3¼ ins. wide and 2 ins. deep and were carried on chairs 3 ft. apart between centres, secured by vertical spikes through the bottom of the grooves. The chairs were laid in concrete, run in with pitch, and the rails were packed underneath

12

with a concrete composed of small broken stone and pitch. The paving consisted of Dalbeattie granite setts, grouted with pitch. The paving was laid on a 2 in. layer of broken stone covered with a layer of ashes.

A different type of rail, designed by the manager, Mr. George Truswell, was used on the extension. This rail weighed 55 lb. per yard and was rolled in 24.4 foot lengths. It was laid and keyed down with oak keys in cast iron chairs, placed at 3 ft. intervals. The joint chairs weighed 37 lbs. and were 6½ inches long and the intermediate ones were 3½ inches long and weighed 25 lbs. The chairs were laid on sleepers of Baltic timber 7 ft. by 12 in. by 4 in. These Truswell rails were 3 in. high and 2¾ in. wide with a one-inch tread and a one-inch groove, plus a guard flange. They were hollowed out enough on one side to receive an oak wedge to fasten them. They stood 2 inches clear above the concrete base and with sufficient room for 5-inch setts for paving and 1 inch of fine screened ashes for bedding. The paving setts were of Clee Hill granite and grouted with melted pitch and tar. There were 46½ chairs per mile of single line; 22 cwts. of coach screws per mile; 7,040 oak trenails and 7,040 coach screws per mile. The cost of the one mile of tramway is given by Kinnear Clark as £4,240.14s. per mile, of which £1,010.10s. was for the steel rails (86 tons), £218.3s. for sleepers, £329.19s. for chairs, £507.4s. for concrete and £1,870 for paving.

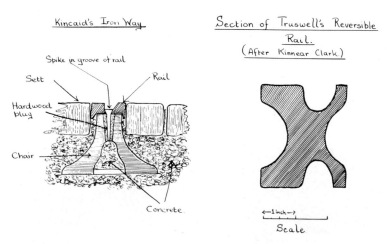

The two types of rail used on the Dewsbury, Batley and Birstal Tramway, copied from "Tramways, Their Construction and Working" by D. Kinnear Clark.   (Author

Tramsheds and stables were erected in Bradford Road, Carlinghow, Batley, and are still in existence, the front of the building proudly displaying the words "Tramway Company, 1874". They became the company's registered office on 4 September 1874. These same premises were later used for the steam trams and for the electric trams which followed. The curious track layout is shown overleaf.

A stud of 40 horses was kept and this was equivalent to eight horses per car in ordinary running, the extra cars being worked by the same stock of horses. The horses were occasionally rested during the week and on every Sunday, there being no Sunday traffic at all. A complaint from the manager of the company about the granite setts used in making the road is mentioned in Kinnear Clark, who states that though it is certainly a good road, there are too many granite setts. He was thinking of the horses of course, and the grip and wear on the horse-shoes. Two horses were used to pull each car and only three pairs were run each day with each car which was in use. One pair was kept in reserve to take the place of sick horses and horses which were having their rest days.

13

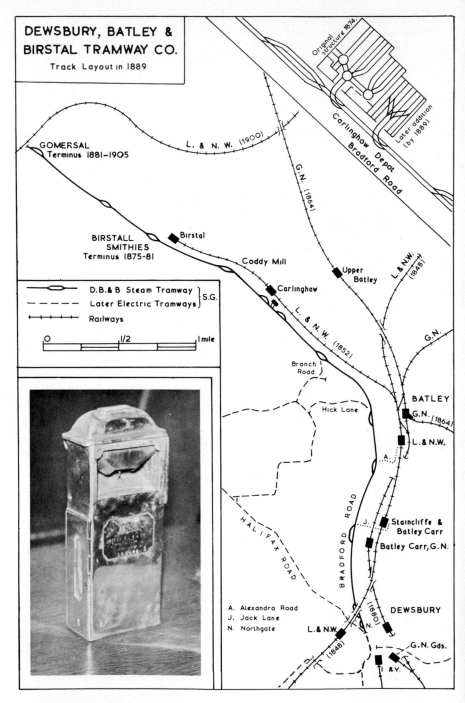

DEWSBURY, BATLEY & BIRSTAL TRAMWAY CO.

Track Layout in 1889

Original structure 1874.

Later addition (by 1889)

Carlinghow Depot

Bradford Road

L. & N.W. (1900)

G.N. (1864)

GOMERSAL
Terminus 1881-1905

BIRSTALL SMITHIES
Terminus 1875-81

Birstal

Coddy Mill

L. & N.W. (1848)

Upper Batley

——◇—— D.B.& B Steam Tramway
— — — — Later Electric Tramways ⎫S.G.
+++++++ Railways ⎭

0   1/2   1 mile

Carlinghow

L. & N.W. (1852)

G.N.

Branch Road

Hick Lane

BATLEY
G.N. (1864)

L. & N.W.

A.

H A L I F A X   R O A D

B R A D F O R D   R O A D

Stainclffe & Batley Carr

J.

Batley Carr, G.N.

A. Alexandra Road
J. Jack Lane
N. Northgate

DEWSBURY

L. & N.W. (1880)

N.

L. & N.W. (1848)

G.N. Gds.

& Y.

The Dewsbury, Batley and Birstal Tramway and (inset) a Kaye's fare box as carried by the company's conductors. This example survived as a forfeit box at the Dewsbury Club and Institute, and is now in the Tolson Memorial Museum at Ravensknowle. (W. Pickles

Figures are quoted in Kinnear Clark for the money spent per year on the horses and the way the animals were cared for:

	£	s.	d.
Provender for 40 horses	1,735	1	3
Renewal of horses, being the cost of new horses, less the amount made on the sale of the old horses	253	17	9
Shoeing	200	16	6
Stablemen, Wages etc.	323	0	0
Veterinary services	30	0	0
General labour	70	16	6
General repairs	15	16	6
	2,629	8	6

Each horse was allowed 17 lbs. of corn per day, composed of oats, peas, maize and bran with 12 lbs. of chopped hay, occasionally mixed with straw. To drink, each horse was given 1½ lbs. of linseed steeped in cold water for 24 hours and stirred about. Mr. Truswell was convinced that it was the finest thing he knew. He believed that a frequent change in the food of the horses gave beneficial results on the road.

The company worked its horses hard, for Mr. Truswell is quoted as saying that "some horses are finished for our purposes in 12 months, whilst others will last five or six years, but we run ours much faster and further in a day than many companies do, which will go a great way to account for their not lasting very long. But I do make it a practice to have them well attended to". The shoes of the horses appear to have lasted on average from eight to ten days. In exceptional instances horses had to be re-shod every four days.

There was no system of punched-ticket fares; the conductor went his rounds of the car at each fare stage, when the passengers dropped their fares into his special brass collecting box. One of these brass boxes still exists, made by Joseph Kaye & Sons of High Holborn, London. It is about twelve inches high, five inches wide and three inches deep, with a slot at the top through which the pennies were dropped. The pennies would deflect a metal wire device which worked the meter dials arranged up one side of the box behind glass. These dials read in units, tens, hundreds, thousands and ten thousands and were read like those of an electric meter in a house. At this point the coins were still resting on two pieces of brass which were hinged, so that at the touch of a knob they parted and the coins then dropped into the container from which they could only be removed by a company official with a key.

Before the conductor pressed the knob and the pennies fell, he was able to count them and then check with the number of passengers in the car and so ascertain whether anyone had not paid their fare. This was really the only way of checking, as no tickets were issued. At the back of the box there is a large brass hook which could be fitted on to a belt or by which the box could be carried by hand. In photographs of the steam cars the conductor can be seen carrying the box in his hand. The box is quite heavy, especially when full of pennies. Presumably officials would go the rounds of the trams and collect the pennies as the day went on.

Before leaving the horse trams, we are given a good picture of the scene at the termini in the *Dewsbury Reporter* of 14 April 1928, when a previous reference to the steam trams brought the following from a correspondent:—"Imagine the sight, every hour of the day of two horses pulling a heavily-laden tramcar along Bradford Road. The funniest recollection one has of the horse trams is of the change round at the termini at Dewsbury and Birstall. The driver dismounted, not nimbly and smartly, but slowly and heavily. He uncoupled the mechanism which attached the horse gear etc. to the tramcar, pulled the horses round to the other end of the tram and yoked them up to the car for the journey in the opposite direction". Evidently the ponderous way in which this operation was done added to the dignity of the scene.

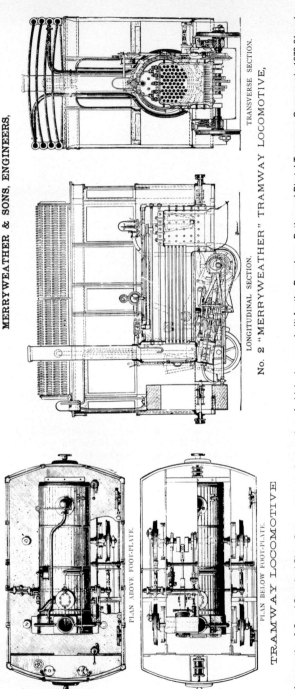

MERRYWEATHER & SONS, ENGINEERS,

TRANSVERSE SECTION.

No. 2 "MERRYWEATHER" TRAMWAY LOCOMOTIVE,

LONGITUDINAL SECTION.

MERRYWEATHER & SONS, ENGINEERS,

PLAN ABOVE FOOT-PLATE.

PLAN BELOW FOOT-PLATE.

TRAMWAY LOCOMOTIVE

Merryweather & Sons' Standard Class 2 steam tramway locomotive, of which nine were built for the Dewsbury, Batley and Birstal Tramways Company in 1879-81 and ran until 1905. The photograph below, taken about 1880, shows one of these engines in Bradford Road, Dewsbury, with three fully laden double deck trailers (Nos. 9, 10 and 2). Since the manufacturer's photographer was present, this may have been a demonstration or test run. In normal service each engine pulled only one trailer, or occasionally two.

(Courtesy Merryweather & Sons, London

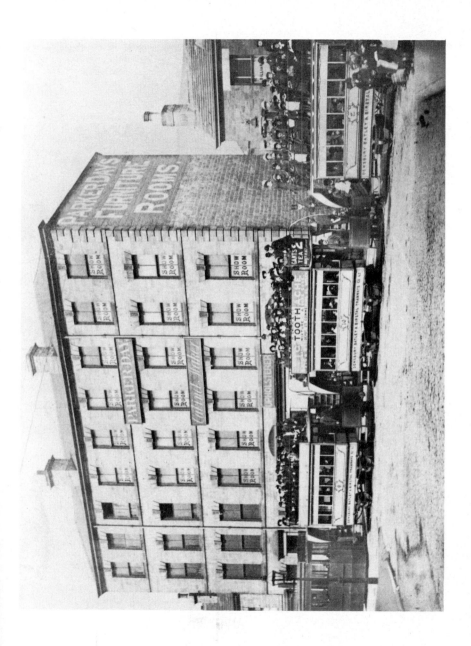

17

Experimenting with Steam traction

Under the terms of the Act the motive power was to be animal; but from time to time, the Board of Trade could sanction the use of steam power or any mechanical power, after a period of seven years from the opening of the line for public use (in this case it was 1880/1881). By this Act the company were given power to experiment with steam as the source of traction, and in due course became the second street tramway, as distinct from a tramway running at the side of the road, to adopt it.

In 1876, two separate trials of steam tramway engines took place on the D.B.&B. Tramways. The reports in the local press give a good impression of what the steam engines were like under working conditions, and are quoted in full. The *Dewsbury Chronicle* of 20 May 1876, after stating that the trials had taken place the previous Wednesday and Thursday, goes on to say that the trials were witnessed by hundreds of people who lined each side of the road from Dewsbury to the points at Coddy Mill between Carlinghow and Birstall. The first took place before a large assembly of people including the directors of the Company, the Mayors of Dewsbury and Batley and also many other people interested in the application of steam locomotion to tramways, from Neath and Liverpool to Edinburgh.

"From a perusal of the prospectus of the firm (i.e. Merryweathers) there was a claim that a saving of at least £300 per annum in the working expenses of each car, was made; an increase in the speed when desirable; a perfect control for stopping and starting quicker than at present whilst the vehicle is on its journey; at each terminus it is disconnected and brought to the front of the car in less time than that taken by the horses. This arrangement without any increase of width to the existing lines, a shorter length is taken up on the road whilst travelling, as it is less than the horse's; a surplus of power is obtained, affording means for erecting a covering on the top of the car for the better protection of outside passengers against the sun and the rain; also for ascending inclines, thus preventing the over-straining of the horses to which they are at present subject; if required (say for example in the country) an extra car can be attached either for merchandise or luggage, thus placing small towns etc. without direct railway communication, on a similar footing to those that already enjoy it; and the engine would also be applicable in winter time when it is often found impossible for horses to travel with the car, owing to the slippery state of the roads, and the snow. In addition they announce that it is noiseless, smokeless and free from any escape of steam; it is perfectly safe and explosion is absolutely impossible, and it is entirely independent so that any car can be attached thus utilising all the present cars without any alterations".

"The engine is a verticular locomotive enclosed in a framework similar in appearance to a small tramcar with a black funnel from which no smoke escapes. The driving gear is placed beneath the floor of the car; in fact the mechanism is hidden from sight. The only part of the machinery to be noticed on taking a peep into the car is a small multi-tubular boiler covered with ribs of oak (the lagging), bound with brass "bands", a water tank and brake appliances. The iron casing of the boiler is protected with felt which effectively prevents the radiation of heat, and thus tends to make the engine house cool even during the hottest months of the summer season. There are four driving wheels with cranks and reversible movements so that the engine can run as well backwards as forwards without any re-arrangement of the driving gear. No cast iron is used in the construction of the machine in any form whatsoever. The upper part of the car is shielded by windows which can be drawn up or let down, as the heat or otherwise of the weather, may require. The boiler has been tested to bear a pressure of 250 lbs. per square inch; but this is at no time required. A coal bunker is made on the near side of the boiler, capable of carrying a day's supply (about 25 lbs.) of anthracite coal. The machinery is well guarded by wrought iron plates on the lower side of the vehicle, all of which as we have before intimated, is hidden from view. A portion of the flooring upon which the engineer stands, however, can be raised; so that no difficulty stands in the way of the cranks, pistons, cylinder and other parts of the works being oiled or cleaned".

"Soon after eleven o'clock, when the above-named gentlemen had assembled, a car was attached to the engine, and the journey from Carlinghow to Dewsbury was commenced in the presence of a large concourse of people. On the suggestion of Superintendent Airton an "advance man" on horseback, carrying a red flag, preceded the car to give warning of its approach, so that there would be but very little possibility of an accident taking place. The traffic on Wednesday (Dewsbury Market day) was usually heavy and therefore the test was unmistakenly a severe one. We particularly noted the horses on the road and were certainly satisfied at the calm way in which those which did take notice of the machine acted. The engine, when run as fast as possible, does not make as much noise as the hoofs of the horses; and no smoke escapes from the chimney. The brake power is almost perfection, and the car can be stopped even when running at full speed much more readily than an ordinary car can with horses. It was tested at various rates of speed with great success, and it took the points in a remarkable manner, in fact there was not so much oscillation in the car as when drawn by horses. The change of metals at the terminus was effected in an almost incredibly short space of time—this being accomplished by means of a very ingeniously contrived coupling. Several runs were made up and down the line on both days, but on Thursday a novelty in the shape of two cars being attached at the same time was introduced".

The *Batley News* of 15 November 1876 carried an account of the second successful trial of a Merryweather engine, this time in competition with a Kitson engine. The Tramway Company invited several members of the Corporations of Dewsbury and Batley and the Birstall Local Board. The party started from the offices of the Company at Carlinghow about 1 p.m., rain coming down pretty freely at the time. The two engines were attached to a car each, Messrs. Merryweather's being the first to proceed down the line in the direction of Dewsbury. After a few stops, the terminus was reached, where the engines were changed to the other end of the car. In order to test the steadiness of each, most of the party changed cars at the terminus and at other points on the return journey. Various opinions were expressed regarding the speed and steadiness of the two cars. Messrs. Merryweather's crossed the points at almost the same speed as when on the straight road. The speed indicator showed the rate at from 8 to 10 miles per hour on some portions of the line, but "we understand it could be increased to 12 or even 15 m.p.h.". The advantages of the steam-worked car over those drawn by horses are then extolled again. Both engines were taken away by their makers after the trial, and no steam engine ran on the D.B.&B. Tramways for the next two years.

At this date, the only British tramway regularly operated with steam traction was the Wantage Tramway, though trials had taken place elsewhere. The Board of Trade was in process of formulating its requirements and recommendations for the use of steam traction on tramways, which were to have a profound effect on such matters as safety, speed, and smoke emission. During 1877 and 1878 various manufacturers produced improved tramway locomotives designed to satisfy the Board of Trade's requirements, and as soon as this stage had been reached, the directors of the Dewsbury, Batley & Birstal Tramways Co. resolved to apply for Board of Trade authority to work their line by steam. A Kitson engine with a roof condenser was hired for the purpose early in 1878, but was not purchased or taken into stock, the company's order being placed instead with Merryweather & Sons of London.

By 1878 the Dewsbury, Batley & Birstal Tramways were ready to ask the Board of Trade for an official inspection of the tramway as a steam operated one. On Thursday 28 March 1878 the chief inspector of railways at the Board of Trade, Col. Hutchinson, came down to Carlinghow Depot, the headquarters of the Company, where he was received by the chairman (Mr. Brooke) and also a number of members of the Board, the manager (Mr. Truswell), and several representatives of Messrs. Kitson & Co. who were the makers of the engine. He was taken to Birstall and on the return to Carlinghow several experiments were made in stopping and starting etc., and afterwards the engine conveyed Col. Hutchinson to Dewsbury. The inspection lasted upwards of two hours. The steam car was then engaged in conveying the general public between Dewsbury and Batley. The following week it then traversed the whole line in general use.

Since there had been no previous case of steam traction being approved for general use on a street tramway, the ensuing formalities took a considerable time and may have been held back to await the passage on 11 August 1879 of an Act which permitted the use of mechanical power on tramways. The Vale of Clyde Tramway at Govan had meanwhile adopted steam traction by virtue of its own less restrictive legislative powers, but the Dewsbury, Batley and Birstal became the first to commence steam operation under the newly enacted general legislation.

The Board of Trade drew up Byelaws under the provisions of the 1879 Extensions Order respecting the use of steam power on these tramways. There were provisions that working parts be concealed and that there should be no steam or smoke visible, that there should be a speedometer geared to 8 m.p.h., and that the engine should be capable of being brought to a standstill at the intersection of cross roads; the engines were also to be free from noise caused through the clatter of machinery and the blast from the chimney.

Once these Byelaws were formulated, regular steam traction was introduced on 10 April 1880 with a Merryweather engine of 1879 (No. 1). The Dewsbury, Batley and Birstal thus became the first regular steam tramway in England to operate along a public thoroughfare. Three more engines (Nos. 2 to 4) arrived in April 1880, but these had to await the prior approval of Batley borough council, whose engineer had to ensure that they were identical with the 1879 machine which the council had sanctioned. In May the company applied for another engine, as they had been advised always to have a spare engine in the yard besides those which were on the road. This was agreed to by the Corporation provided that not more than the four engines agreed to were in use at one and the same time.

On 27 January 1881 the company asked that all their tramways be operated by steam power. Up to this time both horses and steam power were being used, only four steam engines being allowed, and the one horse tram which had to be used in everyday traffic rather hindered the smooth working of the system. Three additional engines were sanctioned, under the same conditions as before, making altogether seven for use and one to be kept in reserve. These three engines (Nos. 6 to 9) were built by Merryweathers in 1881.

The steam engines are described in Merryweathers' 1882 Catalogue of Steam Tramway Engines as "The No. 2 Merryweather Tramway Locomotive, as on the Dewsbury, Batley and Birstal Tramway". The catalogue states that the tramway was worked by nine Merryweather condensing engines having 6½ in. cylinders with 10 in. stroke, and four coupled wheels 2 ft. in diameter. "One of the engines was supplied in 1879 and four more in 1880. The working proved so satisfactory that, on the extension of the line to Gomersal four more were ordered and were supplied in 1881". The catalogue describes the engines in detail:

"The cylinders are placed inside the framing and are joined together in the middle where they form the valve chest, whilst a saddle is placed in each half for the purpose of supporting the boiler at the smoke box end. The guide bars are of steel, the cross head is of cast steel and the cross head slippers are of cast iron, having large wearing surfaces. The guide bars are supported by a cross plate, which they considerably overhang in the direction of the firebox. The guides for the valve spindles are carried by the same plate. The link motion is of the ordinary shifting-link type. The eccentrics and hoops are of cast iron. The coupling rods are made with solid steel ends, having phosphor-bronze bushes. All the oil cups are forged or cast solid on the parts. The wheels and axles are of steel; the crank pins in the wheels are case-hardened. The brake is applied to all the wheels.

The boiler is of the usual locomotive type, of Low Moor iron throughout, double rivetted in the longitudinal seams. It is fed by a feed pump, driven by a special eccentric and by a Gifford's Injector. The whole of the engine work has

20

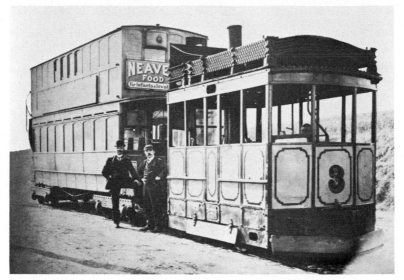

Merryweather engine No. 3 (seen here with trailer 14) entered service on 7 December 1880 and ran for 25 years on the Dewsbury, Batley and Birstal Tramways, until August 1905. This picture was taken in 1902.　　　　　　　　　　　　　　　(Courtesy The Science Museum, London

been made of unusual strength in order to provide for wear and tear by dirt, dust and rough usage. The feed tank, holding 100 gallons, is placed in front of the smoke-box. A fender plate is fixed at each end of the engine to remove obstructions and to obviate any chance of running over any person. Plates are also run along each side to conceal the wheels and the coupling rods. The whole of the work is enclosed in a cab or casing made of sheet iron on angle-iron framing 12 feet in length, 6 feet 4 inches in width and about 8½ feet above the rails.

The condenser, placed above the roof, consists of four longitudinal layers, slightly arched, of thin copper tubes, laid transversely across the roof. The tubes are one inch in diameter outside, No. 28 wire gauge, or 1/55 inch in thickness, and are each six feet in length. There are 60 tubes in each layer or 240 tubes in the four layers, coated with brown varnish to augment their radiating power. They are secured at the ends into three-inch longitudinal pipes, three inches in diameter outside, four on each side and eleven feet long.

The exhaust steam is discharged by two copper pipes one to each side, into the uppermost longitudinal pipe, whence it circulates through the transverse tubes. The condensation water and the remaining vapour are conducted into a separator vessel at the front, whence the water runs down to the feed-water tank, and the vapour passes away into the smoke-box, where it is mixed with and disappears with the products of combustion. So efficient is the condenser that the engine can be worked all day with the one charge of the feed-water tank. This tank holds only 100 gallons and the quantity consumed as the uncondensed steam or otherwise, does not exceed 50 gallons for the day.

The engine is fitted with the apparatus to fulfil the requirements of the Board of Trade. A ball-governor, placed over the foot-plate at one side, is provided for the purpose of shutting off the steam and turning on a steam-brake when the maximum speed allowed (10 m.p.h.) is reached. The steam-

21

brake may also be turned on by means of a small pedal placed near the foot of the driver. Steam levers and reversing levers are fitted in duplicate, one set at each end of the engine, whichever end goes first. A speed indicator is also fitted so that the driver may take his place at the leading end of the engine.

The governor is driven by means of a pitch-chain from the crank-shaft and the speed indicator is driven by a band from the governor spindle.

The working pressure of the boiler is 140 lbs. per square inch. There are two safety valves on the boiler, one of which is a lock-up valve. Steam escaping by the safety valves is conducted to the exhaust pipe, and thence into the condenser. The steam is supplied to the cylinders through a perforated steam-pipe in the upper part of the boiler. The cylinders are, as before stated, 6½ inches in diameter with a stroke of 10 inches. The wheels are 2 feet in diameter, placed at 4½ feet centres. The whole of the machinery is encased from below. The weight of the engine empty is 6 tons, and in working order, with water and fuel 7 tons. The engines cost £750 each''.

The weights of the cars were given as 2 tons 4 cwt. and with eleven passengers which was the average load (16 cwt.) making together a total of three tons. The engines weighed 7 tons each, so that the gross load of engine plus full car would be 10 tons. Occasionally an extra car was added that would make a load of 13 tons and in the case of the engines pulling three cars, 16 tons.

The length of the main line was three and a quarter miles and in the course of the journey, the train, passing through a continuously populated district, was pulled up from 15 to 25 times each way. The double journey of 6½ miles was performed in 66 minutes including stops, making an average speed of 6 miles/hr.

By 9 February 1881 there were complaints about the smoke nuisance from the tram engines, and the Batley Town Clerk was asked to write to the Company asking them to remedy the trouble. This was only one of many requests asking for the cessation of the steam and smoke nuisance from the tram engines. At a later date Dewsbury Corporation was asked by a group of shopkeepers in Bradford Road, Dewsbury that the terminus of the Dewsbury, Batley and Birstal Tramway be moved from its present position in Northgate to a point on the Batley side of the railway viaduct which crosses the Bradford Road a short distance along that road in the direction of Batley (i.e. near Greaves Road). Their request was not granted.

A description of the line as then operating was published in the *Engineer* of 28 July 1882. Steel rails weighing about 70 lb. per yard had replaced the original sections, and there were nine engines in stock, of which six were used each day. Whereas horse traction had cost the company 6.95 pence per car mile, steam traction was only costing 3.92 pence per car mile, a saving of 2.73 pence, and the line had been so worked for a sufficient time to give reliable data.

To provide additional accommodation at busy times, the company in 1886 bought three large covered-top bogie trailers of a type which had by then come into use on most other steam tramways. Covered tops served to protect passengers both from the weather and from smoke and fumes, and the directors soon decided to fit covered tops to sufficient other cars to provide for the basic 15-minute service. One of the converted cars is illustrated on page 29. It was probably at this period that an additional three-track building was erected to house the trailers, shown on the ordnance survey of 1889.

The steam tram era lasted from 1879 to 1905. A ten minute service of cars was substituted for the 15 minute one in 1898, and the company bought two more Merryweather engines in 1900, Nos. 10 and 11. According to the late Dr. H. A. Whitcombe's notes in the Science Museum, they had been built in 1885 for the North London Tramways, and had presumably been kept in store by their makers after the North London lines reverted to horse traction. At the 26th annual general meeting of the company in 1899 the mileage worked in the last year was given as 158,450 (157,207 on weekdays, 1,243 on Sundays). The recent introduction of the ten-minute service had increased the coke bill by £47, the wage bill by £145 and the mileage by 12,950. At this date, the secretary and manager was Thomas Frederick Laxton, who had succeeded George Truswell by 1887. One additional bogie trailer was purchased in 1898.

The B.E.T. takes over

Towards the end of this period interest was growing in the idea of electric tramways in the area. The British Electric Traction Company Ltd., which had been founded by Mr. Emile Garcke in 1896, was interested in expanding the tramways in the Heavy Woollen District, particularly in the adjacent Spen Valley, and began buying shares in the Dewsbury, Batley and Birstal company, soon obtaining control of the company and taking over the management from January 1902. By 1903, the B.E.T. and its nominees held £41,050 in ordinary shares and £4,210 in preference shares. On 24 February 1902 the previous Board (J. Blackburn, H. Brooke, J. J. Carter, H. Chadwick, W. Dawson, J. P. Middlebrook and C. Winterbottom) all resigned, and were succeeded by William Greer (chairman), Emile Garcke, E. A. Paris and C. L. Robertson, of whom E. A. Paris of Crow Trees, Gomersal was resident director; the new secretary was S. Humphrey. The registered office was moved on 10 June 1902 to Donington House, 37 Norfolk Street, Strand, London W.C., the headquarters of the British Electric Traction Company. On the cars themselves, the manager's name was replaced by that of W. H. Fenton, Traffic Superintendent.

In 1899 an Inquiry was held in Dewsbury by the Light Railway Commissioners to investigate the application of the British Electric Traction Co. Ltd. to put down electric tramways in the Heavy Woollen District of Yorkshire, and the opinions expressed in the local newspaper revealed a considerable difference of opinion between the local authorities concerned, namely Dewsbury, Batley, Thornhill, Ravensthorpe, Heckmondwike, Liversedge and Cleckheaton. Some favoured embarking on a municipal system of tramways, but Ravensthorpe and Liversedge in particular were pro-B.E.T. This company in the eyes of these local authorities must have been the natural successor of the Spen Valley, Dewsbury & District Tramways Co. Ltd., which as early as 1883 promoted a Bill for the construction of tramways in the Spen Valley and to Ravensthorpe.

A typical scene on the Dewsbury, Batley & Birstal Tramway at the turn of the century. Merryweather engine and car 11 in Bradford Road, Dewsbury, approaching the L.&N.W. railway viaduct. (F. Hartley)

The *Dewsbury Reporter* for 5 August 1899 stated that the Light Railway Commissioners' decision to grant the application of the British Electric Traction Company Limited (to develop new tramways) had caused a great deal of surprise and evoked hostile criticism. "—Under the Light Railways Act 1896 the company will have a lease of life for 35 years and can then only be bought out at a high figure. We fear that the introduction of the company will put a check on all municipal tramway schemes in this district and that it means a monopoly not only for the route sketched out, but for extensions. The interests of the whole district have been again sacrificed on the altar of local jealousies. Had the six authorities showed a united front against the company the opposition must have triumphed. Each authority appeared to be playing its own hand instead of concerted action".

Apart from these moves by the B.E.T., there was also continual pressure from the local authorities for the Dewsbury, Batley and Birstal company to sell out. Under the Tramways Act, 1870, section 43 gave the local authorities through which a tramway passed the option of buying the concern after a period of 21 years and then at intervals of seven years. By 1894 the first of these options presented itself, but the local authorities did not exercise their option.

By July 1901 the next option came round, and in December 1900 Birkenshaw Urban District Council decided to take advantage of it, intimating to the Board of Trade that they intended to buy the portion of the tramway in their district. The statutory purchase obligation expired on 1 February 1901, so there was very little time to lose. The portion of the tramway in the Birkenshaw Urban area was only about 12 yards, but it was part of the run-round at the terminus, and could therefore affect far more than just that part of the system.

By 3 January 1901 Gomersal Urban District Council had decided to follow Birkenshaw's lead and passed a resolution requiring the Dewsbury, Batley & Birstal Tramways to sell to them that portion of their system which was within their jurisdiction. Gomersal's portion of the system was rather less than 250 yards. An agreement was made with the British Electric Traction Company to grant them a lease of the lines for a period of at least 35 years at a nominal rent of £1 per annum. Birstall Urban District Council followed suit on 16 June 1901, and Batley Town Council on 28 October.

The Dewsbury, Batley & Birstal Tramway Company objected to the purchase of their system, particularly as they had by this time put on a ten minute service, instead of the quarter-hour one run previously. They therefore asked the Board of Trade not to agree to these purchases, stating that it would be impossible for the company to continue in existence and to maintain and work isolated portions of the line. No other objections were received by the Board of Trade to the proposed municipal purchase of the tramways, and in December 1901 a period of fourteen days was given to the Dewsbury, Batley & Birstal Tramway Company to prepare and enter its formal objections.

Negotiations described in the next chapter then ensued between the B.E.T. and the local authorities, resulting in agreements by which the councils would purchase, reconstruct and electrify the tramways and lease them to the B.E.T. In 1903 Batley Corporation served notice on the Dewsbury, Batley & Birstal Tramways Company of their intention to buy the portion of the system within the borough, this being by far the greater portion of the steam tramway system. A referee, Sir Frederick Bramwell, Bt., F.R.S., was appointed to decide the value of this portion of the system.

In the same year the Dewsbury, Batley & Birstal Tramways Act 1903 was passed, which empowered the reconstruction of the tramways in the boroughs of Dewsbury and Batley and the Urban Districts of Birkenshaw, Gomersal, Birstall and Soothill Upper, to enable them to be run by electric traction. Because of a long-drawn-out dispute between Batley town council and the B.E.T., to be described in the next chapter, the electrification was held up and the steam trams kept on running for a further two years. The B.E.T. fare token with D.B.&B. title reproduced on this book's cover dates from this period.

The sale of the relevant portions of the Dewsbury, Batley & Birstal Tramways to the local authorities through whose areas the line ran was eventually completed on 7 June 1905, and the lines were then leased back to the B.E.T. For their last few weeks of operation, the steam trams therefore ran wholly on municipally owned track. In their last full year, the steam trams had run 165,143 miles and carried 1,850,158 passengers.

The work of electrification began at the Gomersal end of the tramway on 10 July 1905, when the steam trams were withdrawn north of Birstall Smithies. Service ceased between Dewsbury and Hick Lane on 8 August 1905; a 15-minute service of wagonettes was instituted, together with a service of electric cars from Dewsbury to Batley via Thorncliffe Road. From 12 September the steam service was suspended between Hick Lane and Branch Road, leaving only the Branch Road—Birstall section, which continued for probably two more weeks (the local newspapers do not give any date). The first section to reopen with electric cars was Dewsbury to Hick Lane on 28 September.

Lt. Col. Druitt inspected the route for electric traction on 23 November of the same year, and sanction was given for public running to commence on the same afternoon, under the auspices of the Yorkshire (Woollen District) Tramways Company Ltd. The Dewsbury, Batley and Birstal Tramway Company went into voluntary liquidation on 1 January 1906, with its secretary S. Humphrey as liquidator, and held its final meeting on 10 May 1906.

Left: Laying the electric tramway feeder cables in Bradford Road, 1905, with a steam tram passing. *Right:* The former steam tram shed at Carlinghow (Batley) when used by a motor trader in 1966. It is now used by a Yorkshire Tweed manufacturer.   (R. Brook, W. Pickles

DEWSBURY, BATLEY & BIRSTAL ROLLING STOCK

Dewsbury, Batley & Birstal steam tram engine No. 9 outside the company's tram depot at Carlinghow. Note the inscription and date (1874) above the entrance and the elaborate carved wooden doors to the entrance seen through the engine windows.

(Courtesy Merryweather & Sons, London

STEAM TRAMWAY ENGINES

Nos.	Date	Builder	Maker's No.	Class	Cylinder Dimen.	Condenser	Wheels Diameter
1	1879	Merryweather	93	Standard Class 2	6½ x 10″	Air (standard)	2′2″
2-5	1880	,,	94, 96, 98	,,	,,	,,	,,
6-9	1881	,,	117-120	,,	,,	,,	,,
10-11	1898	,,	(Built 1885)	Class 17	7½ x 12″	,,	2′4″

All of them remained in use until 1905. They were then sold for £26 each, presumably for scrap, but parts of one engine are thought to have been used by Leeds City Tramways as the basis of an electric rail grinding car; a drawing of it appears on page 33, and the basic dimensions correspond with those of the DB&B engines. There is a one-sixteenth scale model of engine No. 2 with trailer, and another of engine No. 8, both bequeathed by the late Dr. H. A. Whitcombe and housed in the Science Museum, South Kensington.

In the first year when steam was substituted for horse power on the tramway the following mileage was run:—

Engine	Commenced running	Miles run by 22 March 1881
No. 1	10 April, 1880	15,000
No. 2	30 October, 1880	8,000
No. 3	7 December, 1880	6,000
No. 4	11 December, 1880	5,900
No. 5	1 January, 1881	4,800
	Total miles run:	39,700

Engines Nos. 10 and 11 were built in 1885 for the North London tramways, and had been in store, probably at Merryweather's works.

TRAILER CARS

The late Dr. H. A. Whitcombe, in his *History of the Steam Tram* and his notes bequeathed to the Science Museum, stated that all except one of the Dewsbury, Batley and Birstal Tramway Company's passenger cars were built by the Falcon Engine & Car Works of Loughborough. This cannot be correct, because Henry Hughes' Falcon works did not begin tramcar construction until 1877, by which time the D.B.&B. already had the first seven of its cars. Fortunately, an official list of D.B.&B. passenger cars appeared in the *B.E.T. Gazette* for January 1904, listing the fleet as nine cars by Starbuck, three by Ashbury and one by Brush, a total of 13. All cars were normally horse-drawn until 1879, after which the number of horses declined from 46 in 1879 to 37 in 1880, 16 in 1881 and nil in 1882 as working was taken over by steam tramway engines.

The trailer cars were numbered from 1 to 14, including four replacement vehicles. In the absence of any known company papers, the following account of the fleet has had to be based on a study of the Dewsbury Hackney Carriage Register, Duncan's Tramway Manual, the Board of Trade Returns and the available photographs, but some points remain unresolved. In particular, the Hackney carriage licences appear to coincide with fleet numbers up to 1892 but not thereafter, the company having evidently decided to leave three cars unlicensed even though they remained in stock.

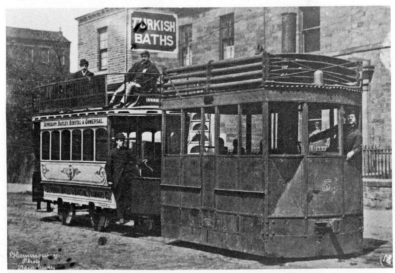

An 1890 photograph of Merryweather engine No. 5 and Starbuck trailer No. 3, one of the five horse cars purchased when the tramway opened in 1874.

(Courtesy The Science Museum, London

Nos. 1 to 5 Built in 1874 by the Starbuck Car and Wagon Company Ltd., Birkenhead, for the opening of the horse tramway from Dewsbury to Batley, but not delivered until 16 September 1874; they entered service two days later. Evidence that the five cars were identical is provided by D. K. Clark's *Tramways, their Construction and Working* (1878) which lists five cars each seating 16 inside and 16 outside and weighing 1¾ tons. The wheelbase was 5 ft. 6 ins., with 30 inch wheels. The cars were of the distinctive Starbuck six-window type also supplied to Bristol, whose cars were 11 ft. 6 in. long over corner pillars, 17 ft. long overall, and cost £180 each. The top deck with its knifeboard seat was reached by a spiral ladder at each end, replaced a few years later by quarter-turn stairways.

A model supposedly of one of these first cars is to be seen in the Dewsbury Museum in Crow Nest Park, Dewsbury. It shows a small five-window car drawn by two horses, but bears only a superficial resemblance to the horse tramcars of the period. The small size, appropriate when horses were used, was a drawback when steam traction began, and four of the cars were soon replaced by larger vehicles, leaving only No. 3 in stock. This car ceased to be licensed after 1893.

Nos. 6 to 10 The company's standard car, of which eight were built, was a large
1(II), 2(II), four wheeled vehicle with eight windows per side, seating 20 inside
4(II) and 20 on the knifeboard, still on a 5 ft. 6 in. wheelbase, and weighing 2 tons 4 cwt. These were quite large cars for a horse tramway, and must have meant hard work for the horses, even on a line whose maximum gradient was only 1 in 200. According to Leeds tramway historian Mr. J. Soper, the first two were acquired second-hand; they had been built by the Starbuck Car and Wagon Company Ltd. of Birkenhead in 1871 or 1872 for the Leeds Tramways Company, but proved too heavy for the horses and were replaced

Large four-wheel trailer No. 9, one of eight similar cars in use on the Dewsbury, Batley & Birstal Tramway. The window bill announces late cars for Dewsbury theatre traffic, and the gentleman on the left is putting his fare into the conductor's brass fare-box.
(Courtesy The Science Museum, London

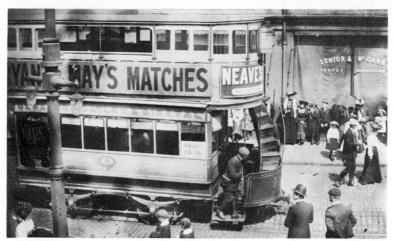

Trailer No. 6 with top cover at Northgate terminus, Dewsbury, on a short working to Batley (Hick Lane). (F. Hartley

from 1874 onwards by single deck cars. Two such cars were lent to the Dewsbury, Batley & Birstal Tramway Company in July 1874 for the inspection and start of service, and were purchased in 1876, presumably becoming D.B.&B. 6 and 7. When D. K. Clark's work was published in 1878 two such cars were in stock, and were used on Saturday evenings and other special occasions, normal traffic being dealt with by the five small cars. Six further cars of the same type had arrived on the D.B.&B. by 1880, of which one may have come from Leeds, the other five being built new. The company's total expenditure on trailer cars to the end of 1880 was subsequently given by D. K. Clark as £2,680.

A model of No. 8 is in the Science Museum, South Kensington. It is described there as a car adapted for steam traction, but is shown with spiral iron ladders, which had been replaced by built-up half-turn stairs before steam working began. There may have been slight dimensional differences between individual cars, because in later years Dewsbury's hackney carriage licences, while always recording the lower deck seating as 20, changed that of the upper deck to 22. After 1890 at least three cars, one of them No. 6, were rebuilt with covered tops similar in style to those of bogie cars 11 to 13, having enclosed ends but an opening portion with sliding windows along each side. Upper deck seating was increased to 24 (26 for car No. 7) but it is not clear whether all five cars licensed to carry 24 outside (1, 2, 4, 6, 8) had been top covered. Cars 9 and 10, whose capacity was unchanged, remained open-topped and were not licensed after 1893. Rebuilt car No. 6 made the last journey, in 1905.

No. 5(II) At some date prior to 1888, the original small Starbuck car of this number was replaced by a slightly larger car of a later type already in use elsewhere. This vehicle had six square-topped windows per side, and was constructed to seat 18 passengers in the saloon and 18 on the knifeboard. The list in the *B.E.T. Gazette* indicates that it was built by Starbuck, which implies a pre-1886 building date, but it is possible that it was either a second-hand purchase or a car from another order left on the manufacturer's hands. By 1895 it was the only small car remaining in use. It is illustrated overleaf.

29

Trailer No. 5 at Gomersal terminus, shortly after the Dewsbury, Batley & Birstal tramway was taken over by the B.E.T. in January 1902. This car replaced an 1874 Starbuck car.
(Courtesy I. S. Smith

Top covered bogie trailer 11 of 1886 outside the Carlinghow tram depot at Batley. The later addition to the depot is seen behind the engine. (Courtesy Mrs. G. Field

30

Nos. 11 to 13 According to Dr. Whitcombe and the Board of Trade returns, these cars arrived in 1886. They were of the large bogie type with covered tops, already adopted on most other steam tramways, and seated 30 in the lower saloon and 36 upstairs. The list in the *B.E.T. Gazette* shows that they were built by the Ashbury Carriage and Iron Company Ltd. of Manchester. The lower saloons had ten fixed windows per side, the upper saloon had sixteen small windows per side of which two sets of three could slide along to give an opening in fine weather. Top deck seating was by a full-length central knifeboard, so the upper saloon had two doors at each end, opening on to a small outside landing. The entrances were at the corners of the car, closed off by a solid gate, and there was a brake rod allowing the car brakes to be applied from the engine.

No. 14 The introduction of the ten-minute service in 1898 had required the acquisition of two more engines, as already mentioned, but only one more car was bought. The *B.E.T. Gazette* gives the builder as Brush, which indicates that the car was built new and not bought at second-hand, since the Loughborough works had previously traded under the title of the Falcon Engine and Car Works. Brush were still using up their stock of Falcon Works enamel builder's plates, and those on D.B.&B. 14 (one of which survives in the collection of Mr. F. Hartley) were identical to those fitted in 1896-7 to the Douglas Southern electric cars. No. 14 arrived in 1898 and was generally similar to 11-13, but had fewer windows per side (nine downstairs, twelve upstairs) and a full height upstairs window on either side of the oil lantern, with only one stairhead door at each

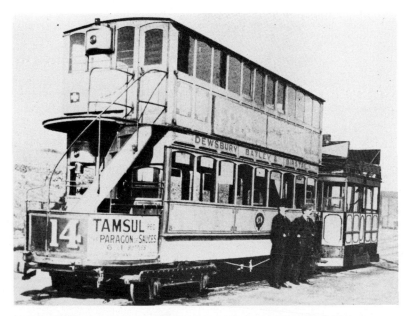

Dewsbury, Batley & Birstal bogie trailer 14, the final addition to the fleet. It was built by the Brush Electrical Engineering Company's Falcon Works at Loughborough in 1898.
(Courtesy The Science Museum, London

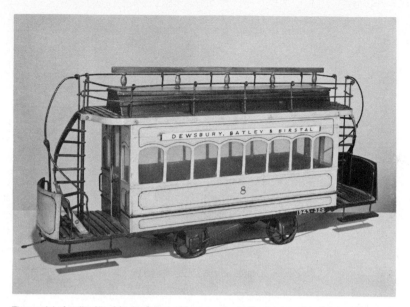

The model of trailer No. 8 in the Science Museum, South Kensington. It is finished in a bright chrome yellow, lined in red and brown. (Crown Copyright, Science Museum, London

end, and no outside landing. By this date the upstairs seating would have been of the transverse (garden) type, but this is not clear from the available photographs. The plate frame bogies were longer and heavier than those of 11-13. With the arrival of trailer 14, the Dewsbury, Batley and Birstal fleet reached its maximum of 11 engines and 14 cars, shown in the *Tramway & Railway World* statistical summary for 1899, but within a year it had become 11 engines and only 13 cars, one of the smaller trailers being withdrawn.

Liveries

The Science Museum model of No. 8 shows the horse tram livery as a bright chrome yellow, lined out in red and brown. So far as is known, the same basic colour was used in steam days, though the rocker panels appear in a lighter colour, probably cream. These panels carried the company title, except in the final years after the B.E.T. take-over, when it was painted out. The route indication "Dewsbury, Batley and Birstal" (to which Gomersal was later added) was painted on each car above the lower saloon windows; the Science Museum model shows it on detachable white boards. Photographs taken at different dates show many minor variations in lining and lettering; originally the cars had elaborate ornamental lining on the waist panel, enclosing the fleet number, but this was gradually simplified over the years. The engines were originally painted an all-over black or dark brown, but from the 1890's they were changed to a livery somewhat similar to that of the cars, with chrome yellow upper parts and chocolate brown lining and skirting.

Disposals

The first trailer cars to be disposed of were the small 1874 Starbuck cars 1, 2 and 4. Two of them were placed end to end, fitted with verandahs and a new roof, and became the headquarters of "Old Sam's" boat hiring business at Ravens Wharf on the River Calder, next to the bridge carrying the main Leeds—Manchester railway over

32

the river. The business ceased in the 1930's, and there is no trace on the site today. After the end of steam tram operation in 1905 the bogie trailer car bodies were sold off for use as garden sheds; the lower saloon of No. 14 was still intact near Mirfield in 1947. Four of the four-wheel trailers appear to have been cut down and sold to the West Riding tramways for use as salt trailers. A reference to "four old steam cars converted into salt cars" occurs in *Tramway and Railway World* in 1908, and Dewsbury was the only likely source of such cars in the area at the date when the West Riding tramways commenced operation.

On 15 August 1905, Dewsbury Corporation received a letter from Mr. E. A. Paris (the local director of the British Electric Traction Company) stating that he had received an offer of £26 each for the steam tram engines and 38s. each for the trailer cars. These prices were accepted by the Dewsbury council, and the Town Clerk was instructed to write to Mr. Paris telling him to go ahead with the sale of the cars and engines. The engines had cost £750 25 years earlier, but now that steam trams were on the way out, they were only worth the scrap price. They were sold to Mr. Smith, metals broker, of Canal Road, Bradford, who took out the boilers, tested them to 120 lbs. per square inch, and offered them for sale. He also appears to have sold one complete chassis to Leeds City Tramways, who used it to build an electric rail-grinding car. In this form, it survived for another fifty years.

This photograph taken in 1906 in Wellington Bridge permanent way yard shows how the Leeds City Tramways built an electric rail-grinding car on the underframe of a steam tram engine, probably from the Dewsbury, Batley & Birstal Tramway. It remained in use until about 1955.
(The Tramway and Railway World

CHAPTER TWO

THE SPEN VALLEY LIGHT RAILWAYS

Once the value of the tramways in the Dewsbury, Batley & Birstall areas had been realised, enquiries were soon being made in the neighbouring Spen Valley as to why better travelling facilities were not available there. The towns of Dewsbury, Batley, Heckmondwike and Cleckheaton (known as the "Heavy Woollen District" from the type of cloths made there for blankets and rugs) already formed a nearly continuous conurbation. The Lancashire & Yorkshire Railway had a branch line up the Spen Valley but perhaps because it had a monopoly there, it gave the minimum of service. To try to break this monopoly the Great Northern Railway Company applied for an extension from Batley into the Spen Valley through Heckmondwike and Liversedge to Cleckheaton.

The first known attempt to provide tramways in the area took shape in 1880, when on 7 September the West Riding Tramways Company Limited was registered to lay tramways between Cleckheaton, Heckmondwike and Dewsbury and between Dewsbury, Savile Town, Ravensthorpe and Mirfield. The promoters included George Truswell, manager of the Dewsbury, Batley and Birstal Tramway Company, with which it shared a registered office. The other promoters were local engineers, contractors and a solicitor (Charles Walker), but the scheme did not proceed. The dormant company was dissolved in 1887.

Two new rival tramway schemes appeared in 1882. Messrs. Goodson, Atkinson and Forde, engineers of Liverpool, asked the Cleckheaton Local Board's consent to make an application for a Provisional Order to lay down a line of tramways in the Board's district to connect Cleckheaton and Dewsbury through Heckmondwike and along Dewsbury Moor to the main Dewsbury—Huddersfield road, where it would meet a branch from Ravensthorpe, terminating about half a mile from Dewsbury Market Place. The company formed to finance this scheme was The Spen Valley, Dewsbury and District Tramway Company Ltd., registered on 22 November 1882, with registered offices at Cleckheaton, and the gauge was to be 3 ft. 6 in.

The second scheme, put forward by Mr. Charles Gott, C.E., of Bradford was to lay down a system of tramways between Cleckheaton and Heckmondwike but via Birstall. Trams would leave Cleckheaton via St. Peg Lane and travel through Gomersal and up Church Lane into Birstall. From there the route would follow the main Leeds—Huddersfield road to Millbridge and then along Flush into Heckmondwike. This scheme was abandoned in September 1882 in favour of that put forward by the Liverpool firm, a more practical proposal, linking the little townships of the Spen Valley with Dewsbury.

There was some disagreement over the siting of the terminus of the Ravensthorpe branch. As proposed in the Bill this was to be at the Bull's Head Inn, near Shepley Bridge, but councillors of Mirfield U.D.C. felt that it should be at the Black Bull Hotel in Mirfield. One councillor thought it should be at the Three Nuns Inn on the Huddersfield road at the County borough boundary. The company was not in favour of taking the tramways through to Mirfield, because of the sparse population and because the road at Snake Hill near Battyeford Station was very narrow.

Discussions continued through into 1883. By March of that year agreement had been reached, the company's view prevailing, so the scheme could be put before the

Board of Trade. The Provisional Order was obtained in December 1883, authorising either animal or mechanical power. The promoters were particularly interested in the idea of a cable system and consequently did not wish to proceed further until the cable tramway at Highgate Hill in London had proved itself. The line was to be single track with passing places and a length of double track at each terminus. It would start at the point where Hunsworth Lane meets the main Bradford Road in Cleckheaton, and then pass along the latter road through Cleckheaton Market Place and along the main road leading from Cleckheaton to Heckmondwike (A638), through Rawfolds and Littletown, Liversedge, up Frost Hill and along the Flush to Heckmondwike Market Place. From there it was to continue along Walkley Lane, through Dewsbury Moor, round the western boundary of Crow Nest Park and then down the steepest gradient of the line (1 in 10) on Temple Road before turning into Huddersfield Road, meeting at this point the branch up Scout Hill from the Bull's Head Inn in Ravensthorpe. The line was then to terminate in Dewsbury at the junction of Huddersfield Road with Cemetery Road, by the side of the R.C. Chapel.

All the fifteen passing places were to be constructed equi-distant of the centre line of the tramway except the one at the bottom of the Moor End Lane, Dewsbury Moor, which was to be built on the west side of the centre line. The scheme however came to nothing, and the company was dissolved in 1890. The gradients would probably have been beyond the capabilities of steam tramway engines. Further progress had to await the development of electric tramways.

The B.E.T. Arrive

The British Electric Traction group founded in 1896 by Mr. Emile Garcke, decided to try and obtain tramway powers in this area, since it consisted of several modest-size towns, which could be linked to form an extensive company-operated network. Between 1899 and 1901 the group entered into agreements with all the local authorities in the area, except Batley, as to the conditions under which the Company might build and operate electric tramways.

In commencing the story of the electric tramways in and around Dewsbury, we must first record our appreciation of the work of local photographer Fred Hartley, who recorded every important event that occurred in his town during the Edwardian years, and many years later entrusted his tramway negatives and copyrights to R. B. Parr. In this view of Church Street, Dewsbury, car 32 from Thornhill awaits the passing of a funeral procession entering All Saints Church, with a Ravensthorpe car bringing up the rear. (F. Hartley

35

In 1898, the British Electric Traction Co. Ltd. deposited the Spen Valley Light Railway Order, proposing a tramway from Ravensthorpe (at the western end of Huddersfield Road, at a point 370 yards to the east of Church Lane Bridge) northwards through the centre of Dewsbury and then along Halifax Road through Staincliffe, Heckmondwike, Liversedge and Cleckheaton, to Bradford Road at its junction with Hunsworth Lane and Whitechapel Road (Moor End). This system was described as three railways:—

Railway No. 1: 2 miles 2 furlongs 9 chains from Ravensthorpe to Northgate, Dewsbury.

Railway No. 2: 5 miles 0 furlongs 1 chain from a junction with the above railway to Hunsworth Lane, Cleckheaton.

Railway No. 3: 1 chain in length connecting Railway No. 1 with the lines of the existing Dewsbury, Batley and Birstal Tramways at the southerly extremity (i.e. at the Dewsbury terminus).

A public enquiry was held by the Light Railway Commissioners in August 1899. The Commissioners agreed to grant the order, although the final order was not handed over to the Board of Trade for confirmation until 14 May 1900. Meanwhile the Company had deposited a further application for substantial extensions to the proposed system. Four additional lines were proposed:

a) a branch from Leeds Road, Millbridge, at the junction with Huddersfield Road, along Gomersal Road and Oxford Road to Birkenshaw, and thence to the Tong Cemetery terminus of the Bradford Corporation lines within that city.

b) A branch from Millbridge, along Huddersfield Road, Station Lane, Halifax Road to Hightown before turning back to Moor Bottom and thence to Westgate, Cleckheaton joining the main line again at The Green.

c) A branch off Batley Road, Heckmondwike along Healey Lane, Clerk Green and Wellington Street to a terminus in Hick Lane.

d) A line from Church Street, Dewsbury to Thornhill.

A further enquiry was held on 7 June 1900 and these extensions were granted by the Commissioners despite representations made against the application by Batley Corporation, which had proposed a rival bill. The Commissioners stipulated however that the Company line concerned could not be constructed if the Batley Corporation Bill was subsequently made law.

The B.E.T. had written to Batley Town Council, in July 1898, stating that they proposed to seek powers for the construction of tramways connecting Ravensthorpe, Dewsbury, Staincliffe, Heckmondwike, Liversedge and Cleckheaton. In December, Batley Town Council gave notice of objection to the application, and this was the beginning of a period of discord between the Council and the B.E.T. which led to delays in the opening of part of the system and in the electrification of the Dewsbury, Batley and Birstal Tramways. Batley Council wished to operate tramways itself, even though they would probably form part of a larger network. The Council lodged its various objections to the B.E.T. scheme from 1898 onwards, and in April 1900 the Board of Trade decided to sanction the tramway scheme of the Batley Council, subject to a clause conferring on the Spen Valley Light Railway promoters running powers over such portions of the tramways as coincided with the Spen Valley Light Railway system, on terms to be settled in case of dispute by arbitration. The gauge of all the lines was to be 4 ft. 8½ inches.

On 14 June 1900 The Town Clerk of Batley reported that a Bill had been introduced into Parliament to confirm the Provisional Order granted by the Board of Trade authorising the Batley Corporation to construct and work tramways. The Corporation's application, which had been granted, included a stretch of line in Halifax Road which would be controlled jointly by the Company and the Corporation. The company would build the down line (towards Heckmondwike) while the Corporation would build the up line (towards Dewsbury).

The Spen Valley Light Railways Order, made by the Light Railway Commissioners, was approved by the Board of Trade on 22 April 1901. Major

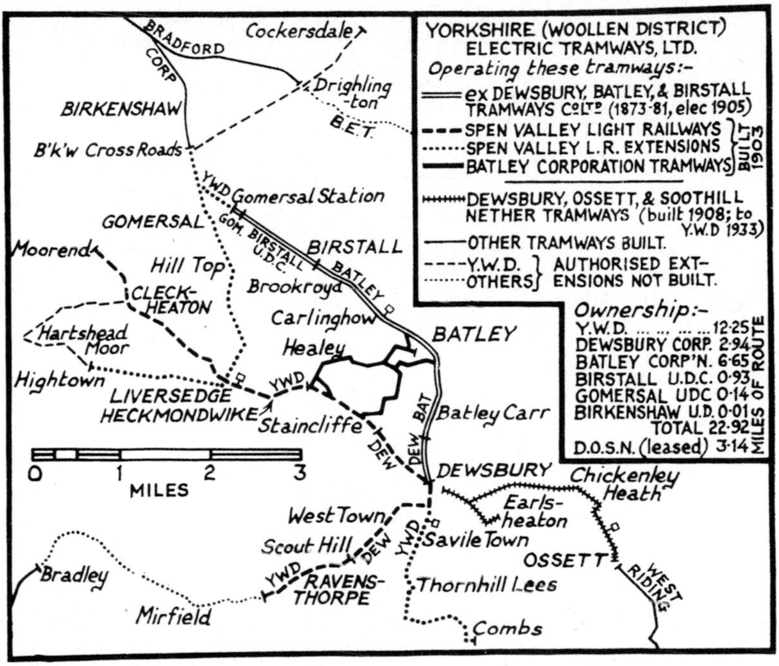

YORKSHIRE (WOOLLEN DISTRICT) ELECTRIC TRAMWAYS, LTD.
Operating these tramways:-
ex DEWSBURY, BATLEY, & BIRSTALL TRAMWAYS Co.Ltd. (1873-81, elec 1905)
SPEN VALLEY LIGHT RAILWAYS
SPEN VALLEY L.R. EXTENSIONS
BATLEY CORPORATION TRAMWAYS
BUILT 1903
DEWSBURY, OSSETT, & SOOTHILL NETHER TRAMWAYS (built 1908; to Y.W.D 1933)
OTHER TRAMWAYS BUILT.
Y.W.D.
OTHERS
AUTHORISED EXTENSIONS NOT BUILT.
Ownership:-
Y.W.D. ... ... 12·25
DEWSBURY CORP. 2·94
BATLEY CORP'N. 6·65
BIRSTALL U.D.C. 0·93
GOMERSAL UDC 0·14
BIRKENSHAW U.D. 0·01
TOTAL 22·92
D.O.S.N. (leased) 3·14
MILES OF ROUTE
BRADFORD CORP
Cockersdale
Drighlington
B.E.T.
BIRKENSHAW
B'k'w Cross Roads
YWD
Gomersal Station
GOMERSAL
GOM.
BIRSTALL U.D.C.
BIRSTALL
BATLEY
Moorend
Hill Top
CLECKHEATON
Brookroyd
Carlinghow
Hartshead Moor
Healey
BATLEY
Hightown
LIVERSEDGE
HECKMONDWIKE
Staincliffe
DEW
BAT
Batley Carr
0 1 2 3
MILES
DEWSBURY
Chickenley Heath
Earlsheaton
West Town
Scout Hill
Savile Town
OSSETT
Bradley
RAVENSTHORPE
Thornhill Lees
WEST RIDING
Mirfield
Combs

The Spen Valley Light Railways (built and authorised) and other tramways in the area of the Yorkshire (Woollen District) Electric Tramways, showing ownership of tracks. (J. C. Gillham

Druitt held a local inquiry into the Corporation's application to borrow £52,451 for the purpose of the Batley Tramways Order of 1900, and on 2 May 1901 it was reported that the Board of Trade had sanctioned the borrowing of the money. There was also an application to delay the commencement of the works thus authorised until 6 February 1902 and 6 August 1903. An extension was granted until 2 February 1902, but in September 1901 the Council were informed that the promoters of the Spen Valley Light Railway would shortly commence breaking up the road etc., in the Borough, for the construction of their railway, and forwarded the plans for approval. The Council would not agree to the proposals because of their own tramway scheme.

On 13 November 1901 the Town Clerk of Batley was instructed to tell the British Electric Traction Company that the committee was willing to discuss the question of a lease of the Corporation tramways and would consider any proposal which the company might like to make to them. Engineers were instructed to value the portion of the D.B.&B. Tramways which were situated in the Borough of Batley. Further negotiations were prolonged into 1902 and the Board of Trade was asked for an extension of time.

On 19 November 1901 the B.E.T. registered a new subsidiary Company, the Yorkshire (Woollen District) Electric Tramways Limited, to build and operate the system authorised under the Spen Valley Orders. This Company entered into an agreement with the B.E.T. to buy the whole of the undertaking authorised by the Spen Valley Light Railways Orders. The Managing Director at the formation was Mr. E. A. Paris, AMIEE, and the company's first address was Crowtrees, Gomersal (evidently Mr. Paris's residence). In 1903 the company's address was changed to the newly built Frost Hill depot at Liversedge.

Mr. Stephen Sellon, the chief engineer of the B.E.T., attended a meeting on 6 February 1902, and discussed proposals for the terms of a lease by Batley Corporation to the company of the tramways proposed to be constructed as well as the portion of the existing tramways (i.e. the D.B.&B. Tramways). Meanwhile work on the construction of the B.E.T.'s system had begun on 15 April 1902. Batley had also gone ahead with construction, and by September 1902 £3,288 had been spent on permanent way, contracts, wages and materials. In November 1902 the Town Clerk of Batley was able to submit a draft Agreement with the B.E.T. for a lease of the 1873 tramways and those being constructed under the 1900 Order, and also the Halifax Road tramways.

In December 1902 the Batley Council were informed by the B.E.T. that they intended to start work in Halifax Road, Batley in January the following year and they enclosed a statement of materials. The company intended to use granite setts and the Batley Corporation required the use of Yorkshire setts. Elsewhere on the system sufficient progress had been made for B.E.T. to apply in January 1903 for a Board of Trade inspection.

On 3 January 1903 of that year a trial trip was made on the Halifax Road section and this was not without its teething troubles. Prior to the formal inspection of the line by the Board of Trade inspector, the B.E.T. were already testing their cars and equipment along the Thornhill route and on the Halifax Road line. Everything went well until on one occasion at the Dewsbury Infirmary (now the Municipal Buildings) the trolley pole was knocked off the wire by the branch of an overhanging tree. With the object of making a fresh start up the hill, which is steep, (about 1 in 9 gradient) the driver reversed the car and proceeded to run down the hill towards Dewsbury. A short distance behind the car there was a G.N.R. lorry and behind that a grocer's trap belonging to Mr. Pearson of Church Street, Dewsbury. Soon after setting the car in motion, the driver noticed that the line was obstructed by the lorry and applied his brakes. These caused the wheels to lock during the heavy rain and the car skidded out of control, carrying the grocer's trap before it until it smashed into one of the overhead standards.

Soon after 9 a.m. on 18 February 1903, two double-deck cars were run out of Savile Town depot and conveyed the officials of the company and the contractors as far as Thornhill Station, where they met the two inspectors from the Board of Trade who had arrived from London, Major Druitt (for rolling stock) and Mr. A. P. Trotter (for electrical equipment). The party mounted the cars and proceeded along Brewery Lane at a smart speed. The inhabitants turned out in large numbers to witness the trip. On reaching the junction of Brewery Lane and Lees Hall Road, the cars were brought to a standstill and the party dismounted. Members of the Thornhill U.D.C. drew the attention of Major Druitt to the dangerous nature of this curve, which had been the centre of a great deal of argument by both Council and Board of Trade, as there was hardly room for a person to pass between the wall of the building and a car. Major Druitt stated that as the lines were now laid there was little that could be done, and that the U.D.C. should have submitted their objection to the Board of Trade at an earlier date. It was pointed out by some of the councillors that the curve was shown differently on the plans they had seen, but Major Druitt refused to accept this and said that they should have seen the original plans. In any case he decided that he would make a ruling for a speed limit of 2 miles per hour round this corner, and this appeared to satisfy the councillors. The car then proceeded along Lees Hall Road and up the hill below the Council Offices, before arriving without a hitch at the terminus of the line at Combs Pit gate, where the party was greeted by large crowds. Except for a couple of high-spirited horses in Brewery Lane, which took fright at the sight of the car, the return journey was equally successful.

On reaching the Savile Town tram sheds the party transferred to single deck cars; two low railway bridges precluded the use of double-deckers on the Ravensthorpe section. Near Dewsbury Parish Church the cars were boarded by members of the Dewsbury Corporation and other officials of the tramways undertaking. The cars then proceeded along Aldams Road and up Webster Hill.

This hill has a gradient of 1 in 15 and on the drawings shown to the Dewsbury Council double track was indicated; when the work was under way, however, the B.E.T. had started to lay interlaced track on this portion between Aldams Road and Webster Hill, and there was correspondence about this point between the Town Clerk of Dewsbury and the Board of Trade during September 1902. However, two separate tracks were finally laid and the road straightened out a little. The cars then proceeded smoothly to the Borough boundary near the bottom of Scout Hill, close to the Lancashire and Yorkshire Railway Company's bridge over the Huddersfield Road.

Returning from Ravensthorpe to Dewsbury Market Place, double-deck cars were boarded again and these proceeded to Halifax Road as far as the "Shoulder of Mutton" Inn (the borough boundary on this line). The hill beyond this Inn was the steepest on the system, with a gradient of 1 in 8, and was no doubt discussed, even though not yet submitted for formal inspection. Major Druitt and Mr. Trotter appeared satisfied with the inspection and at once granted the company a temporary certificate to run cars for the public between Dewsbury and Thornhill until official sanction was granted by the Board of Trade.

Major Druitt in his report on the inspection made certain stipulations as regards speeds and compulsory stops. The maximum speed on any section was fixed at 10 miles/h, with many more severe restrictions. The slipper brake or other track brake was to be applied before moving off from the compulsory stopping place on Webster Hill, Dewsbury at the "Stag and Pheasant" public house on the descending journey. Two vehicles were not to be allowed to pass each other on the portion of the route in Halifax Road, Dewsbury between Wellington Road and Willans Road.

Major Druitt expressed himself in favour of single deck cars for the Halifax Road service, owing to the steepness of the route, but double deckers were authorised.

YWD car 66 in Webster Hill, Dewsbury, waiting at Pinfold Hill, for a procession to pass. This 1845 railway bridge was one of the two that made single deck cars necessary for the Ravensthorpe route, and the gradient in Webster Hill required the use of track brakes. Note the double overhead wires installed to reduce voltage drop. (F. Hartley

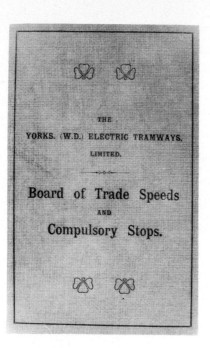

THE

YORKS. (W.D.) ELECTRIC TRAMWAYS,

LIMITED.

Board of Trade Speeds

AND

Compulsory Stops.

BOARD OF TRADE SPEEDS AND COMPULSORY STOPS.

Thornhill Route.

In Wilton Street, Dewsbury, 10 miles an hour.
On Savile Bridge, 4 miles an hour.
In Savile Road, 10 miles an hour.
In Railway approach, 8 miles an hour, except from Railway Station, Thornhill, to Brewery Lane, where 4 miles an hour is allowed.
In Brewery Lane, 10 miles an hour.
In Lees Hall Road and in Dewsbury Road, 10 miles an hour, except on the portion of double line from the Board School Offices in Dewsbury Road to the Chapel, Lees Hall Road, when 6 miles only is allowed on the downward journey.
Round the corner from Brewery Lane into Lees Hall Road, 3 miles an hour on the inside curve and 4 miles an hour on the outward curve when coming from Lees Hall Road into Brewery Lane.
A COMPULSORY STOP is required before passing the Board School Offices in Dewsbury Road on the downward journey.

Ravensthorpe Route.

In Huddersfield Road, 10 miles in each direction except on Ravenswharfe Hill on the downward journey, when 6 miles an hour is allowed, and when crossing Temple Road in each direction speed must not exceed 4 miles an hour.
On Webster Hill, 4 miles an hour on the downward journey and 10 miles an hour on the upward journey.
In Aldams Road, Dewsbury, 8 miles an hour.
In Church Street, Dewsbury, 8 miles an hour.
In Westgate and Market Place, Dewsbury, 4 miles an hour.
In Northgate, Dewsbury, 6 miles an hour.
Round corners Aldams Road into Church Street, and Church Street into Westgate, 4 miles an hour.
A COMPULSORY STOP is required at the Stag and Pheasant, on the downward journey, where slipper brakes are to be applied before going down Webster Hill.

Spen Valley.

In Halifax Road, Dewsbury, from Northgate to St. Mark's Church, 6 miles an hour.
From St. Mark's Church to Highfield House, 10 miles an hour.
From Highfield House to Track Road, 6 miles an hour.
A COMPULSORY STOP before crossing Eightlands Road on downward track, and before crossing Oxford Road on downward journey.
No two cars on opposite tracks are allowed between Wellington Road and Wilians Road at the same time.
In Halifax Road, Batley, from Thorncliffe Road to Hirst's Buildings, 8 miles an hour.
From Hirst's Buildings to Batley Boundary, 4 miles an hour on descending journey, 8 miles an hour on ascending journey.
A COMPULSORY STOP at Hirst's Buildings.
From Common Road to Batley Boundary, 6 miles an hour on descending and 10 miles an hour on ascending journey.
In High Street, Heckmondwike, from Batley boundary to Market Place, 6 miles an hour on descending and 10 miles an hour on ascending.
A COMPULSORY STOP in High Street, Heckmondwike, at Bath Road on descending journey.
Along "The Green" and in Westgate, Heckmondwike, 8 miles an hour, except between Hill Street and Wood Street, where 4 miles an hour may be allowed.
On Frost Hill, from Wood Street to Car Depôt, 8 miles an hour, from Car Depôt to Swan Inn, 6 miles an hour.
In Littletown Road, 8 miles an hour.
In Watergate, Liversedge, 8 miles an hour.
Round corner at "The Green," Liversedge, 4 miles an hour.
From "The Green" to Liversedge boundary, 10 miles an hour.
In Dewsbury Road, Liversedge, 10 miles an hour.
In Bradford Road, Cleckheaton, 10 miles an hour.

Hightown.

8 miles an hour, but 4 miles an hour round curves and through facing points.

Batley.

The speed on these tramways must not exceed 8 miles an hour.
In Hick Lane, on downward journey, 4 miles an hour.
In Wellington Street, from Purlwell Lane to Providence Street, on downward journey, 4 miles an hour.
In Purlwell Lane, on downward journey, 4 miles an hour.
In Track Road, 10 miles an hour.
Speed must not exceed 4 miles an hour round the following corners:—

Between Purlwell Lane and Track Road.
,, Track Road and Thorncliffe Road.
,, Thorncliffe Road and Halifax Road.
In Healey Lane at 4 miles.
Between Healey Lane and Mayman Lane.
,, Mayman Lane and Upper Commercial Street.
,, Upper Commercial Street and Henrietta St.
,, Henrietta Street and Branch Road.
,, Clayhill and Mayman Lane.
,, Clarke Green Road and Purlwell Lane.
In Healey Lane.
From Bellevue Street to Borough boundary, and from Town Gate Road to Mayman Lane on downward journey, 4 miles an hour.
In Henrietta Street, on downward journey, 4 miles an hour.
In Halifax Road, from Thorncliffe Road to Common Road, 12 miles an hour.

COMPULSORY STOPS.

In Healey Lane, at Town Gate Road on the downward journey.
In Wellington Street, at the Wellington Inn, on downward journey.
In Purlwell Lane, at Oxford Street, on the downward journey.
In Upper Commercial Street, before turning into Henrietta Street.

Cars must come to a dead stop at all poles painted with TWO white bands.

J. V. Isherwood, Printer, Bond Street, Dewsbury.

Board of Trade Regulations applicable to the Yorkshire (Woollen District) Electric Tramways, issued as a card folder to each driver.
(Courtesy C. C. Hall, FCIT

All the objections of the various authorities were now settled and the cars commenced running in the afternoon of 18 February 1903, the day of the inspection, on the first section of the system, 2½ miles between Combs Hill, Thornhill and Dewsbury Market Place. Five cars maintained a ten minute service. Because work at the Dewsbury Electric Light and Power Station had not been completed, the Halifax Road route and the Ravensthorpe section could not be used and the subsequent opening was delayed. Even then, on the latter route running would only be possible as far as the L.&Y.R. Ravensthorpe Station at the Dewsbury Borough Boundary, as beyond that point difficulties had arisen with the overhead equipment and the telegraph wires, and this section was not yet ready for inspection. In addition, the inspector required certain alterations to be made to the single deck cars, the effect of which was to delay the start of the Ravensthorpe service until Sunday 15 March 1903.

Soon after the opening the company requested permission to lay a third track in Dewsbury Market Place. Major Druitt thought that if there were cars standing on all three lines at the same time they would obstruct the traffic. In practice, the westernmost track (nearest to the pavement) was used as the terminus of the Dewsbury to Ravensthorpe route, which the company worked as a separate branch, and the easternmost track was used as the terminus of the Dewsbury to Cleckheaton route, the middle track being used mainly for depot journeys. The turning of trolley poles caused excessive vibration to the overhead, and the company wanted to erect two more poles to give extra support; the Corporation claimed compensation, but were overruled by the Board of Trade.

By April 1903 it had become apparent that the Spen Valley Light Railways would have to be operated in the initial stages as two physically separate sections, one at Dewsbury, the other based on Frost Hill depot at Liversedge. The reason was a dispute between the B.E.T. and Batley Corporation, details of which are given later in this chapter. On the trunk line of the system from Dewsbury to Heckmondwike and beyond, a portion about 0.9 miles in length (along Halifax Road, Staincliffe) lay in the borough of Batley. The B.E.T. was authorised to build and own part of this line, but about 800 yards of it (from Thorncliffe Road to Common Road) coincided with Batley's own proposed circular route, and could not be completed or opened until the dispute was settled.

Work was therefore concentrated on the section of the Spen Valley Light Railway between Quarry Inn, Staincliffe and Moorend. A car was taken on a bogie from Dewsbury, put on the track and run to Cleckheaton on Tuesday, 7 April. Further cars were later transferred to Frost Hill depot in readiness for the start of service.

On 24 April 1903 Major Druitt inspected the trunk line of the system from Quarry Inn, Staincliffe, down High Street through Heckmondwike, Liversedge and Cleckheaton to Moor End. He was accompanied by officials of the company and the chairmen of the three U.D.C.'s concerned. The Hightown section had not yet been completed and the line between the Swan Inn, Liversedge and Birkenshaw, via Gomersal had not been begun. Mr. T. F. Firth J.P. had some strong comments to make about the speed limits which Major Druitt proposed along the section on the Flush at Heckmondwike. The Chairman of the Liversedge U.D.C. called attention to various detailed matters in the Council area whilst Cleckheaton U.D.C. had no objection to raise at all. The party returned from Cleckheaton as far as the Quarry Inn and then walked to Thorncliffe Road, because on this section only one track had been laid (on the south side of the road), the other was to be laid subsequently by Batley Corporation. At Thorncliffe Road they boarded another car (sent from Dewsbury) and inspected the section along Halifax Road to Carr Top, Batley Carr. The lines inspected were approved, and service began on the same day, between Heckmondwike Market Place and Moorend. Owing to a shortage of cars, no service could be run from Heckmondwike to Staincliffe.

Major Druitt's next visit of inspection was on 28 July 1903, the main purpose being to inspect the Batley Corporation Tramways. While in the area, he went on to inspect the Hightown section of the Spen Valley Light Railways, and sanctioned it. He also sanctioned the section in Halifax Road at Staincliffe which comprised one Batley track and one B.E.T. track, and the remaining section of the Ravensthorpe route to Fir Cottage, which opened next day, 29 July 1903. The completion and opening of the line through Staincliffe enabled a through service to be instituted next day from Dewsbury to Moorend, and meant that the Spen Valley system was no longer in two isolated portions.

By October 1903 the Millbridge, Gomersal and Birkenshaw section of the Spen Valley Light Railways was ready for inspection, which took place on 13 October. Suggestions were made by members of the Gomersal U.D.C. regarding speed limits in the village, due to the nearness of the school to the tram route. A great deal of interest was shown in the inspection along this route and when in the afternoon, cars commenced running for public use, many of them were well patronised in spite of bad weather. Through cars were run by this route from Dewsbury to Birkenshaw.

The only portion of line constructed under any of the extension Orders was a short length connecting the former terminus of the Dewsbury, Batley & Birstal Tramways with the Millbridge to Birkenshaw section near Birkenshaw terminus. This was constructed under the Spen Valley and Morley Light Railways (Extensions) Order 1901 and opened on the same date as the electrified steam tramway, 23 November 1905, after lowering the roadway at Gomersal Station bridge.

Constructional details. (YWD lines).

The contractors for the permanent way and overhead equipment were Dick, Kerr & Co. The cables in the Dewsbury area were laid by British Insulated Wire Co., and in the Cleckheaton area by W. T. Henley. The gauge of the track was 4 ft. 8½ inches, and the grooved girder rails weighed 94 lb. per yard (100 lb. per yard on curves). The sharpest curve on the system was one of 45 feet radius. The overhead wires were suspended both from side poles with bowstring brackets, and from span wires. The poles carried a flat finial and an octagonal ornamental base which was not moulded as part of the complete pole as were those used by Batley Corporation, which latter carried the Batley Borough Coat of Arms within a "garter". The ornate bases on the former were later removed as it was found that the separate base encouraged corrosion. Parts of the three Dewsbury routes were equipped with twin trolley wires to relieve the feeder cables of extra load at peak times.

The contractors were instructed to pave the metals with granite setts, and this cause quite a lot of delay. The councils wanted soft Yorkshire stone on gradients as it was feared that the granite would be too slippery for the horses' feet and much correspondence took place on this subject between the local authorities, the Tramway Company and the Board of Trade. It was also suggested that as an alternative to the complete paving of the space between the metals with setts, it should be macadamised with a single row of setts on the inner side of each line and this was actually done in the section under the control of the Birkenshaw Urban District Council.

In two portions of the system, wood setts were used instead of granite. One section was by the Roman Catholic Chapel in Huddersfield Road, Dewsbury and the other was Westgate, Heckmondwike, where Jarrah wood blocks were used. There was also considerable trouble due to the narrowness of the road between the tramway depot at Frost Hill and the Green at Heckmondwike. The Company insisted on double track along the Flush at this point, and the Council and the owners of the property, particularly Mr. T. F. Firth who owned the mill along the Flush, thought that a double track would obstruct the free flow of traffic into and out of his mill. The Council suggested that single track should be laid on the north side of the road along Westgate Road and the Green. This would have created a bottle-neck on the main line of the system and was opposed by the Company. This was amicably settled later and a double track constructed.

The two western routes of the Spen Valley system (Moorend and Hightown) were operated for many years by small single-deck cars, but for the first three years, 1903-5, double deck cars were used, as shown in these photographs. The upper view is of car 35 at Moorend terminus on the service to Heckmondwike (before the through service commenced to Dewsbury) and the lower view shows car 37 descending the hill from Hightown towards the Huddersfield Road at Liversedge. The trolley ropes were later replaced by bamboo poles.

(H. Tolson collection and R. Brook

The steepest gradient was 1 in 8 at two points, in Halifax Road, Batley for four chains above the Shoulder of Mutton Inn, and for 1.56 chains near Popely Fields on the Heckmondwike—Gomersal—Birkenshaw route. There was also a gradient of 1 in 8.6 for 1.75 chains in Healey Lane, Batley. The system thus ran some of the steepest routes, if not the steepest in the country. It was certainly the steepest in the area, as can be seen from this table:—

	Maximum Gradients
Huddersfield	1 in 9.3
Halifax	1 in 9.5
Mexborough & Swinton	1 in 9.0
Bradford	1 in 9.8
Leeds	1 in 8.4
Dewsbury & Ossett	1 in 12.0
West Riding	1 in 15.5
Barnsley	1 in 10.0

The narrow arch of the L.N.W.R. bridge on the Halifax Road section of the Spen Valley main line at Dewsbury caused the Board of Trade considerable anxiety, being at the foot of a steep gradient (1 in 9). The Board insisted on double track or interlaced track instead of single track. In fact interlaced track would still have been a source of worry, as a car which got out of control down the hill could still meet an on-coming one in collision. In the final double-track layout, the near-side track was very near the causeway at this point and cars could easily be touched by passers-by.

The tram sheds at Liversedge and Savile Town were built by Messrs. Sam Drake & Garforth Bros. The Frost Hill depot at Liversedge had a fan of ten tracks, one of which further divided into two. Savile Town depot had a fan of six tracks into the car shed, and there was a single line in the yard between the tram sheds and the River Calder. It was a B.E.T. custom at this period to lay Vignoles rail in the depots instead of grooved rails, and there are pictures which show this, including one of No. 11 in Savile Town depot yard standing on ballasted open track as in railway permanent way. At least one length of this remained at Savile Town until the

No. 27, now top-covered, passing the Shoulder of Mutton Inn in Halifax Road, Batley, at the Dewsbury boundary. The steepest gradient on the system, 1 in 8, is to the left of the tram. The tram standard carries a white disc showing the number of the fare stage.   (F. Hartley

44

When the Dewsbury—Ravensthorpe route was extended to Fir Cottage (on 29 July 1903) cars showed "Fir Cottage" or "Shepley Bridge" to distinguish the new Ravensthorpe terminus from the original terminus at Scout Hill. Later all cars ran to the new terminus, displaying "Ravensthorpe".
(R. B. Parr)

extension to the sheds was made to accommodate the buses, in the early 1920s, but the depot was eventually relaid wholly in grooved rail. A paint shop and repair bay was added at the Frost Hill depot in 1904. The Frost Hill property was freehold, Savile Town was on a 999-year lease.

INSPECTION DATES

Route	Inspection Date	Date of Opening
Dewsbury to Thornhill	18 February 1903	18 February 1903
Dewsbury to Ravensthorpe (as far as the L.&Y.R. Station)	18 February 1903	15 March 1903
Dewsbury to Batley boundary (Halifax Rd.)	18 February 1903	18 April 1903
Moorend to Heckmondwike	24 April 1903	24 April 1903
Thorncliffe Road to Batley Borough boundary	24 April 1903	24 April 1903
Heckmondwike to Quarry Inn	24 April 1903	29 July 1903
Quarry Inn to Thorncliffe Rd.	28 July 1903	29 July 1903
Swan Inn Liversedge to Hightown	28 July 1903	29 July 1903
Ravensthorpe L.&Y.R. Station to Fir Cottage (terminus)	28 July 1903	29 July 1903
Batley Corporation Tramways	28 July 1903	26 October 1903
Swan Inn to Birkenshaw	13 October 1903	13 October 1903
Dewsbury to Hick Lane	23 November 1905	28 October 1905
Hick Lane to Gomersal (Bradford Rd./Oxford Rd. jn.).	23 November 1905	23 November 1905

BATLEY CORPORATION TRAMWAYS

As already mentioned on page 36, Batley Council wished to operate tramways itself, even though they would probably form part of a larger network. Plans for tramways to serve the borough were prepared, and in April 1900 the Board of Trade decided to sanction Batley Council's tramway scheme, subject to certain running powers for the Spen Valley Light Railway. Parliamentary sanction was obtained by the Batley Corporation Act 1901.

Details of the lines authorised to Batley Corporation are given in the Batley Corporation Tramways Order 1900. The system was to be a circular route from Hick Lane along Wellington Street, Purlwell Lane, Track Road and Thorncliffe Road to a junction with the Spen Valley Light Railway at Halifax Road. There was disagreement about the section in Staincliffe, where the tramway as originally planned by Batley Corporation would run parallel to the lines laid down by the B.E.T. as far as Common Road. As first mooted, each track was to take traffic working in both directions. Eventually an agreement was reached so that the Batley Corporation track would take the traffic going towards Dewsbury and the B.E.T. Company's track would take that going from Dewsbury to Heckmondwike, with suitable compensation for wear and tear on each set of metals. From Halifax Road the Batley Corporation system was to go along Common Road and then Healey Lane, Mayman Lane and Commercial Street with one branch to Batley Market Place terminus and the other via Henrietta Street and Branch Road to join the Bradford Road tramway. A depot was to be built in Mayman Lane.

The Corporation also wished to purchase, electrify and operate its portion of the (by then B.E.T.-owned) steam tramway in Bradford Road. The B.E.T., for its part, was only willing to sell if the Corporation would lease the lines back for the Company to operate. Batley countered this in November 1902 with an offer of mutual through running powers. The B.E.T. was to pay the Corporation 3d. for each time that one of the Company's cars passed over the Corporation's lines and the Corporation would pay 3d. for each time that one of their own cars passed over the Company's Light Railway. This sum was to cover the cost of the current supplied and the renewal of the rails and overhead equipment. After payment of these liabilities each party was then at liberty to take the whole of the receipts taken on their own cars. However, when an Agreement was drawn up the Company refused to sign it.

When agreement seemed near towards the end of 1902, the B.E.T. had promoted the Dewsbury, Batley and Birstal Tramways Bill. This would authorise the reconstruction and electrification of the (steam) tramways in the boroughs of Dewsbury and Batley and the Urban Districts of Gomersal, Birkenshaw, Soothill Upper and Birstall and their lease to the B.E.T. for 30 years. It also empowered Batley to construct a generating station at Valley Mills, estimated to cost £23,100, in addition to Batley's share of the tramway reconstruction cost, estimated at £44,100. The same Bill authorised a standard-gauge line from the Ravensthorpe terminus to the Huddersfield Corporation Tramways at Bradley.

There were many unresolved differences between the company and Batley Corporation, and in January 1903 the Electricity Committee of the Batley Corporation decided to make preparations to run their own municipal tramways. The lines already laid belonged to the Corporation, they would have a depot, and sample tramcars were to be inspected by a Committee, so if negotiations with the B.E.T. for a lease of the tramways fell through completely, the Council would be in a position to run its own cars. Alderman Hirst, Councillor Bagshaw and Councillor Ben Turner formed a deputation to go to Manchester and Preston to inspect tramcars with a view to selecting the best and most suitable cars for the district. The Company approached the Batley Corporation to try and induce it to withdraw its opposition to the Bill, but without avail, and it had to be fought out before a House of Lords Committee.

The Corporation's decision to purchase eight tramcars was announced in *The Light Railway and Tramway Journal* for 3 April 1903. Tenders were to be submitted to the Corporation's consulting engineers, Messrs. Lacey, Clirehugh and Sillar of Westminster, by 18 April. The successful tender was that of the Westinghouse company, who on 30 April were awarded a contract to supply eight electric tramcars with complete equipment, British Electric Car Co. Ltd. bodies and Brill trucks.

On 5 May 1903 five peers, with Lord Clifford of Chudleigh presiding, commenced sitting as a committee of the House of Lords to consider certain Parliamentary Bills, among them the Dewsbury, Batley & Birstal Tramways Bill promoted by the B.E.T. This sought powers to enable the local authorities of Dewsbury, Batley and Birstall, Soothill Upper, Birkenshaw and Gomersal to buy their respective portions of the tramways in Bradford Road and then lease them to the Company. The Company hoped that they would be able to come to terms with the Batley Corporation and obtain a lease of the tramways in the Borough, but the Corporation announced their intent to ask Parliament for the necessary sanction to enable them to run the tramways themselves. If the British Electric Traction Company then desired to run through the Borough on their lines, they must pay Batley Corporation for this privilege and also grant it running powers to Dewsbury and Birstall.

The breach between the two parties was now wider than ever, and the B.E.T. intended to hold their position without yielding anything to the Corporation. To do this they stated to the Lords' Committee that a connection could be made from Dewsbury to Gomersal and Birkenshaw without traversing the Bradford Road through Batley, i.e. via Halifax Road and the Spen Valley through Heckmondwike, and also that the distance would be no greater than that of going through Batley. There was further dispute about the purchase of the electrical energy to run the trams. The British Electric Traction Company maintained that they were allowed by law to purchase their power where they liked, whilst Batley Corporation maintained that it was against all justice for the company to be able to buy its power from anyone except the local authority through whose area the trams were to run, especially when that authority had gone to the expense of putting down the plant to supply that power.

Agreement was eventually reached, and the Bill was allowed to proceed; it received the Royal Assent on 11 August 1903. The agreement was that Batley Corporation would re-construct that portion of the Bradford Road tramway which passed through the Borough of Batley, i.e. from Batley Carr to a point opposite the gasworks at Birstall. They would lay a double track and equip the lines electrically. After completion, the whole undertaking would be leased to the B.E.T. for a period of 28 years. During the arguments there was a mention not only of the proposed extension towards Huddersfield, but also of another possible line through Liversedge to Clifton and almost to Brighouse, and other extensions from the Birkenshaw terminus.

There was also the question of the lines already laid in Batley and the eight tramcars which Batley Corporation had already bought. The B.E.T. agreed to take the latter into their own fleet without monetary loss to the Corporation. The B.E.T. were asked to run a 15 minute service of cars throughout the whole town. On this point Batley had to make a concession, this being that the British Electric Traction Company would run a service which must suit the convenience of the public. If this could not be met by the Company then the Batley Corporation would appeal to the Board of Trade.

A further point in the agreement made between the Corporation and the B.E.T. was that the B.E.T. was to provide and erect the electrical equipment of both the Light Railway and the Corporation Tramway in the Halifax Road section where both were to run side by side. This was to be on the span wire method in use on the Batley Corporation system. Each undertaking was to pay half the cost. The revised estimate of the proposed Batley Corporation Tramways was £50,644 and the Corporation was authorised to borrow £51,000 to cover the same. The total Batley Corporation mileage when completed would be 6.53 route miles (10.47 track miles).

When the agreement was reached with the Tramway Company the tracks had already been laid in Common Road; they were stated by the B.E.T. to be of no use to them, but the Company agreed that the Council should not bear the whole loss and agreed to contribute £2,000. The Company also agreed to pay the Corporation £1,150 in cash towards costs, to be paid when the Bill received the Royal Assent.

The Batley Corporation tracks were laid with steel girder rails 7 ins. deep and weighing 104 lb. per yard in 45 feet lengths. These latter figures are from the Board of Trade correspondence, but Garcke's Manual quoted Walter Scott and Co.'s rails at 102 lb. per yard in 60 feet lengths. Tiebars were of wrought iron, 8 feet apart, and rolled steel fishplates were used, on 3 ft. steel soleplates. Most paving was in granite setts, but some sections were wood paved with 6″ x 4″ Karri blocks, close joined by hot mastic. Rail bonds were supplied by Chicago, Crown and Columbia, with Cooper & Howard Smith's patent anchor rail joints. The overhead equipment was by British Insulated and Helsby.

The Batley system was mainly single line with passing places, with stretches of double line in Thorncliffe Road, Healey Lane, and Wellington Street. The radius of the sharpest curve on the system was 40 feet.

By July 1903 the lines were complete and awaiting inspection by the Board of Trade. There was some delay in the delivery of the Batley trams and this would delay starting the services unless the B.E.T. company would use some of their cars from Frost Hill or Savile Town depots, to help out. A trial run was made with a car from Savile Town depot on 22 July, and the official inspection was arranged for Tuesday, 28 July.

Arrangements had been made for two B.E.T. cars to start from the bottom of Hick Lane, Batley at 2 p.m., this being the most convenient spot for Major Druitt to board the cars after leaving the London train at Batley Station. There was as usual a large gathering of people to watch the proceedings. The Mayor of Batley (Alderman J. W. Turner) and the Town Clerk accompanied the Inspector from the railway station to Hick Lane, where they were met by representatives of Batley Town Council, municipal officials, representatives of the B.E.T and the companies who had carried out the various contracts.

However, the two cars which had been detailed to carry the inspector did not appear. News soon came through that they had been in collision in Purlwell Lane. As they descended Purlwell Lane the first car had slowed down, or was stopped, near the bottom of the hill, and the following car ran into it. It was thought that the Westinghouse magnetic brake had not acted quickly enough. The conductor of the first car was pitched into the road and broke his collar-bone, and both the drivers were badly shaken. Both cars were damaged and were not able to proceed on the tour of inspection; they were taken back to Frost Hill depot at Liversedge.

Two other B.E.T. cars were sent, one from the Halifax Road section and the other from Frost Hill, and the inspection finally got under way at about three o'clock, one hour late. Major Druitt rode on the top deck of the first car, together with the Mayor and several officials. The car came to a stand halfway up Hick Lane, because the sand boxes were not working satisfactorily, but was re-started by throwing a few handfuls of sand under the wheels. The same thing happened again near the junction of Clerk Green with Wellington Street, but the cars thereafter mounted Purlwell Lane easily, and even the steep hill leading to the Junction Inn was negotiated safely. Major Druitt suggested various road-widenings and the moving of a gas lamp, and imposed numerous speed limits. He was concerned that on some parts of the route there was only about ¾ in. clearance between the motor and the setts, which meant that with a heavy load of passengers there would be a risk of damaging the car or even throwing it off the rails. It was explained that service would not be commenced in Batley until the delivery of the new cars which were on order, the wheels of which were 1½ in. larger than those of the cars used in the trial. On the return journey, the cars traversed Healey Lane into Clerk Green, encountering a herd of cows, reversed back to the junction and followed Mayman Lane, Upper Commercial Street, Henrietta Street and Branch Road. Further rough riding was encountered, but it was due to the grooves not having been cleaned out.

The works specified by Major Druitt were carried out, but it was not until 26

October 1903, after the delivery of the Corporation's eight tramcars, that services could be commenced. The eight cars were included in the lease to the B.E.T., and although retaining Batley's own livery of green and cream, were numbered in the company's fleet and carried the B.E.T. magnet-and-wheel device. Until the steam tramway was electrified, together with Carlinghow depot, the eight Batley cars were kept at Frost Hill, Liversedge. Batley council had earlier planned to build a new depot in Mayman Lane, but it was altered during construction to serve as a fire station. The single line in Clerk Green would have given Hick Lane cars access to this depot.

So ended the feud which had served only to hold up the electrification of the Bradford Road lines, and which also delayed the opening of the Halifax Road section of the main line of the Spen Valley Light Railways. Contracts could now be placed for the conversion of the steam tramway, and work began early in 1905. Work that could be carried out without stopping the steam tram service was done first, and a photograph exists of a steam tram passing a gang digging a trench in which to lay the feeder cables under the pavement. Work on the track had to await its purchase by the local authorities in mid-1905, after which the steam trams ceased in stages as the final reconstruction began. The old steam tram sheds which the Dewsbury, Batley & Birstal Tramways had used at Carlinghow were taken over to house the electric trams, and were reconstructed for electric traction, reopening in time for the start of the full electric service on 23 November 1905. The eight Batley trams, which had been working from Frost Hill depot, were transferred to Carlinghow and thereafter provided the bulk of the service along the former steam tram route. In the intervening months, a special service of electric cars at a twopenny fare had been operated between Dewsbury and Batley via Halifax Road, using a double track curve laid in May 1905 from Halifax Road into Thorncliffe Road, but this presumably ceased when electric service commenced between Dewsbury and Hick Lane on 28 October, in advance of the throughout opening.

If Batley Corporation had become a tramway operator in its own right, Y.W.D. car No. 8 seen here leaving Dewsbury (Northgate) terminus for Birkenshaw would have been on a jointly-operated route shared with Batley cars, each operator granting running powers to the other. The shaded headlamp shows that this photograph was taken during the 1914-18 war.
(F. Hartley

The Yorkshire Woollen District electric tramway system was now complete, and no extensions were ever made. However, the routes as constructed left unserved the western part of the Borough of Dewsbury (known as Westborough) and the district along the main Dewsbury to Leeds road, to Shaw Cross.

Even when the first routes had only been open for a few weeks, the public were quick to see the advantages of this form of transport and on 16 May 1903 (which was before all the lines were built) there was a meeting of the ratepayers at Westborough, Dewsbury asking for an extension of the tramways to the Westborough and Dewsbury Moor areas of Dewsbury. The ratepayers suggested several different routes for consideration.

These routes were:—

(1) From Dewsbury Market Place up Willans Road, Moorlands Road, Boothroyd Lane and along Staincliffe Road to terminate at the Borough boundary there.

(2) As above, as far as Staincliffe Road, then along Healds Road to join the trunk line of the Spen Valley Light Railway near the Shoulder of Mutton Inn.

(3) Along the Ravensthorpe route as far as Temple Road and then along that road, round the western boundary of Crow Nest Park to Heckmondwike.

(4) As in (3) as far as Temple Road and along it and round the Borough Park and then along Staincliffe Road to the Butcher's Arms Inn in Halifax Road (Batley). This would have made a circular route.

(5) Along Halifax Road as far as Birkdale Road and up there to Westborough; this according to the report in the *Dewsbury Reporter* was the route most favoured.

Some of these routes were proposed in the Dewsbury Corporation Tramways Provisional Order of 1900, the earliest mention of new electric tramways in the Dewsbury Borough, in particular those in Birkdale Road, Temple Road and Heckmondwike Road. It is interesting to compare the routes proposed in the 1900 Order with the routes later proposed for the Dewsbury Corporation Tramways. The two sets of proposals are shown in map form on page 188.

From 1901 there was almost continuous agitation for trams to serve Westborough. The proposal for this tramway was later to get entangled with another for a tramway from Dewsbury Market Place to Shaw Cross on the main Dewsbury to Leeds Road. These two places which were situated on opposite sides of the town were to be connected by the same tramway running through the centre of the town.

In the meantime on 15 November 1903 a deputation from Soothill Upper Urban District Council appeared before the Dewsbury Town Council asking that they should co-operate in building a tramway from Dewsbury Market Place to Shaw Cross via Crackenedge Lane, and another from the Market Place to Shaw Cross along the main Dewsbury to Leeds main road as far as the Borough boundary. These two tramways would have provided a circular route. At this meeting a resolution was passed to apply to the Board of Trade for a Provisional Order under the Tramways Act 1870. No action appears to have been taken, in spite of the fact that the Soothill Upper Urban District Council were ready to adapt their scheme to anything which the Dewsbury Council put forward, to advance the construction of the tramway. They were finally to be disappointed.

As part of this scheme, the Soothill Upper Council decided that it would ask the Board of Trade for powers to construct a semi-circular tramway from the Dewsbury borough boundary at Shaw Cross through Hanging Heaton and along Crackenedge Lane to the Dewsbury boundary in that road. However it was suggested to the Council that the Crackenedge Lane section was impracticable due to the narrowness of the road. Dewsbury Town Council was so impressed by the objections put forward that it decided to withdraw the offer of co-operation, which left the Soothill Upper Council in a curious position. A line from Dewsbury to Shaw Cross, whilst offering facilities to many, would not be of much value to a large number of ratepayers in the Hanging Heaton and Crackenedge districts, and so Soothill was not able to proceed with its scheme. Another inspection of the route was made and they decided to ask the Board of Trade to grant powers to lay the circular line in the form originally suggested, leaving out the portion in Crackenedge Lane which was outside their area. It was hoped by this move to provide at least some public transport for inhabitants of Shaw Cross and Hanging Heaton, but in the event they had to wait until the advent of motor buses.

During 1903-4, at least three Yorkshire (Woollen District) cars were lent to the Barnsley and District Electric Traction Company, which was under the same local management. Photographs (taken in Barnsley) exist of Y.W.D. car 19 in open top state and of cars 20 (above) and 29 with top covers. (Commercial postcard, courtesy R. Brook

CHAPTER THREE

THE YORKSHIRE WOOLLEN DISTRICT TRAMWAYS, FROM 1904 TO 1934

By the start of 1904 the Spen Valley Light Railways, operated by the Yorkshire (Woollen District) Electric Tramways Company, had been completed and a total of seventeen miles of track was now being served by 58 cars.

Once the Y.W.D. cars were on the lines, there were a few teething troubles, mainly with cars which got out of control, and these accidents sometimes led to renumbering of cars, thereby helping to confuse the fleet list. This happened with No. 55 of the Batley Corporation fleet when still in open-top condition. This accident occurred on 16 January 1904 in Track Road on the Thorncliffe Road section of the system. The car left the rails at the sharp curve which forms a "T" junction between Thorncliffe Road and Track Road Batley. As soon as the car left the rails it careered into a stone wall which it demolished and it finished up in the grounds of a house, with its front end smashed in. The driver and two passengers were injured. The car was soon brought back to the rails and before any of the mechanism had been touched, the Westinghouse magnetic brake was tested as it had been presumed that the accident was caused by the failure of this brake to act in time. In spite of the fact that the controller was dislocated and the front of the platform, dashboard, etc. badly broken up, it worked perfectly. Later Major Druitt,

Batley car 55 in the garden of "Hurstlands" after the runaway of 16 January 1904. The car left the rails at the corner of Thorncliffe Road and Track Road. This car later carried the number 60.
(Courtesy Mrs. G. Field

Y.W.D. car No. 7 after its accident in Dewsbury on 20 May 1904. This was one of the first cars to be fitted with a top cover.   (F. Hartley

the Board of Trade inspector, carried out an investigation of the accident and in his report published later stated "Taking all the evidence available into consideration I do not think there was any failure of the Westinghouse brake, but the car got out of hand owing to the motor-man approaching the corner at too high a speed and failing to apply the brakes in sufficient time to check the car". Another report says that the driver made the wrong brake connections. The car after renovation was renumbered 60, and one of the short single-deck cars took the number 55. This interchange of numbers occurred on other systems, due to superstition after a serious accident.

Another accident occurred on 20 May 1904 when car No. 7, which by this date had received a top-cover, got out of control in Halifax Road Dewsbury at Carlton Road on the downward journey. Though this car was fitted with hand brakes on the wheels, Westinghouse electric brake and Spencer Scotch brake the car careered down the hill and collided with several carts and drays in succession and finally with a Birkenshaw car which was proceeding down Northgate. By the Rose and Crown Inn some distance below Carlton Road the trolley came off the wire. The presence of the Birkenshaw car at the Market Place end of Northgate is interesting, as these cars later turned back clear of the junction, near Bradford Road. At the first collision the driver was thrown off the car but the passengers were unhurt although two tram drivers, two conductors and the driver of one of the drays were more or less severely hurt.

Again Major Druitt attributed the accident to the driver of the tram losing his head and not to the failure of the braking mechanism which was found to be in perfect order. He stated that a much higher standard of training was required to operate an electrically worked brake than for those who had to use a purely mechanical one. This point needed attention. The report gave the impression that an electric brake would take longer to act than a mechanical one and drivers need not be troubled with the theoretical side of the working so long as they could use them. Neither a mechanical nor a power brake would bring a car which is out of control to rest immediately.

There were several other minor collisions and one or two people were injured by the cars in the early days. There was also considerable antagonism between the old

The junction of Halifax Road and Northgate in Dewsbury, with a car for Cleckheaton climbing the gradient in Halifax Road down which car No. 7 ran away on 20 May 1904. The Bradford Road car in the distance under the railway arch is going to Birstall or Birkenshaw after reversing at its terminus at the crossover just visible in this photograph, beneath the crossover wire.
(F. Hartley

horse cab men and the new electric cars. This went on for a considerable time after the trams were underway. We read that in August 1906 Edward Farrance, a very well-known "cabby" in Dewsbury, was fined for obstructing a tram up Halifax Road Dewsbury. He chose to drive his cab very slowly up the steepest part of the hill in front of the tram and took no heed of the driver ringing his bell. The car was going so slowly that it was in danger of sliding back. Once on the level and at a point where the road was wider the car overtook the cab and as it did so the "cabby" lashed out at the conductor with his whip. This was not the first time that this sort of thing had happened. Eventually these people settled down and accepted the trams.

By September 1904 the Y.W.D. were thinking of using double-deck cars for the Ravensthorpe route and wrote to the Board of Trade to this effect. The trouble was the clearance of the L.N.W.R. bridge in Webster Hill; this had the least clearance of the two bridges on the route. The minimum height from the rails at the upper end of the bridge was 15 ft. 2 ins. and the height of the trolley wire 14 ft. 7 ins. The clearance between the top deck and the underside of the bridge would only be 5 ft. 3 ins. whereas the Board of Trade required a minimum of 6 ft. 6 ins.

Preparations were made for running double-deckers through the bridge, and at least one car had its trolley standard and destination boards lowered for this purpose. This was probably the illuminated car used for the Dewsbury County Borough celebrations, as a photograph exists of this car with a very low trolley standard and with the destination boxes fitted between the hand rail and the decency panels at each end of the car, instead of being fitted on stands above the handrail. In addition suitable notices were to be placed on the upper deck of the car and also on the bridge warning passengers not to touch the trolley wire, and the conductors would be specially instructed to be on the upper deck of the cars while they were passing under the bridge (it does not say whether they would be seated or otherwise) to warn passengers of the danger. However the Board of Trade would not sanction the use of double-deck cars on this route and so it remained a single-deck route throughout its existence.

In the early months of 1905 there were continual grumbles by the draymen about the granite setts used in the tramways and another plea for the use of Yorkshire setts was made. Also there were complaints that the existence of the tram tracks prevented draymen "zig-zagging" their way up Webster Hill and other hills with their loads.

In May 1905 a letter was sent from the Y.W.D. to the Board of Trade asking for permission to run a demi-car, and enclosing a blueprint giving details. The system of control was Raworth's Regenerative and in addition there were both wheel and mechanical track brakes. It was to seat 22 passengers, 14 inside and 8 outside. The hinged bar between the platform seats and driver's compartment is shown. The Board insisted that the car be fitted with a special electric brake to prevent run-backs, and wished to make sure that the lifting of the hinged bar at the driver's platform would cut off the current from the motors as in the Southport demi-car. These details were attended to later the same month and a new life-guard had been fitted. On 22 May 1905 the Board gave its official sanction for the car to be put into use. This car was the only one on the Y.W.D. to have vestibules and be fitted with windscreens. It appears only to have run until September 1905 on the Y.W.D. system, before being transferred to Barnsley.

It would seem in fact that the demi-car had already been running for the best part of the year, for the directors on 28 September 1904 recorded their approval of the economies it offered in power consumption and decided to place an order for eight sets of Raworth's regenerative equipment. This arose from a dispute between the company and Heckmondwike Urban District Council about the supply of electricity from the Council. The company were entitled to take a maximum of 100 kilowatts, and the power station breaker was apparently set at this load, but at busy times when the load increased the breaker tripped leaving the trams without any power. In view of the steep hills and the Board of Trade requirement that the cars should be fitted with an electric run-back brake, the company considered this a safety hazard and the Board wrote to the Council, but the Council refused to give way. The company then decided to fit regenerative equipment to the six single deck cars used on the Hightown route, and J. S. Raworth joined the Y.W.D. board. By November 1905 Heckmondwike power station was complaining about erratic readings on their meters due to the use of regenerative control on the trams, and

Demi-car 59 on the Heckmondwike to Hightown service in 1905, photographed in Bradford Road, Millbridge where cars on this service had to reverse before proceeding to Hightown. This car was sold to Barnsley later in 1905. (Courtesy C. Wood

Dewsbury Corporation asked the company to indemnify them against damage to their plant from the same source. The company maintained its position until Heckmondwike gave way in 1909 on the question of maximum load, after which the directors on 13 October 1909 decided that the cars would be reconverted to series-parallel control. J. S. Raworth resigned his Y.W.D. directorship in the same year. The original cause of the dispute was a mistake by the consulting engineer, who had underrated the maximum demand, an error which limited the Hightown service to one car uphill and one downhill at any time. From 1912, economy in power consumption was assisted by fitting certain cars with Venners meters.

Small regenerative-control car 55 at Moorend terminus. This car was originally numbered 60, but exchanged numbers with Batley car 55 after the latter's accident at "Hurstlands" in January 1904.

(Commercial postcard, Jackson & Son

As stated in previous chapters, the route of the Dewsbury, Batley and Birstal company was purchased in 1905 by the local authorities through which the line ran and then leased to the B.E.T. who in turn transferred the lease to the Yorkshire (W.D.) Company. There were now 69 tramcars operating on 22 miles of track and the main line extended from Thornhill in the south (at Combs Pit) through Thornhill Lees, Dewsbury Market Place, Halifax Road, Staincliffe, Heckmondwike Market Place, Liversedge, Littletown, Cleckheaton Market Place to Moorend. Two routes branched from Liversedge, one westwards past the Council Offices to Hightown (Board Schools) and the second north through Five Lane Ends, past California Works, High Top Gomersal and Moor Lane to Half Way House Birkenshaw to connect with Bradford Corporation Tramways. The electrified D.B.&B. line, referred to above, left the main line at Dewsbury Market Place and passed through Batley Carr, Soothill, Batley, Birstall and Gomersal, before linking with the Birkenshaw line. The Batley Corporation lines linked the main line with the D.B.&B. line at Heckmondwike, Staincliffe, Branch Road and Hick Lane.

The extension to Tong Cemetery was not proceeded with as Bradford Corporation acted first in extending their own tramway from Tong Cemetery to Birkenshaw, and through running was not possible because of the change of gauge, the Bradford gauge being 4 ft. 0 in. The Bradford tramway to Birkenshaw was opened on 30 September 1903, a fortnight before the Y.W.D. tramway from Cleckheaton on 13 October. In July 1904 the B.E.T. Gazette reported the introduction of through tickets from the Y.W.D. system to Bradford, and on 1 January 1905, arrangements were made for a joint parcels service with Bradford City Tramways, parcels being exchanged between cars at Birkenshaw terminus. This was later extended to the Dewsbury & Ossett and West Riding tramways, and Bradford's 1909 tramway handbook quotes parcel rates to Y.W.D. and West Riding destinations, but not to Leeds. The Leeds tramways did not at that time offer parcels facilities, but Mr. Paris stated at a conference that tramway parcels could be sent between Bradford and Leeds via Dewsbury and Wakefield. It is doubtful whether this through facility was much used.

In August 1905, the B.E.T. asked leave to abandon the proposed extensions of the line from Cleckheaton to Hartshead Moor and Hightown Heights. Despite protests from the Cleckheaton Tradesmen's Association, it would seem that the Cleckheaton end of the system was not very profitable. The most profitable section was the Dewsbury one. The Gomersal section (Liversedge to Birkenshaw) after a capital expenditure of approximately £41,000 showed a profit for the six months ending 30 June 1905 of only £146 (without provision for depreciation). The company was therefore losing heavily on this section of the tramways. The profit for the whole concern was not good during 1903 and 1904, being respectively £5,184 12s. 1d. and £1,906 13s. 2d. The company had expended a capital of about £300,000 and the profit for 1903 was only 2½% and for 1904 less than 1%.

Late in 1906 the problem came up of the payment of rates by the Y.W.D. to the various local councils. Thornhill and Heckmondwike councils were in the front of the attack. They had to wait until a decision was made in the case of the Wakefield & District Light Railway, as to what exactly was the position of these tramways in law. It was decided that a Light Railway was to be regarded as a railway and not as a tramway, and was therefore assessed at a quarter of the nett amount of the district rate.

The question of the overcrowding of the cars was under consideration as early as January 1907, and also the lack of a queue system at the boarding points. As it was, the crowd simply rushed on the tram when it had disgorged its passengers at the terminus. On 5 January 1907 Mr. Tom Myers (a Thornhill councillor) said that shortly before the previous Christmas he had travelled on a car carrying 75 passengers which number included the Thornhill Prize Band with all its instruments! Mr. Myers went on to state sarcastically that the Council ". . . would judge that the car was in a very "comfortable" state (laughter!)".

By July 1907 the Y.W.D. gave official notice that application would be made to the Board of Trade for the transfer of the undertakings authorised by the Morley & District Light Railways (Extensions) Order 1902, and such portion of the undertaking authorised by the Spen Valley Light Railway (Extensions) Order 1902 which had not been constructed, from the B.E.T. to a new Company to be known as the Leeds & Bradford District Tramways Ltd. It was proposed that the new company should have running powers over the lines of the Y.W.D. system from Cleckheaton and Hightown to Heckmondwike and through Gomersal to Birkenshaw, to enable the company to connect with the unconstructed portions of the railways authorised by the Spen Valley Light Railway (Extensions) Order 1901, which would be transferred to them. The intention was to proceed with the construction of the lines from Leeds to Morley and from there to Drighlington in the first instance. It was further proposed that the new company should apply for extension of the authorised Morley Tramways through Birstall by a line joining the authorised Hartshead Moor line and then by another extension to Brighouse. Drighlington and Gildersome councils approached the Leeds City Corporation asking that it continue its tramways from the city boundary along Whitehall Road and Gelderd Road to Drighlington and Gildersome. None of these lines was built and in July 1910 the Y.W.D. company obtained powers to abandon the unconstructed portions of the lines comprised in the Spen Valley and Morley and Spen Valley (Extensions) Order.

There was considerable trouble about workmen's fares in the early days. To get workmen's fares the workmen had to look like workmen, as the following story

Two Dewsbury to Thornhill cars on the single track approaching South Street in Savile Road, Dewsbury. This track was laid off-centre and doubling was proposed in 1909, but not carried out. On the right behind the cars is the Savile Hotel, which stood at the corner of the approach to Savile Town depot. The photograph was taken from another tram waiting to enter the single line. (F. Hartley

illustrates. Two workmen were travelling on the car from Thorncliffe Road to Batley, one wearing a collar and the other a handkerchief round his neck. The man with the collar paid 1d. and the man with the handkerchief was let off with ½d. And they were both colliers! Clerks wearing white collars were also charged full fares, though in many cases they were drawing less wages than the manual workers.

In July 1907 the question arose concerning the duty on hackney carriages and whether the cars running in Dewsbury were such. After considerable discussion it was decided that these light railways should be regarded as street railways and not tramways and the conclusion arrived at was that this was a railway within the meaning of the Act and that these carriages not being propelled elsewhere than on a railway, were not subject to payment of duty.

In May 1909, after the opening of the Dewsbury, Ossett and Soothill Nether Tramways connecting Dewsbury and Ossett, Mr. Paris agreed to contact the other tramway managers in the area about the possibility of arranging for the issue of circular tour tickets. There was now a circular route of tramways from Dewsbury to Wakefield via Ossett, from Wakefield to Leeds and on to Bradford. From Bradford a car could be boarded for Birkenshaw where contact was made with the Y.W.D. From Birkenshaw a tram could be taken back to Dewsbury. These circular tours were quite popular, but as remembered by the author six separate bookings had to be made.

There was a proposal in June 1909 that part of the land which was not being used as car sheds at Savile Town be let off as a roller skating rink, but nothing appears to have come of the suggestion. In October it was proposed that the tram track between the Savile Hotel Dewsbury and the Cricket Field be doubled but nothing ever came of it.

In March 1910 there was some discussion of possible through-running to Bradford, in spite of the difference in gauges of the tracks of the two systems.

Special cars would have had to be built so that at Birkenshaw the wheels of the trucks could slide to accommodate themselves to the other gauge, as did happen at Stanningley on the Leeds—Bradford route, but the suggestion was allowed to lapse.

Soon after this an increase in tram fares led to many people walking to their work rather than pay the extra money. As one correspondent to the local paper stated, "The B.E.T. has put its fares up and Dewsbury people walk. Emile Garcke has learnt one thing, and that is that to increase fares is one thing, but it is another to get them". This trouble even caused Thornhill Urban District Council to approach the Lancashire & Yorkshire Railway to introduce a penny fare between Dewsbury and Thornhill, so as to secure better facilities from the Y.W.D. Tramway Co., but eventually Dewsbury people accepted the increased fares which the people of the Potteries protested against successfully. All this happened during the early months of 1910, under the aegis of the B.E.T. "Fair Fare" system.

So many letters were published by the local press about the increase in tram fares that Mr. Arthur Forest was prompted to write suggesting that "Instead of all this fault finding, snarling and cavilling, let us work together for a "Tramways Sunday" with collections at all the churches and chapels throughout the district on behalf of these benefactors of mankind". It is hardly likely that the religious bodies referred to would have been pleased to donate a Sunday's collections to help the tramways! During this year there was correspondence in the local paper urging protection for the drivers of the trams. In spite of the experience gained by the demi-car, none of the other cars of the fleet were ever vestibuled and the conditions of the men at the front remained as before, very grim in winter.

In May 1911 the question of through-running from Thornhill to Batley and Thornhill to Heckmondwike came up. There were two reasons for not doing this. Ignoring the Ravensthorpe route, where only single-deck cars could run, the rest of the Y.W.D. system was more or less in the shape of a letter "Y" with Thornhill at the foot and Moor End on the left "arm" and Birkenshaw on the other. It was

The standard Yorkshire Woollen District tram had 56 seats (34 on top, 22 inside) but this pre-1914 picture of No. 17 on a Sunday School outing at Gomersal shows nearly eighty children, teachers and parents, plus the crew. Private hire, then as now, was a useful source of revenue.   (F. Hartley

59

Although the Thornhill and Cleckheaton routes met end-on at Dewsbury Market Place, and were worked by similar cars, there was no through running until Savile Town depot closed to trams in 1931. Thornhill and Ravensthorpe cars turned back on the west track and Cleckheaton cars on the east track. The photograph dates from 1904-6, before the hinged doors to the top covers were replaced by sliding doors. (F. Hartley

argued in the Council that because of the distance of the Batley/Birkenshaw terminus from that of the Thornhill cars in Dewsbury, cars were often missed and great delay ensued. But the argument against the through running was that cars running through from both Birkenshaw and Cleckheaton to Thornhill would give the latter about a 5-minute service which it did not warrant. There was no mention of the fact that the Bradford Road cars were not fitted with track brakes. Councillor McCann brought to light another point, that the moment a car left the Bradford Road and proceeded into Northgate it ceased to travel on a tramway and was now on a light railway. Cars and men were both licensed differently for these two types of traffic.

On 8 March 1913 the Manager of the Bradford Corporation Tramways again wrote to the Y.W.D. Company to see if it would be willing to participate in through-running between Dewsbury and Bradford. The Dewsbury Town Council had no objection to this scheme provided that if and when it did take place, the present terminus of the Batley and Birkenshaw cars would be moved from Northgate into the Market Place. This was rather an "about face" for the Town Council as hitherto their policy was against "cluttering up" the Market Place with trams.

Negotiations between Dewsbury Corporation and the National Electric Construction Company were entered into for working the proposed Dewsbury Moor to Shaw Cross routes in October 1913. Four 16-seat Daimler motor buses were purchased in 1913, and inaugurated a service from Cleckheaton to Scholes, and a link between Ravensthorpe tram terminus and that of the Huddersfield tramways at Bradley. A garage was erected at the Savile Town Depot to accommodate them. Two more Daimler buses were ordered in March 1914, and in July of that year an offer was made by the Yorkshire Woollen District tramways to run a bus service between Golcar and Milnsbridge (Huddersfield) for £5 a day. If this venture had matured this small bus service would have been in complete isolation from the tramway routes. Instead, a service was introduced from Morley to Cleckheaton and

Most Yorkshire Woollen District double deck cars had received top covers by about 1913, but a few remained open-top until 1923. One is shown in this view at Dewsbury Market Place, in which car 35 has the headlamp hood fitted during the 1914-18 war. (F. Hartley

Brighouse, on which a bus overturned at Clifton Common on 16 October 1915, causing three deaths. During 1915 the six buses carried over 807,000 passengers, and in 1917 the vehicles were altered to run on coal gas carried in a bag on the roof.

In December 1914 the local tramways contract tickets were withdrawn and the Ravensthorpe special workmen's trams were stopped. This was presumably an early effect of the War. In May 1915 a Halifax tram overturned and there were complaints about the speed of the Y.W.D. trams descending Lees Hall Road from Thornhill. There were statements that 30 miles/h was reached and that the cars rocked and swayed dangerously. This was denied by drivers who pointed out the Board of Trade compulsory stop at the top of the hill. Women conductors were also authorised at this time.

The Company like the Dewsbury and Ossett suffered a severe shortage of manpower due to the war, but not to the same extent as the latter company. On 5 March 1917 there was a fire at Frost Hill Depot, causing severe damage to two single-deck cars. By August 1918 they were compelled to reduce the number of cars in service and as far as possible cater for the long distance travellers, and with this aim in view all short-distance fares were increased from 1d. to 1½d. after 7 p.m. and after 2 p.m. on Saturdays and 1 p.m. on Sundays. Despite this, the number of passengers rose to 14,863,000 in 1918, two million more than in 1916. From April 1919 all penny stages were abolished on the tramways. The new fares were confirmed by an Order issued on 21 July 1920 under the Tramways (Temporary Increase of Charges) Act 1920.

Later that year in August came the plea from Sir Eric Geddes to conserve coal, and with this end in view Batley Town Council met Mr. Paris, asking that the tram services be cut so as to operate from 9 a.m. to 10 p.m. each day with no Sunday services. It does not seem that this was done.

Just after the war there was a brief revival of interest in tramway extensions, possibly because the Y.W.D. tramways were now quite profitable (paying a 6 per cent dividend in 1919), whereas the motor buses were still experimental. *The Tramway and Railway World* for 5 June 1919 records that Dewsbury town council had agreed to support a Y.W.D. proposal for a tramway link between Dewsbury and Leeds, but the plan does not seem to have survived a subsequent decline in profits.

Six more buses were ordered on 15 April 1919, but the Board then changed its mind and decided on 19 October to dispose of its bus operation to the Barnsley & District Traction Co. Ltd., together with a lease of part of Savile Town depot. Instead, the bus services were closed down completely on 27 February 1921, and two of the buses were rebuilt as maintainance vehicles for the tramway permanent way and overhead. The tramways, in contrast, carried their highest-ever traffic in 1920. (16,506,293 passengers, half as many again as in 1914).

Between December 1919 and July 1920, twelve single deck cars were purchased by Y.W.D. from Sheffield Corporation. These cars took over the Batley local service (Hick Lane—Thorncliffe Road) releasing some double-deck cars, which enabled the Cleckheaton—Moorend section to be incorporated in the main through service from Dewsbury. The Sheffield cars also took over the Heckmondwike—Hightown service, releasing the small former regenerative cars, which were offered for sale (without result). From March, 1922 the Thorncliffe Road—Hick Lane cars were extended through to Dewsbury via Bradford Road each afternoon and evening, sometimes with double-deckers.

A new manager, Major J. F. Chapple, DSO, succeeded Mr. E. A. Paris in July 1921. As on most tramways, the rolling stock was in a very poor state after the War and the new manager had the job of getting the fleet back into good order again. The variations of livery will be dealt with under another heading, but here let it suffice to say that under Major Chapple complete restoration of the fleet took place and a new standard livery introduced, maroon lined white and black and a very light

Twelve single-deck cars were purchased by Yorkshire Woollen District from Sheffield Corporation in 1919 and 1920. They were kept at Frost Hill depot and were used on the Batley—Thorncliffe Road and Heckmondwike—Hightown routes. This view of No. 76 still in its Sheffield livery of navy blue and cream also shows the distinctive overhead poles adopted by Batley Corporation. (J. G. D. Whitaker

Y.W.D. No. 26 in all-grey livery soon after the 1914-18 war. The scene is in Halifax Road, Dewsbury, at the Board of Trade compulsory stop opposite St. Mark's Church. The driver is applying the track brake before descending the 1 in 9 gradient from Oxford Road towards Dewsbury. (J. G. D. Whitaker

Y.W.D. No. 26 in final livery at Heckmondwike Market Place, about 1930. The third track was used as the terminus of the Heckmondwike—Hightown service. (Lilywhite Ltd

On a system as hilly as that of Yorkshire (Woollen District) Electric Tramways, runaways were bound to happen from time to time. This one involved a car of the 66-69 class on the Ravensthorpe route in the 1920s. The company's strictest disciplinarian, Inspector Tolley, is standing alongside. (F. Hartley

chrome yellow (custard) unlined and edged black. A rail grinder was purchased by the company in April 1922 at a cost of £250, and motor bus operation was reintroduced with new Leyland vehicles in the same month.

During 1924 there was further trouble about overcrowding of cars and at a Dewsbury Town Council meeting it was explained that one of the sources of trouble was that some of the tramways in the County Borough were built under the Tramways Act 1870 which forbade standing passengers and others were constructed under the Light Railways Act of 1896. It was finally agreed to limit the standing passengers to one-third of the seating capacity of the lower deck.

Because the fleet included insufficient long single-deck cars to cope with the traffic on the Dewsbury—Ravensthorpe route, two more were built at Frost Hill workshop in 1924-5 by using parts of four small cars, as described in Chapter Four. One of these was decorated and illuminated for Dewsbury Shopping Week from September 3 to 10, 1925. Several cars received new Brush trucks at the same period, and the year 1925 also saw the doubling of the track in Huddersfield Road from Quarry Road to Scout Hill. On completing the work, Dewsbury Corporation charged Y.W.D. an increased rent.

The company's receipts for 1924 were £514.980, against £451,778 in 1923. There were suggestions that the company should reduce fares, but a new agreement was reached with Batley Corporation under which Batley would not oppose the continuance of the existing Y.W.D. fares for so long as Y.W.D. continued to pay Batley 0.25 pence per unit more for electricity than the price specified in the lease.

The motor bus side of the undertaking was now expanding steadily. In 1924, the 11 buses carried 2,467,656 passengers, compared with 15,294, 169 passengers carried by the 80 trams. The company was less troubled by competition than were its neighbour undertakings, since Major Chapple was able to demonstrate to the local councils that the indiscriminate granting of bus licences could adversely affect the revenue which the councils derived from the tramways. A joint bus service with Huddersfield Corporation was instituted on 15 March 1926 from Dewsbury to Huddersfield, following a route once proposed for a tramway. This caused the company to press for permission to run its buses into Halifax instead of being forced to deposit passengers at the Hippersholme terminus of the Halifax tramways.

The expansion of the bus fleet required suitable premises to house and repair the vehicles. Extensions were made at Savile Town in 1925 and 1928, and a new bus garage was built at Swallow Street, Heckmondwike. Where further space was required in 1931, a decision was taken to concentrate the tram fleet at the large ten-road depot at Frost Hill, Liversedge and hand over Savile Town to the buses (the former tram depot became a bus repair shop). Since the ex-steam depot at Carlinghow could only accommodate a maximum of 15 cars, this meant that the Ravensthorpe and Thornhill cars would now be based at Liversedge, and through running was therefore instituted in the autumn of 1931 from Cleckheaton to Thornhill via Dewsbury to reduce the need for depot journeys.

This transfer caused considerable hardship for the drivers and conductors, and one man, Sam Wood, who lived at Ravensthorpe had to walk across the fields to the Frost Hill depot at Liversedge, some three miles away, before starting his day's work at 5.30 a.m. and when on late shift he had the same distance to trudge back from the depot to Ravensthorpe after the last car at night, there being no staff buses.

The last five open top Y.W.D. cars were given top covers in 1923-24. Two of them, 10 and 30, received top covers with four windows instead of flvo, each with a hinged ventilator. This view shows No. 30 in Heckmondwike Market Place on October 3, 1931, shortly after through running had commenced between Cleckheaton and Thornhill.   (S. L. Smith

The Final Days of the Tramways

As the last years of the second decade of the twentieth century were approaching, both the company and the local councils were aware that the time was drawing near when the leases would expire. The Company was operating 22.7 miles of tramways of which 11.82 were owned by it and 9.75 were leased to it from local authorities under five leases, three of which were due to expire in 1933 and two in 1940. The track was fast wearing out, and complaints began to appear in the local press as to its condition.

At a meeting held in Dewsbury on 19 April 1929 the directors of the Company told the local authorities that they might be willing to dispose of the whole of the tramway and omnibus undertaking, subject to terms and conditions being satisfactory and mutually arranged. Meanwhile in December 1929 the London Midland and Scottish Railway and the London & North Eastern Railway had acquired a joint interest in the Yorkshire (W.D.) Electric Tramways and a working agreement was entered into with the railway companies for the co-ordination of rail and road interests in the area covered by the Company.

Frost Hill depot, Liversedge, in 1932, with three of the single deck cars from the Dewsbury—Ravensthorpe route, based here after the closure of Savile Town depot. Nos. 6 and 55 were Y.W.D. rebuilds from older vehicles.   (Dr. Hugh Nicol

In January 1930 the question of taking over the Dewsbury and Ossett Tramways was discussed and in April an agreement with the National Electric Construction Company was drawn up in which the Y.W.D. would pay a due proportion of the receipts to N.E.C. who would credit Y.W.D. with average operating expenses. An agreement between the two companies was completed in July 1930 and the settlement of the capital charges at ½d. per mile was agreed upon. In 1930 the Dewsbury Corporation asked the Company if it would still be prepared to sell the undertaking, but the Company stated that due to the fact that the railway companies had now become interested and were substantial shareholders, and had appointed nominees to the Board of Directors, the circumstances had changed considerably and the Company now declined to sell. The Dewsbury Council had "missed the boat" by a few months.

On 22 September 1930 in a letter to the Town Clerk of Dewsbury, the Company put forward its proposals for a gradual changeover from tramways to omnibuses and suggested that these should form a basis for discussion. There were protracted negotiations between the company and the local authorities and it was finally agreed that the local authorities would support a Parliamentary Bill to be promoted by the Company, providing for the abandonment of the tramways and for the substitution of a service of buses being operated by the Company. Meanwhile there was correspondence between the Town Clerks of Dewsbury and Batley to determine whether the authorities should take over and retain the tramways. At the Conference of local authorities meeting on 3 October 1930 it became clear that of all the local authorities affected, Batley was the only one which could run a tramway system, if need be, as it was the only one which had the cars as well as a depot, electrical equipment and lines. In November 1933 when the lease expired, Batley would find itself in the position of possessing a more or less self-contained tramway system with sufficient rolling stock, depots and equipment to come within the definition of "a local authority operating a tramway undertaking". On that date the Company would cease to have power to run tramways anywhere else in the Borough of Batley except along the Company's Light Railway lines in Halifax Road. So the position of Batley both from a legal and practical point of view offered few difficulties.

With Dewsbury this was not the case. A substantial proportion of the tramways in the County Borough were owned by the Company, namely Scout Hill to Ravensthorpe and practically the whole of the line from Savile Bridge to the Thornhill terminus. There were also several lengths of light railway in Heckmondwike, Spen Valley and Birkenshaw which depended for their usefulness on being connected with other light railways in the County Borough area belonging to the Corporation and the Company. The Company could not be compelled to sell their lines in the County Borough area to the Corporation. If the Dewsbury Corporation refused to renew the lease of the Corporation lines to the Company and the Company desired to continue working their light railway system through to Heckmondwike and Cleckheaton after the expiration of the lease in 1933, the Corporation must grant it running powers over the light railways of the Corporation upon such terms and conditions as may be "fair and reasonable between the Corporation and the Company". As the Dewsbury lease did not include any depot nor was there any provision for the taking over of any of the rolling stock, a depot, rolling stock etc., would therefore have to be provided unless arrangements could be made with Batley for the joint use of that Corporation's depot and rolling stock, assuming that Batley Corporation were willing.

Dewsbury Corporation was left with the following alternatives:

(1) To purchase by agreement the lines in the County Borough area which belonged to the Company and make arrangements to run them themselves, obtaining their own rolling stock and depot. In this connection it was assumed that should Batley become a local authority operating a tramway, then it would be possible for Dewsbury to arrange with Batley (and possibly Birstall) for through-running powers and interchange of traffic.

(2) Not to purchase any further tramways but to buy rolling stock (or with the help of rolling stock of the Batley Corporation and by suitable arrangements with that Corporation) to provide tramway services between Scout Hill and/or Savile Bridge and the Borough Boundary in Halifax Road and Bradford Road. This could be taken as making the Corporation a "tramway operating authority" for the purposes of the Act.

There seemed nothing to prevent Birstall U.D.C. becoming, on the expiration of the lease in 1933, a local authority operating a tramway in respect of the lines within the U.D.C. area. They would have to provide rolling stock, depot etc. Here again some arrangement between Birstall U.D.C. and Batley Corporation would be a way round Birstall's difficulty in providing a depot and rolling stock. Birkenshaw's lease of line (about 18 yards) did not expire until 1940 but being so short it is difficult to see how this authority would have been able to put forward any workable scheme to become a local authority operating a tramway.

Even if Dewsbury did take the steps indicated, the length of lines operated would be considerably smaller than those worked by the Company. In any case Ravensthorpe would be cut off from Dewsbury as far as tramway transport was concerned. Even if all the authorities were willing to become tramway operating local authorities, it did not follow, as a matter of course, that they would be able to run buses under the Road Traffic Act of 1930. However keen the local authorities showed themselves to be to run an omnibus service, there appeared little prospect of the existing vested interests of the Company in the matter being extinguished or restricted merely because the local authorities decided to take the necessary steps to invest themselves with powers to run omnibuses.

The company's Bill was deposited in Parliament in November 1930. During the early part of 1931 there was a great deal of disagreement and dissention among the members of the Dewsbury Town Council as to that Council's attitude. One section supported the company's Bill, but the other opposed it and was of the opinion that the Corporation should seek powers to operate its own transport. The Council eventually decided that it would support the company's Bill, but this was not to be the end of it. A number of members of the Council who were opposed to the Bill formed a "splinter group" which was led by Mr. Ben Riley, the Labour M.P. for

Y.W.D. car 34 outside Frost Hill depot, about a year before the closure of the service from Birkenshaw to Batley Market Place via Heckmondwike in March, 1934.
(Science Museum, Whitcombe Collection

Dewsbury at that time. Mr. Riley gained some support from fellow members of the House of Commons and was successful in delaying the second reading of the Bill.

Despite all the opposition, the company's Bill was passed and received the Royal Assent on 8 July 1931, as the Yorkshire (Woollen District) Transport Act 1931. This Act scheduled an agreement dated 16 April 1931 by which the Corporations of Batley and Dewsbury were entitled to share in the profits of certain services operated by the Company and on certain fixed dates to require the Company to sell to them at a fair market price a defined portion of the undertaking. The financial provisions of this agreement proved increasingly lucrative to the local authorities during the next thirty years or more in which they have operated, and were still in force when this book was written. No action has ever been taken to exercise the option of purchase.

With the passing of the Yorkshire (Woollen District) Transport Act 1931 the way was now open for the abandonment of the tramways and the substitution of a bus service. The tramways were closed down in stages. First to go was Hightown to Liversedge and the Birstall and Birkenshaw sections, on 19 March 1932. The last car from Dewsbury to Carlinghow Depot was run on 3 April 1932 and this was car No. 14. Dewsbury to Thornhill closed on the same day, 3 April, with the last car leaving Thornhill terminus at 11.10 p.m. 31 December saw the end of the Ravensthorpe section and car No. 68 was the last car. Ten lowbridge double-decker buses replaced the trams on this route. By January 1933 the bus fleet numbered 193. On 30 April 1933 the Thorncliffe Road section of the tramways was abandoned and on 4 March 1934 Batley to Birkenshaw via Liversedge and Gomersal Top was closed to tramway traffic.

The last section to remain open was Dewsbury to Cleckheaton, the trunk route of the system, and this line was abandoned on Wednesday, 31 October 1934. The last tram was No. 11, which left Dewsbury at 11.30 p.m. with the Mayor of Dewsbury, Councillor Herbert F. Shaw at the controls. On arriving at the Borough boundary in Halifax Road he handed over the controls to the Mayor of Batley, Councillor Mrs. Elsie Taylor, who drove the car to the Heckmondwike boundary.

Here the Chairman of the Heckmondwike U.D.C., Councillor T. W. Crowther took over amidst great cheering and a considerable amount of bandying. When the Heckmondwike boundary was reached, Councillor Crowther handed over to Councillor Andrew Stott J.P. (Vice Chairman of Spenborough U.D.C.). He took command and the journey was continued to the Frost Hill Depot, where in addition to several hundred residents, employees of the Company who had finished duty earlier heralded the approach of the "ghost tram" with a "peal" of bells from all the available bells in the depot. Refreshments were served to the "mourners" and the General Manager, Mr. D. E. Bell (who had formerly been West Riding's electrical engineer, and continued as Y.W.D. general manager until the 1950s) presented the civic heads with chromium plated tramcar bells to mark the occasion. The bells were the ordinary handbell type which (as in Bradford) were fitted to all the cars of the fleet, there being no footgongs. They were hung from the canopy in the case of the single-deckers and the underside of the stairs in the case of the double-deckers.

These bells deserved being honoured, as throughout their lives they had taken part in a very solemn ritual each time the car arrived at one of the termini. As the passengers made their way out of the back of the car, the driver with the bell in one hand and the controller key and sand pedal in the other, solemnly followed them to the other end of the car. As he did so the oncoming passengers would have caught up with him and were dutifully and slowly following him to their seats. This solemn procession was in marked contrast to the activity of the conductor who was running round the outside from one end of the car to the other, with the trolley boom held by means of a bamboo pole; later, automatic trolley reversers were installed at all the termini, except at the short workings.

Left: Car No. 27 in Halifax Road, Dewsbury (at Carlton Road) on the last route of the Y‑ (Woollen District) Tramways to remain in operation, from Dewsbury to Cleckheato‑ took over on November 1, 1934.   (Dr. F‑

Right: Some inhabitants of Liversedge had their own reasons to regret the pas‑ tramways! The scene is in Frost Hill, at Cooke's Mill.   (D‑

69

Conditions of Work

Except for demi-car 59, which stayed for less than a year, no Yorkshire Woollen District cars were ever fitted with vestibules, and so the conditions under which the drivers worked could be grim. But in many ways they were like the old railway engine drivers who objected to cabs being built on the locomotives; many preferred the open front to a partly enclosed vestibule.

Like other tramway systems of the time, the conditions of work were not good. The hours were long, from 5.30 a.m. to 2 p.m. and 2 p.m. till 11.30 p.m. or midnight. Meal-breaks were unknown and meals had to be taken as and when possible, the can of tea standing on one of the steps of a double decker whilst the sandwiches were being eaten as the man was driving. A typical example is given by Mrs. E. M. Hepworth, niece of driver Sam Wood. On cold winter nights Sam's sister would say to her about 9.45 p.m. or so, "Here, Edith, go meet your Uncle Sam's tram and give him this ("this" being a can of hot soup or tea) and then wait for him coming back from the terminus and bring the can home". While he was at the terminus he would swig the soup or tea and hand the empty can to his niece as he passed her at the point where she was waiting. Another way of getting a "meal break" unofficially was on busy days like Saturdays, when a following tram would arrive at the terminus almost immediately after the one in front, the driver of the first tram would take the second driver's place so that he could have a longer break and then when they arrived at the other terminus, they would change places once more.

It has been said also that in severe wintry weather, if a car was approaching Thornhill, either empty or with passengers whom the driver knew, he would set the car going up the hill and step inside and close the doors and get warm, leaving the car apparently running driverless. In those days there was so little other traffic that it was fairly safe to do this. Such were some of the "tricks of the trade" which made the driver's life more bearable. Men with a tendency to lung trouble would be advised to get a job as a tram driver as the open air life helped them, and judging from results it did, as some drivers who took the job because of this, lived to a ripe old age.

One employee with an unusual job was Pat White. He was the pointsman who stood by the Dewsbury Parish Church where the Ravensthorpe route left that going to Thornhill. He commenced work with the company in 1916. His job was to turn the points and switch the overhead frog. This latter was a spring one and with one car he had to hold the connection in position and for the other he let it go. The track points were not spring points and he moved these with a points rod for each car as it passed. He had no hut or protection from the weather. As far as the author is aware he and his young assistant were the only pointsmen employed though there were other places where routes diverged; at this particular spot the Ravensthorpe cars when going towards Dewsbury ran against the traffic for about 50 yards and the pointsman helped to direct the traffic. For those days the narrow street here was quite busy with horse drays and early motor lorries in the War period and the early 1920's. The junction was eventually doubled, probably in 1925.

After the Tramways

It is not the intention to deal in this book with the later history of Yorkshire Woollen District as a bus operator after the closure of the tramways in 1932-34, which has in any case been completely outlined in the Y.W.D.'s Jubilee book issued on the occasion of the company's seventy-fifth anniversary in 1978, but a brief survey is merited. A fleet of 51 buses had been built up by the end of 1926, and that year the buses carried 4,500,000 passengers and ran 1,500,000 miles. Expansion continued, and in 1930 the buses for the first time carried more passengers than the trams. The passing of the Yorkshire (Woollen District) Transport Act 1931 authorised the use of buses to replace the trams, and after its own trams in 1932-34 and those of the Dewsbury & Ossett in 1933, the bus fleet rose to 224 buses in 1935, the year in which the company's title was

70

changed to Yorkshire Woollen District Transport Company Ltd. The fleet rose to 289 vehicles in 1939, with an average seating capacity of 37, and in 1963 it stood at 276 vehicles with an average capacity of 52. Y.W.D. became one of the most successful bus companies in the B.E.T. group.

The sixtieth anniversary in 1963 was celebrated in unusually lavish style. A luncheon took place at Dewsbury Town Hall on 18 February 1963, presided over by the company chairman, Mr. Raymond W. Birch, and a Leyland double-deck bus was rebuilt for the occasion to resemble an open top tram, with reversed stairs, fenders, lifeguard, headlamp, quarter-lights, controller, and handbell, and finished in the original dark red and cream livery lined in gold and bearing the B.E.T. magnet-and-wheel device. It took guests from Savile Town depot on a tour of the first Y.W.D. tram route to Thornhill and back. Later that year, a jubilee exhibition was held at Batley Central Library, opened by the Y.W.D. general manager, Mr. G. W. Battensby, with model trams, photographs, and a set of tramway rail sections presented to a former Batley borough surveyor by the manufacturer of Batley's tram track.

In 1968 the Y.W.D. along with the 25 other B.E.T. bus companies in Britain became part of the nationalised bus industry, and the depot at Frost Hill, Liversedge now serves as the chief office of National Travel North-East. There has been some decline in both fleet and services, in common with other areas, but traffic is still heavy and in 1977 half the mileage was still crew-operated as opposed to one-man operation. The Y.W.D. system today consists of a network of through bus services linking Leeds, Dewsbury and Wakefield with Bradford, Halifax, Brighouse and Huddersfield along the ex-tramway and other routes, and these buses also provide the bulk of the local service formerly performed by the trams. The trams, confined as they were by breaks of gauge and gaps in the network, could not have survived in this pattern of working, but if the proposed links with Leeds and Huddersfield had been built and the handicap of the different gauges had not existed, the story might have been different—if the many local authorities had been prepared to work together.

The former head office of the Yorkshire (Woollen District) Electric Tramways Co. Ltd. at Frost Hill, Liversedge. The tram depot in rear became a bus garage in 1934, and when the Y.W.D. management was merged with that of West Riding Automobile Co. Ltd. in 1969, Frost Hill became the headquarters of National Travel (North East) Ltd. (W. Pickles

71

Today, the undertakings forming the main subject of this book are worked as one, with headquarters at the West Riding depot at Belle Isle, Wakefield, but the separate titles and fleets of Yorkshire Woollen District and West Riding are still retained.

General Managers—Yorkshire (Woollen District) Electric Tramways

E. A. Paris, 27 January 1903 to 13 July 1921
Major F. J. Chapple, 14 July 1921 to 9 January 1927
D. E. Bell, 10 January 1927 to 31 March 1953.

Yorkshire (Woollen District) Electric Tramways

Owned by Y.W.D.	12.25 miles
Owned by Batley Corporation	6.27 miles
Owned by Dewsbury Corporation	2.94 miles
Owned by Birstall U.D.C.	0.93 miles
Owned by Spenborough U.D.C.	0.14 miles
Owned by Birkenshaw U.D.C.	0.01 miles
Total	22.54 miles

Y.W.D. Tram Services as operated 1922-31

Dewsbury and Thornhill (double deck)
Dewsbury and Ravensthorpe (single deck)
Dewsbury, Batley, Birstall and Birkenshaw (double deck)
Dewsbury, Cleckheaton and Moorend (double deck)
Dewsbury, Hick Lane and Thorncliffe Road (single deck)
Batley (Market Place), Heckmondwike and Birkenshaw (double deck)
Heckmondwike and Hightown (single deck)

Extracts from Board of Trade (later Ministry of Transport) Returns, 1903 to 1933
Yorkshire (Woollen District) Electric Tramways

	Capital expenditure to date	Net surplus on year	Miles open	Number of cars	Passengers carried
1903	£289,870	£5,889	21.12	58	4,442,119
1904	£310,813	£4,896	21.11	58	7,152,004
1905	£314,280	£10,421		69	8,342,575
1906	£326,766	£17,441		69	8,855,828
1907	£328,073	£16,556		69	9,757,922
1908	£328,473	£15,965		69	8,796,612
1909	£328,909	£16,624		69	8,887,327
1910	£329,479	£19,214		69	9,540,988
1911	£332,360	£21,131		69	10,266,696
1912	£336,139	£23,377		69	10,448,186
1913	£336,803	£25,197		69	10,970,896
1918	£338,788	£50,397		68	14,726,984
1919	£339,227	£49,898	22.76	68	15,717,076
1920	£340,683	£50,648	22.63	79	16,506,293
1921	£340,868	£37,556	22.63	79	14,059,430
1922	£340,930	£46,674	22.63	79	14,512,339
1923	£341,512	£49,337	22.63	79	14,870,269
1924	£344,961	£47,433	22.54	79	15,294,169
1925	£345,940	£40,708	22.54	77	15,001,723
1926	£346,639	£33,750	22.54	77	13,904,585
1927	£343,636	£32,000	22.54	72	14,563,884
1928	£344,189	£27,428	22.54	72	14,501,145
1929	£341,398	£24,642	22.54	72	14,190,714
1930	£343,666	£25,403	22.54	72	13,669,052
1931	£120,043	£16,904	11.27	39	13,123,652
1932	£103,584	£7,591	9.85	39	8,469,440
1933	£99,163	£7,701	5.31	17	4,696,651

CHAPTER FOUR
YORKSHIRE WOOLLEN DISTRICT ROLLING STOCK

During its 31 years of electric tramway operation, the Yorkshire (Woollen District) Electric Tramways Limited operated a total of 82 electric tramcars, including eight which were owned by Batley Corporation but numbered in the Y.W.D. fleet. Details of the horse and steam tramcars have been given at the end of Chapter One; this chapter will describe the electric cars. Almost all were built by the Brush Electrical Engineering Company Ltd. of Loughborough, both this company and Yorkshire Woollen District being part of the British Electric Traction group throughout the years concerned. The first 48 cars were delivered in time for the opening of the Spen Valley tramways in 1903, including six single deckers for the Dewsbury—Ravensthorpe route with its two low bridges.

Nos. 1-6   Single deck four wheel cars with five windows per side, built 1902.
Bodies built by Brush Electrical Engineering Co. Ltd., Loughborough.
Dimensions: 19 ft. 6 in. long over corner pillars, 28 ft. 5½ in. long overall, width 6 ft. 6 in., height to trolley plank 10 ft. 7½ in.
Seating for 26 passengers plus four on platforms, total 30.
Electrical equipment supplied by Brush Electrical Engineering Co. Ltd.
Two Brush 1000B motors of 30 horse power each. Two Brush type HD2 controllers.
Truck: Brush A of 6 ft. 6 in. wheelbase, later modified to type AA (probably at Loughborough) by fitting altered springing and wide wing axleboxes.
Braking: hand wheel brake, mechanical track brake, rheostatic brake.

Yorkshire Woollen District No. 5 at Ravensthorpe terminus, painted in the unlined green and cream livery adopted for certain cars during the first world war in place of the standard crimson lake. By this time cars 1-6 had been rebuilt with type AA truck and longitudinal seats, but still had offset bulkhead doors.   (Courtesy R. Croughan

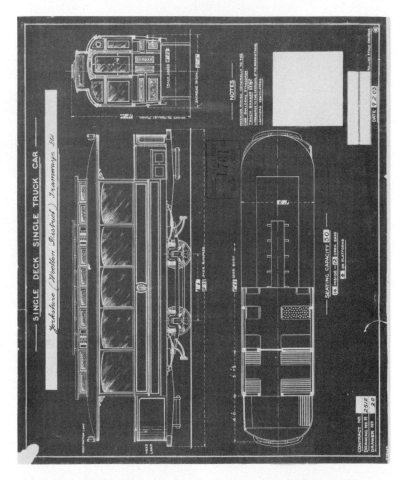

An official B.E.T. blueprint of Yorkshire Woollen District combination single deck cars 1 to 6, deposited with the Board of Trade on 11 February 1903. As built, these cars had transverse seating and offset bulkhead doors; seating was drilled plywood in the central saloon and wooden slat in the end compartments, with a seat for two on each platform. They were rebuilt before entering service with longitudinal seats in a full-length saloon.
(Reproduced from document MT6/1653 in the Public Record Office, by permission of the Controller of H.M. Stationery Office. Crown Copyright reserved.

These vehicles were built as 30-seat combination cars with a central 14-seat saloon, flanked by two semi-open six-seat smoking sections, plus a seat for two persons on the locker on each platform. Seating was two-and-one transverse, with offset gangway and bulkhead doors. They had arrived at Savile Town depot by December 1902, and were stored there until the completion of the Dewsbury—Ravensthorpe route early in 1903. A photograph of No. 2 as built, posed in the entrance to Savile Town depot, appeared in *The Light Railway and Tramway Journal* for 6 March 1903, showing the semi-open end and the absence of a track brake wheel. The inspector, however, insisted on slipper brakes for the Ravensthorpe route, and may have required that passengers be separated from the driver. The opening was delayed, and by the time cars 1-6 entered service they had been fitted with slipper brakes, and the bulkheads separating the central saloon from the end smoking compartments had been moved to the car ends, creating a single large saloon with longitudinal seating. Two extra thick window pillars per side showed where the bulkheads had been. From this time smokers were supposed to travel on the rear platform, but this accommodation was not sufficient and in 1911 there were complaints in the local press that smokers in the saloon were inconveniencing other passengers. No. 6 was extensively rebuilt in about 1923 after a depot fire, as described later.

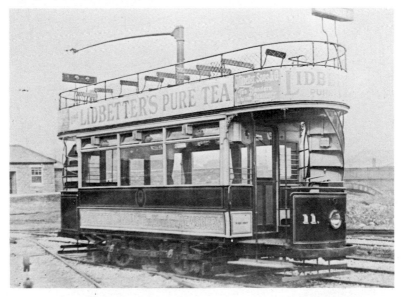

Yorkshire Woollen District No. 11 standing on the non-grooved rail in Savile Town depot yard. Fittings later removed included bulkhead oil lamps, curtains, and the Leather's Patent Ventilators above the windows.   (Courtesy Lidbetters, Dewsbury

Nos. 7-48   Double deck open top cars with three window saloons, built 1902-3. Bodies built by Brush Electrical Engineering Co. Ltd., Loughborough. Dimensions: 16 ft. 0 in. over corner pillars, 27 ft. 5 in. long overall, width 6 ft. 6 in., height to trolley plank 9 ft. 10 in. 90 degree reversed stairs.
Seating for 22 passengers inside and 26 outside (total 48), later increased to 22 inside, 34 outside (total 56) by using double in place of single seats on the upper deck.
Electrical equipment supplied by Brush Electrical Engineering Co. Ltd. Two Brush 1002A motors of 32 horse power each. Two Brush HD2 controllers.

Y.W.D. car No. 15 after being fitted in 1904 with the first type of top cover, in which the upper saloon doors were hinged and the trolley standard projected through the roof. The upper deck railings were left in place.   (Courtesy W. B. Stocks

Truck: Brush A of 6 ft. 0 in. wheelbase, later modified to type AA (probably at Loughborough) by fitting altered springing and wide wing axleboxes. Some of the AA trucks were new 6 ft. 6 in. replacements.

Braking: Hand wheel brake and rheostatic brake. First few cars delivered with Westinghouse magnetic track brake and Spencer electric Scotch, all cars later fitted with mechanical track brake.

These cars, which formed the majority of the Y.W.D. fleet, were of a standard Brush/B.E.T. design also supplied to other tramways such as Barnsley and Peterborough; at least three cars (Y.W.D. 19, 20 and 29) ran at Barnsley on hire during 1904.* Longitudinal slatted seats were fitted inside, and transverse wooden two-and-two seats upstairs. When new, the cars had wire mesh lifeguards, which were later replaced by the gate-and-tray type. Ten cars were delivered to Savile Town depot by December 1902 and were used to start the service early in 1903, the other 32 arrived during the summer of 1903. They were delivered with chilled iron wheels, but a decision was taken in February 1904 to replace these with 31-inch steel-tyred wheels as and when they wore out.

The Woollen District tramways began to fit covered tops to their cars within a year of the opening. The *B.E.T. Gazette* for April, 1904 reported that several Y.W.D. cars now had top covers resembling those at Huddersfield, and that one of them had earned an extra £2 8s. 10d. in a week. These were lightly built covers with six opening windows per side, which fitted inside the existing upper deck sides and railings, and left the end balconies uncovered. There were two types of cover, the later batch having a stronger roof, with a wooden strip above the windows. They did

---

* It has been suggested that two of these may have remained there, being numbered into the Barnsley fleet and replaced by identical new cars on Y.W.D. though there is no documentary evidence to support this.

76

Y.W.D. No 26 at Thornhill with the other type of short top cover, modified with sliding doors to the upper saloon. These covers were replaced by a later type with covered balconies after the 1914-18 war. (F. Hartley

not have to carry the weight of the trolley standard, as it was retained from open-top days and projected through a hole in the roof. An exception was car 33, whose top deck rails were removed and the top cover mounted flush with the original decency panels; this cover carried a dwarf trolley base, replacing the trolley standard. About half of the class received the original Bellamy type of top cover, but the rest remained open top until an improved type of top cover was evolved in 1908.

The illuminated tramcar to celebrate Dewsbury becoming a county borough in 1910. This was one of two cars altered in the hope that double deck cars might be run to Ravensthorpe. The trolley standard was lowered, and the destination boxes were fixed to the guard rails. Permission to run the cars to Ravensthorpe was however refused. (F. Hartley

Y.W.D. No. 27 at Thornhill terminus, fitted with the 1908 type of top cover. The wire mesh on the balconies has been replaced by plain metal strip. From this period, the foot-gong was replaced by a hand bell suspended from the stairs at the driver's end of the car and transferred by the driver when he changed ends at the terminus. (Courtesy R. Brook

The 1908 top covers were made by William Rouse & Sons of Heckmondwike, and were of the balcony type with five opening windows per side, of which those at each end were smaller than the central three. A canopy projected over the end balcony, and the side panels replaced the former decency boards and railings, except at the ends. On these cars the trolley base was of the dwarf type, carried on the roof. Further covers of this type were obtained in sufficient numbers to replace the 1904 Bellamy type covers, but five cars remained open topped until 1923-24.

In 1910, two cars which had not yet been top covered were altered to fit under the low railway bridges on the Ravensthorpe route. The trolley standard was lowered, and the destination boxes were fitted to the guard rails of the upper deck instead of projecting above them on stanchions. Permission to run the cars in this form was refused, probably because passengers would have been in too close proximity to the wire beneath the bridges, and the cars did not enter service. One car, still on its original Brush A truck, was decked out with coloured lights and flags to celebrate Dewsbury becoming a county borough in 1910, and both cars probably went direct to top-covered state after the experiment. One is thought to have been No. 9.

To complete the top covering of the fleet, the company in October 1922 ordered five top covers from Charles Smith of Barnsley, generally similar to those which Smith had made for the Barnsley cars. They had four equal windows per side, and the last two covers had half-light ventilators; these were fitted to Nos. 10 and 30. No. 10 was the last open top car to receive its cover, and resumed service in this form on the Thornhill route on Good Friday, 1924. During postwar overhauls all cars in series 7-48 received a waist-high solid curved panel to part-enclose each balcony, with a solid curved wooden seat inside it. One such car is illustrated on page 91.

Track brakes were considered essential for the hilly Y.W.D. system, save only on the former steam route. The first cars of series 7 to 48 were fitted with Westinghouse magnetic track brakes and the Spencer Scotch, but after a 1904 runaway accident to car 7 in 1904 a gradual change was made to the hand-operated Spencer slipper brake. In 1907, car 42 (which had by then received a Brush AA 6 ft. 6 in. truck) was fitted with the Freund self-winding axle brake after 1906 trials with an earlier version, and in September 1908 this car was taken to Nottingham and demonstrated on the Mapperley route to the members of the Municipal Tramways Association during their conference. The laden car could be stopped quickly from 20 miles/h on a gradient of 1 in 12, but despite this the Spencer slipper brake remained standard. The Spencer Scotch of 1903 must have been a short-lived experimental device, for no later references have been found.

Car No. 52 at Hick Lane terminus, Batley, with a steam tram passing. The eight cars of this type (49 to 56) were owned by Batley Corporation and leased to Y.W.D.
(Reproduced from an early Y.W.D. souvenir brochure

Nos. 49-56 Double deck open top cars with three window saloons, built 1903. Bodies built by British Electric Car Co. Ltd., Trafford Park, Manchester.
Dimensions: 16 ft. 0 in. over corner pillars, 27 ft. 6 in. long overall, width 6 ft. 6 in., height to trolley plank 9 ft. 9 in. Reversed stairs.
Seating for 22 passengers inside, probably 33 outside, total 55.
Electrical equipment supplied by Westinghouse Electric Company Ltd., Trafford Park, Manchester. Two 35 hp Westinghouse 200 motors, two Westinghouse 90 controllers.
Truck: Brill 21E of 6 ft. 6 in. wheelbase.
Braking: hand wheel brake, Westinghouse magnetic track brake, rheostatic brake.

Batley Corporation B.E.C. car 49 with top cover but retaining the ornamental ironwork on the balconies. Note the 180 degree reversed stairs and the absence of the track brake wheel. Although originally green, this was the first Batley car to be repainted in Y.W.D. red.

(F. Hartley

These were the cars owned by Batley Corporation, painted in Batley's own green livery and operated by Y.W.D. on Batley's behalf, mainly on the ex-steam Bradford Road route which had only slight gradients and did not require a mechanical track brake. Until this route opened, they were used on the other Batley routes, where No. 55 came to grief in a runaway accident on 16 January 1904 and when repaired exchanged numbers with single deck car No. 60. The magnetic brakes were removed (or omitted) from the cars used on Bradford Road. Nos. 49-56 differed in several ways from the Y.W.D.'s own cars, having Brill 21E instead of Brush trucks, half-turn reversed stairs, cane rattan instead of wooden slat seating inside, off-centre twin leaf doors to the lower saloon (never used by B.E.C. elsewhere) and ornamental upper deck scrollwork instead of the plain diamond-pattern wire mesh of the Brush cars. The waist panel was deeper than on the Brush cars, and projected above the line of the dash rail. They were delivered in open top condition, though top covers had been discussed and rejected because of the extra weight of 18 cwt. per car. Unlike the Brush open top cars, they had two lighting standards on the upper deck.

These eight Batley cars, by then 49-54, 56 and 60, did not receive the Bellamy type top covers, and went direct after 1908 from open-top to balcony-top condition, receiving the five-window type of cover with extended canopies. The seats on the balconies were curved wooden ones, not garden seats. The original shallow weather-boarding and deep scrollwork was retained on the balconies, but some (including No. 52, shown on the cover) carried enamel advertisements which also offered better protection against wind and weather.

A further rebuilding of these cars took place in 1919-24, when the original weather-boarding and B.E.C. scrollwork at the ends was replaced by the waist-high solid curved panel which was the standard practice of the Y.W.D. company at that time. Each one was then fitted with a Spencer slipper brake, enabling them to be

Batley Corporation car 53 at Thorncliffe Road terminus, Batley, in 1920, now fitted with mechanical track brake and high balcony panels, but retaining its half-turn reversed stairs. The car is painted in all-over battleship grey.   (J. G. D. Whitaker

used on the Dewsbury to Thornhill route. In subsequent overhauls they also received standard 90 degree reversed stairs of Brush design, and were then painted in standard Y.W.D. livery. The only remaining feature which distinguished them from the Brush cars was the deep waist panel.

Single deck car 57 in Huddersfield Road, Ravensthorpe. The two cars of this type are described overleaf.   (F. Hartley

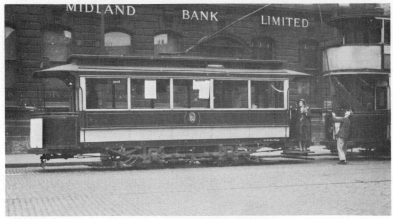

A car of the 57-58 class in final condition at Dewsbury Market Place about 1930, mounted on a Brush 7 ft. 6 in. wheelbase truck. These cars originally had full-drop opening windows.
(Dr. Hugh Nicol

Nos. 57-58 Single deck four wheel cars with five drop windows per side, built 1903.
Bodies built by Brush Electrical Engineering Co. Ltd., Loughborough.
Dimensions: 21 ft. 0 in. over corner pillars, 30 ft. 0 in. long overall,
width 6 ft. 6 in. height to trolley plank 10 ft. 9½ in.
Seating for 30 passengers.
Electrical equipment supplied by Brush Electrical Engineering Co. Ltd.
Two Brush 1002A motors of 25 horse power each, two Brush HD2
controllers.
Truck: Brush A of 6 ft. 6 in. wheelbase (later replaced by Brush 21E
wide wing of 7 ft. 6 in. wheelbase).
Braking: hand wheel brake, mechanical track brake, rheostatic brake.

Traffic on the Dewsbury—Ravensthorpe route developed quickly and the six
original single deck cars did not suffice, with the result that two more cars were soon
ordered. They differed from 1-6 in having five flat topped (instead of round topped)
windows, and were built without internal bulkheads. In the early 1920s the opening
windows were replaced by plain fixed windows, and platform stanchions were
added. New 7 ft 6 in. Brush trucks were fitted at the same time.

No. 59(I) Single deck vestibuled four wheel one-man demi-car, built 1904.
Body probably built by British Electric Car Company, Trafford Park,
under sub-contract to Brush Electrical Engineering Company and/or
Raworths Traction Patents Ltd.
Dimensions: length 20 ft. 6 in. overall, width 6 ft. 6 in.
Seating for 20 passengers (14 inside, six on platforms).
Electrical equipment supplied by Raworths Traction Patents Ltd. Two
shunt wound Brush motors of 17 hp, two Raworth controllers.
Truck: rigid frame suspension of 6 ft. 0 in. wheelbase.
Braking: hand wheel brake, mechanical track brake, regenerative
brake.

In the face of what were considered to be excessive charges for electricity
bought from Heckmondwike council's power station, the Y.W.D. decided to
experiment with Raworth's system of regenerative control with the aim of
minimising power consumption on the sections concerned. As a first step the
company bought one Raworth regenerative demi-car, the order being announced in
the *Dewsbury Reporter* for 30 April 1904. Raworth drawing No. 162 deposited with
the Board of Trade shows the Y.W.D. demi-car with the distinctive canopy brackets
used by the Brush company, who were the originally intended builders, but later

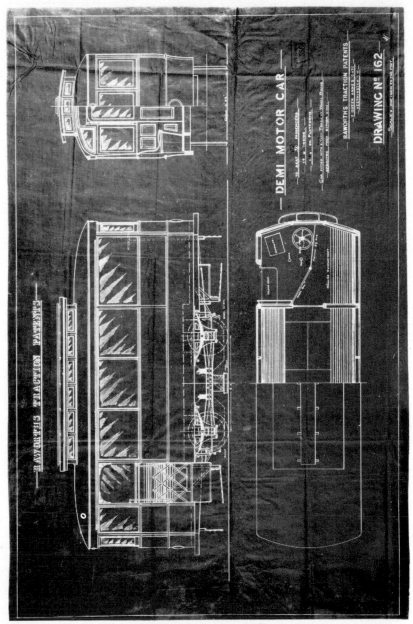

Raworth drawing No. 162, attached to the application to the Board of Trade for permission to run a demi-car as the Yorkshire (Woollen District) Tramways. On the original, the seating figures have been amended in red ink to read 20 inside, 6 on platforms, and the braking data altered to read "Car fitted with both track and wheel brake".
(reproduced from document MT6/1654 in the Public Record Office, by permission of the Controller of H.M. Stationery Office. Crown Copyright reserved

83

research by I. A. Yearsley recounted in *Tramway Review* suggests that the car was built under sub-contract by the British Electric Car Company Ltd. of Trafford Park, Manchester. The patented features included a lifting bar on each platform which if raised would cut off the power and apply the electric brake.

The demi-car entered service later in 1904 on the Heckmondwike to Hightown route, and the economy in power consumption offered by the regenerative system must have been judged worthwhile, for the directors on 28 September 1904 decided to place an order for eight sets of Raworth's regenerative equipment. Six were for the new two-man single deck cars for the Hightown route, the other two sets were fitted to double deck cars, one of them being No. 26.

By September 1905 the demi-car was no longer required on the Y.W.D. system and it was lent to the Barnsley and District Electric Traction Company (managed, like Y.W.D., by Mr. E. A. Paris) and was sold to them for £500 two months later, becoming Barnsley 13. No vestibuled tram ever ran again on the Y.W.D. system.

No. 59(II)   Single deck parcels car, built 1903 as a water car, rebuilt in 1905 as parcels car and numbered 59 after the sale of the demi-car to Barnsley. Original body built by Brush Electrical Engineering Co. Ltd., Electrical equipment supplied by Brush Electrical Engineering Co. Ltd. and thought to be standard with that of the first 48 passenger cars, namely two Brush 1002A motors of 32 horse power each and two Brush HD2 controllers.
Truck: Brush A of 6 ft. 0 in. wheelbase.
Braking: hand wheel brake, mechanical track brake, rheostatic brake.

This vehicle began life as a 2000 gallon water car of Brush standard design. The introduction of through parcels service with the Bradford tramways via Birkenshaw evidently created a need for a specialised vehicle. The directors on 18 December 1905 considered a suggestion by Mr. Paris to buy a steam lorry, but this was deferred and it was decided to convert the water car. The tank was removed and replaced by a van-type body, with an upright trolley standard. It continued to be recorded each year as a parcels car, but in later years spent most of its time towing a small four wheeled wagon loaded with sand or ballast. Passenger car 1 was often used on similar work.

Nos. 60-65   Single deck four wheel cars with four windows per side, built 1904.
(later 55   Bodies built by Brush Electrical Engineering Co. Ltd., Loughborough.
and 61-65)   Dimensions: length over corner pillars 14 ft. 8 in., overall length 22 ft. 2 in., width 6 ft. 6 in., height to trolley plank 10 ft. 6 in.
Seating for 20 passengers.
Electrical equipment supplied by Raworths Traction Patents Ltd. Two shunt wound Brush motors of 17 horse power each, two Raworth controllers.
Truck: Brush A of 5 ft. 6 in. wheelbase, later modified to type AA.
Braking: hand wheel brake, mechanical track brake, regenerative brake.

These small cars with regenerative equipment spent most of their time working on the Heckmondwike—Hightown and Cleckheaton—Moorend routes, where they entered service on December 10, 1904, permitting restoration of the full service which had been reduced since August due to a dispute over power supplies. By November 1905 Heckmondwike power station was complaining about erratic readings on their meters due to the use of regenerative control on the trams. The company, who had adopted regenerative working in response to the onerous terms imposed by Heckmondwike for supplying electric power, maintained their position until Heckmondwike gave way in 1909, after which the directors on 13 October 1909 decided that the six cars were to be reconverted to series-parallel control. Details of the re-equipment are not known for certain, but it seems likely that six pairs of Westinghouse 35 hp motors were bought and mounted in some of Nos. 7-48, releasing Brush 1000B motors for the six small cars.

Short car No. 63 at Moorend terminus in 1905, one of six cars fitted with Raworth regenerative control to reduce power consumption in the Heckmondwike district. Note the brake staff outside the dash. Four of these cars were rebuilt in 1924-25 into two long cars.

(Courtesy Yorkshire Woollen District Transport Co. Ltd.

After the accident of 16 January 1904 to double deck car 55, this car exchanged numbers with single deck car 60. After the arrival of the ex-Sheffield single deckers, five of the 20-seat cars were offered for sale in August 1923, but without result.

By this time, the company needed two more large single deck cars for the Dewsbury—Ravensthorpe service. It was decided to convert four of these small cars

One of the two spliced cars (55 and 61) decorated and illuminated to celebrate the Dewsbury Shopping Week in September 1925. These cars were created by joining pairs of the short cars illustrated on the previous page, to cope with increased traffic on the Ravensthorpe route.

(F. Hartley

to form two long ones, and the car works superintendent, Mr. Griffith, explained to the late Walter Gratwicke in 1927 how this had been done (probably in 1924-25). Each car was produced by taking one body with one platform, less the other and one bulkhead, and splicing it with part of another body (one platform, one bulkhead, and three windows) and mounting the assembly in a new angle underframe, carried on a new Brush 21E 7 ft. 6 in. truck.

This conversion produced two seven-window single deck cars, numbered 55 and 61, 25 ft. 0 in. long over corner pillars, 32 ft. 6 in. long overall, 6 ft. 6 in. wide and 10 ft 4 in. high, seating 36 inside on longitudinal wooden seats, and powered by two Brush 1202B 35 hp motors. Spencer slipper brakes, obligatory for the Ravensthorpe route, were fitted, and one of the two lengthened cars was decorated for Dewsbury's Shopping Week in 1925.

Yorkshire (Woollen District) long car 68 as originally built, with 8 ft. 6 in. wheelbase Lycett and Conaty radial track, standing at Fir Cottage terminus, Ravensthorpe.   (Courtesy Mrs. G. Field

Nos. 66-69   Single deck four wheel cars with six windows per side, built 1905. Bodies built by Brush Electrical Engineering Co. Ltd., Loughborough. Dimensions: 26 ft. over corner pillars, 32 ft. 6 in. long overall, width 6 ft. 6 in., height to trolley plank 10 ft. 4 in. Seating for 36 passengers. Electrical equipment supplied by Brush Electrical Engineering Co. Ltd. Two Brush 1002B motors of 32 hp each, two Brush HD2 controllers. Truck: Brush Conaty radial of 8 ft. 6 in. wheelbase.
Braking: hand wheel brake, mechanical track brake, rheostatic brake.

The busy Ravensthorpe route presented a unique problem to the B.E.T. engineers. The low railway bridges necessitated single deck cars, the traffic carried required cars of ample capacity, and the gradients required mechanical track brakes. Similar problems at Burnley and Dundee had led to the use of expensive four-motor single-deck cars with track shoes mounted in Brill equal-wheel trucks, but the Board of Trade was known to prefer slipper brake cars to be four-wheeled to lessen the chance of derailment. The Spencer slipper brake could only be fitted to rigid or semi-rigid trucks, which excluded most of the radial types then available.

Car 69 of class 66-69 photographed at Ravensthorpe terminus in the 1920s, remounted on a Brush 7 ft. 6 in. wheelbase truck with extension struts to reduce the effect of the excessive overhang. Several pictures exist of Ravensthorpe cars with soap advertisements at one end only. (F. Hartley

The Conaty and Lycett truck, which could take a track brake but which allowed some deflection of the axles, seemed to offer a solution, and its wheelbase of 8 ft. 6 in. would give fairly good support to the long body. YWD 66-69 took shape as the longest four-wheeled single-deck tramcars hitherto built in Britain. In order to give maximum seating capacity, the end platforms were particularly narrow, and this

Car 66 in final condition with dwarf trolley base and fixed end windows, photographed about 1930 at Dewsbury Market Place. (Dr. Hugh Nicol

gave rise to a court case in 1915 in which a lady fell into the road while alighting from No. 66. The *B.E.T. Gazette* for September 1906 reported that Conaty trucks were giving trouble on other B.E.T. tramways, but Y.W.D. persevered with them until the early 1920s, when they were replaced by Brush 21E type trucks of only 7 ft. 6 in. wheelbase, which left about 10 ft. of unsupported tram fore and aft of the truck springs. In later overhauls, the opening end windows were replaced by fixed panes, and the brake staff was remounted outside the dash plate.

Nos. 70-73   Single deck four wheel cars with five windows per side. Purchased in December 1919 from Sheffield Corporation Tramways, Sheffield numbers 91, 93, 103 and 211. Renumbering sequence not known.
Bodies built in 1900 by Brush Electrical Engineering Co. Ltd., Loughborough (211 by Sheffield Corporation in 1902).
Dimensions: 19 ft. 11 in. long over corner pillars, overall length 28 ft. 11 in. as new, width 6 ft. 9 in., height to trolley plank 10 ft. 2½ in. Certain cars had been given extended platforms, increasing the overall length to 30 ft. 4 in. For dimensions of Sheffield 211, see next entry.
Seating for 28 passengers inside. Y.W.D. added two seats on each platform.
Electrical equipment supplied by British Thomson-Houston Ltd. Two GE58 motors of 35 horse power each, two B.T.H. B13 controllers.
Truck: Brill 21E of 5 ft. 6 in., wheelbase, later extended by Sheffield to 6 ft. 0 in.
Braking: hand wheel brake, mechanical track brake, rheostatic brake.

In 1919-21 Sheffield Corporation sold most of their remaining single deck cars to other tramways, twelve of them (in three batches) to Yorkshire Woollen District, where they ran for some years in Sheffield livery before being repainted. Sheffield's hills had always required mechanical track brakes, and these were retained by Y.W.D.

Nos. 74-81   Single deck four wheel cars with five windows per side. Purchased in
(later 65   1920 from Sheffield Corporation Tramways, Sheffield numbers 101
and 74-80)   and 204 in February, Sheffield numbers 40, 44, 45, 47, 49 and 128 in August. Renumbering sequence not known.
Bodies built by G. F. Milnes & Co. Ltd. in 1899 (40 to 49), by Brush Electrical Engineering Co. Ltd. in 1900 (101), by Sheffield Corporation in 1902 (128) and 1903 (204).
Dimensions: 20 ft. 0 in. long over corner pillars, 32 ft. 4 in. long overall, width 6 ft. 9 in., height 10 ft. 1¼ in. (for dimensions of Sheffield 101, see previous entry).
Seating for 28 passengers inside. Y.W.D. added two seats on each platform.
Electrical equipment supplied by British Thomson-Houston Ltd. Two GE58 motors of 35 horse power each, two B.T.H. B13 controllers.
Truck: Brill 21E of 5 ft. 6 in. wheelbase, later extended by Sheffield to 6 ft. 0 in. One car (Sheffield 45 or 47) when sold to Y.W.D. still had a Peckham cantilever 6 ft. 0 in. wheelbase truck.
Braking: hand wheel brake, mechanical track brake, rheostatic brake.

The first four Sheffield cars having given satisfaction, Y.W.D. bought a further eight in 1920, and again placed them in service before repainting. Nos. 40, 44 and 49 had been vestibuled by Sheffield Corporation in 1914-15, but the platform vestibules were removed at Y.W.D.'s request before the cars were despatched from Sheffield, presumably due to Y.W.D.'s practice of allowing smokers to travel on the open rear platform.

The arrival of these cars brought the Y.W.D. fleet to its maximum strength of 81 cars, but when Y.W.D. car 65 was dismantled about 1924 for use in lengthening another car, the Sheffield car bearing the highest number (81) was renumbered 65.

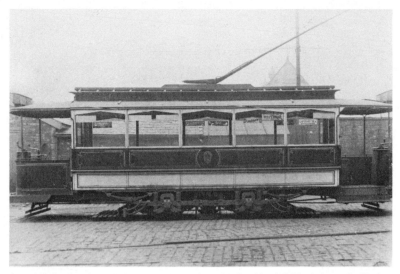

Two of the twelve single-deck cars purchased from Sheffield in 1919-20, photographed before and after being repainted in Y.W.D. livery. The upper picture is at Frost Hill depot, the lower one at Savile Town. (Yorkshire Woollen District Transport Co. Ltd.

No. 6(II)   On 5 March, 1917 a fire occurred at Frost Hill depot, in which (according to newspaper reports) two cars were "practically destroyed". Their fleet numbers are not known, but it seems likely that one was a small single-decker of the class originally numbered 60 to 65 (which would explain why only five such cars were offered for sale in 1923, instead of six) and that the other was 1902 single-decker No. 6. The latter car was reconstructed in the company's own workshops about 1923 with a new body having five rectangular windows per side, and extended platforms. Dimensions were 19 ft. 6 in. long over corner

Ex-Sheffield car 74 and rebuilt Y.W.D. single-deck car 6 in Frost Hill depot yard in 1933. No. 6 was rebodied after a fire and was given extended platforms with a seat for smokers.
(Dr. Hugh Nicol

pillars, 31 ft. 0 in. long overall, 6 ft. 6 in. wide and 10 ft. 4 in. high to trolley plank, with seating for 24 in the saloon and three on each platform. The car was mounted on a Brush 21E truck of 7 ft. 6 in. wheelbase and according to the late Walter Gratwicke had B.T.H. electrical equipment, though since no such order appears in the B.T.H. records this would probably have been purchased from Sheffield. The new No. 6 had a dwarf trolley base instead of the upright type.

The Steam Lorry

In December 1905 Mr. Paris suggested to the Y.W.D. board that a steam lorry be bought for parcels and goods transport. Nothing was done until October 1908, when a quotation from the Yorkshire Patent Steam Wagon Co. Ltd. of Leeds for a steam lorry at £500 was submitted. In February 1909 the board decided to hire a steam lorry from the Yorkshire Patent Steam Wagon Co. Ltd. for a trial period of six months, with option to purchase, and it was delivered at the end of July 1909. The hire was extended by six months in January 1910 and for a further six months in July 1910, but no later references occur in the minutes.

Liveries

The original Y.W.D. livery was crimson lake and cream, both lined out, with the B.E.T. magnet and wheel device on the waist panel, and the fleet number repeated on either side of the headlight, a practice adopted by several B.E.T. companies. The eight cars owned by Batley Council were in a distinct livery of green and cream, also lined out; the intention had been that they should bear Batley's own coat of arms, but a photograph taken of car 55 after the 1904 runaway shows it with the B.E.T. magnet and wheel.

During the 1914-18 war, shortage of paint and transfers brought several changes in car liveries. Several double deck cars and Nos. 66-69 were repainted in unlined red and cream with a single fleet number above the headlamp, but others including 2 to 6, 10, 45 and 46 were repainted in unlined green and cream, perhaps with paint held in stock for the Batley cars. Y.W.D. 26 ran for a while painted battleship grey all over, as did Batley cars 50, 51 and 53, and Batley car 49 appeared after the war in Y.W.D. red. The parcels car was painted all-over unlined green, which it retained to the end.

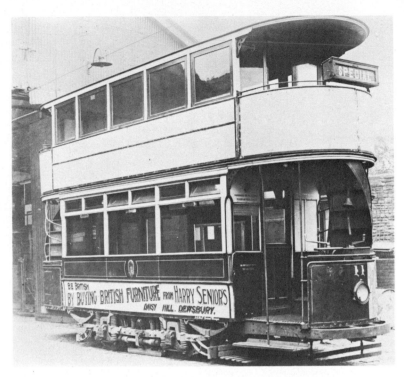

Y.W.D. car 11 in the postwar livery of maroon and primrose. The car is shown in its final form with high balcony panels and a Brush AA type truck. (Science Museum, Whitcombe Collection

In 1922, car 35 emerged from overhaul in an all-over unlined dark red, with two fleet numbers on each waist panel. This dark red, referred to by Y.W.D. as maroon and identical with the shade used in later years at Leicester, was adopted as the new Y.W.D. standard colour for trams and buses, with primrose for those parts of the car formerly painted cream, the dark red being lined black and white and the primrose being bordered in black. The Sheffield cars were among the last to receive it, running until then in their Sheffield livery, navy blue on those recently repainted and somewhat darker shades on those which had weathered; on Y.W.D. 74 the blue had become almost black. In the first few postwar overhauls of Y.W.D. cars the fleet number was repeated twice on the waist panel, but this was soon discontinued.

This "maroon and primrose" livery, using paint supplied by T. R. Williamson of Ripon, continued in use on the buses, though with gold lining on the maroon. The primrose was later replaced by Yorkshire Cream, and in 1953 the maroon was replaced by a lighter shade of red. Thus altered, the livery continued until the adoption of National Bus Company red livery in 1973. To mark the company's 75th anniversary in 1978 two buses were repainted in the livery of the 1920s, using Williamson's Monarch Maroon paint and Dulux coach cream enamel.

91

CHAPTER FIVE

THE DEWSBURY & OSSETT TRAMWAYS

At the beginning of the century, when the Spen Valley Light Railway was laid down, hopes were entertained that a tramway would be constructed to link Dewsbury and Ossett with Wakefield. The Dewsbury and Castleford extensions of the Wakefield & District Light Railways Order 1901 were to be the answer to these hopes, but the period of time granted for the construction of the lines lapsed and it was 1908 before trams actually ran from Dewsbury to Ossett and to Earlsheaton, after seven years of talk and argument and abortive attempts to get something done. The Dewsbury & Ossett Tramways, to abbreviate the somewhat unwieldy title, were run by the National Electric Construction Company which also owned the Mexborough and Swinton and certain other tramways.

The Wakefield and District Light Railway Company applied in 1901 for powers to construct a light railway from Dewsbury to Wakefield, passing through Ossett, with a short branch to serve the village of Earlsheaton from a junction at the bottom of the Wakefield cutting in Dewsbury Bank. The application was supported by a petition signed by 153 persons in the borough of Ossett. There were immediate objections from the two railway companies concerned, the Lancashire & Yorkshire and the Great Northern, both of which ran services from Dewsbury to Wakefield. The L. & Y. line took a more southerly route than the proposed light railway, and this company objected mainly because the proposed light railway would pass in front of its station in Dewsbury Market Place. The G.N.R. ran through Earlsheaton, Chickenley and Ossett, and was the route usually taken by passengers to and from Dewsbury and Wakefield. The Wakefield & District Light Railway now hoped to serve each of these townships with its light railway.

The G.N.R. claimed that 69,735 passengers were carried in a year between Wakefield Westgate Station and Dewsbury, with receipts totalling £1,574 8s. 9d. and that 281,011 passengers were carried in a year between Ossett and Dewsbury with receipts of £2,304 4s. 6d. The Lancashire & Yorkshire Railway's figures for passengers and receipts between Dewsbury and its own station of Horbury & Ossett were given as 45,764 passengers and £1,300 receipts. The G.N.R. thought that the district was well provided with travelling facilities by them, as there were stations at Dewsbury, Chickenley Heath and Earlsheaton as well as Ossett. The G.N.R. also objected that the proposed light railway was to pass over the bridges at Chickenley Heath and Wakefield Road, Dewsbury, just above the Market Place. The company maintained that these bridges were not constructed to carry such heavy loads as tramcars, and that an increase in the cost of maintenance would result if permission were given for the light railway to be constructed. If the light railway authorities also thought fit to use electricity as a motive power, serious consequences might result if the electrical apparatus were to interfere with the railway's telegraphic signalling apparatus. The good travelling facilities at Chickenley Heath mentioned by the G.N.R. amounted to four trains a day on the branch line from Ossett to Batley, and the residents had to go either to Ossett by one of these trains and change there for Dewsbury, or go via Batley. That its fears were very real was shown by the fact that soon after the Dewsbury & Ossett Tramways commenced running in 1908, the G.N.R. withdrew the Chickenley Heath passenger service altogether.

Apart from the promoters of the light railway and the Mayor of Ossett, Mr. Walter Townend, the principal supporters of the scheme were two Ossett

Councillors, Wilson and Wilkinson. They held an open-air meeting in October 1901 ro rouse some enthusiasm for the light railway amongst the ratepayers, claiming that Ossett could build the lines and lease them to the company at a substantial profit. They had heard that Soothill Upper Urban District Council had paid £230 for some 65 yards of tramway line in their district and that this line was to be leased to a company at £231 per year. Their mathematical minds set to work and they proclaimed to the meeting that at this rate a mile of tramways was worth £6,231 10s. 0d., and the value of the 1¼ miles from Ossett Market Place to the boundary with Soothill Nether would be £7,778; moreover if the tram lines were taken to Wakefield via Roundwood (Flushdyke) the total value of the system in Ossett would be £20,250. Their enthusiasm was obviously outstripping their common sense, or they were counting their chickens before they were hatched!

Despite the railway companies' objections, the Wakefield Syndicate succeeded in its application and powers to build the lines were granted in the Wakefield & District Light Railways (Dewsbury & Castleford Extensions) Order 1901. However, there was a clause in the Bill that if the light railways were not completed within three years, the powers would lapse. This is precisely what happened; they were not completed, or even begun, within three years, and so the powers lapsed. This set off another round of tramway applications by other parties, and enabled the National Electric Construction Company to negotiate with the three local authorities to operate tramways to be laid by them. This lapsing of the light railway company's powers also caused the tramways to be constructed under the Tramways Act 1870 and not the Light Railways Act of 1896.

Meanwhile the two Soothill Urban District Councils (Upper and Nether) each had their own ideas for constructing tramways and were seeking powers to that end. Soothill Nether's proposals differed from those of Wakefield & District in that they would be confined to a district which was virtually without a railway station. Granted the G.N.R. had a station called Earlsheaton, but as so often the case it was a long way from the village which it was built to serve, out on the road between Earlsheaton and Ossett, and people wishing to use it had to walk in the opposite direction from Dewsbury in order to get a train going to that town.

Soothill Nether Urban District Council decided to promote their own Bill under the Tramways Act 1870 for authority to construct tramways in the Urban District, and as the boundary was so near to Dewsbury Market Place (a matter of a few hundred yards) it was decided to include Dewsbury in it and put the terminus at the bottom of Wakefield Road, Dewsbury, adjacent to the Town Hall. It would run from there in an easterly direction along the main Wakefield to Dewsbury road, as far as the boundary with the Borough of Ossett. From the bottom of Wakefield Cutting at the junction of High Road with the main Wakefield to Dewsbury Road a

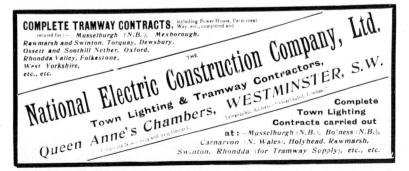

A 1910 advertisement by the National Electric Construction Company Ltd., lessees and operators of the Dewsbury and Ossett Tramways.   (The Light Railway and Tramway Journal

loop was to lead off to serve Earlsheaton, to go along High Road, Town Street, Syke Lane and rejoin the main Wakefield Road line by the Earlsheaton Cemetery. Land for a generating station was to be bought just to the east of the cemetery, for the Council intended to generate their own electricity for the tramway system. In Town Street and along Syke Lane property was to be demolished and the road widened so that the track could be laid, most of the property on both sides of the road having to be set back.

Ossett Town Council likewise decided to apply to the Board of Trade for powers to construct a tramway for Ossett residents and not for the privilege of laying a light railway from Dewsbury to Wakefield passing through Ossett. Ossett's point of view was a particularly parochial one—Ossett for the Ossetters so to speak. The difficulties of running a small tramway system did not enter their heads. Ossett Council apparently did not realise that it was cheaper for a large company like the Wakefield and District syndicate to construct one mile of line (for that was what the Ossett proposals amounted to) than would be the case for a small municipality like Ossett. Such a line would cost Ossett £17,000 and it was estimated that it would have cost £7,500 for the Wakefield Syndicate to construct. Ossett Town Council thought that if they constructed the lines then they might grant running powers over them to the Wakefield Syndicate. However, the town clerk of Ossett thought differently, stating at the enquiry which was held, "We are quite willing to sail our own boat". Mr. Morris, representing the Wakefield Syndicate then retorted "Yes, but it will be such a miserable little boat" (laughter).

Meanwhile, a new company calling itself the Dewsbury & District Light Railway Company applied for authority to construct a light railway from Dewsbury to Ossett, to link up with the already constructed Spen Valley Light Railway in Church Street, Dewsbury, and then follow Vicarage Road round the front of the Town Hall before continuing along the Dewsbury to Wakefield Road through the Urban District of Soothill Nether. Its lines would go through Chickenley Heath along Ossett-Street-Side and along the main road towards Wakefield as far as Palesides, before turning up Dale Street and into Ossett Market Place (where a connection was to be made with the lines already laid in the Market Place by the Wakefield Light Railway Company) and terminate at the junction of Bank Street and Station Road. A site at Palesides on the main Dewsbury to Wakefield Road was earmarked for a generating station and car shed. The cost of construction of this light railway is given on the deposited plans as £17,434 11s. 6d., of which £480 was for land for the generating station and car sheds. It is not known what connection this company had with the B.E.T. interests whose lines it would have joined, but in any case the application was withdrawn when it became clear that the local authorities intended to build the lines themselves.

Another point which had to be considered by the Councils was that once the tramways were constructed, there were only two companies who were willing to lease them and they were the Wakefield & District Light Railway Company and the British Electric Traction Company. Neither of these two companies was prepared to undertake the construction of the branch lines proposed in the Bill through Earlsheaton Village from Wakefield Road by Earlsheaton Cemetery and through the village to join the main Wakefield Road again at the bottom of the Wakefield Cutting, nearer to Dewsbury.

The Soothill Nether Tramways Bill, together with the Provisional Order to confirm the Orders made by the Board of Trade, was passed in June 1904. All three schemes were considered together—those from the Dewsbury and Ossett Corporations and the one from Soothill Nether U.D.C.—and they were again opposed by the Great Northern Railway, on grounds that, together with the existing Wakefield & District's Light Railway scheme, they would form a continuous line of tramways for passenger service from Wakefield to Dewsbury via Ossett and Horbury. The G.N.R. also objected to the carriage of goods, parcels, minerals etc., as stated in Clause 25 of the Ossett Order, and considered that only passengers, mails and luggage not exceeding 28 lbs. should be carried. Ossett Corporation was adamant that the clause should be retained, as they felt that a station at Chickenley

94

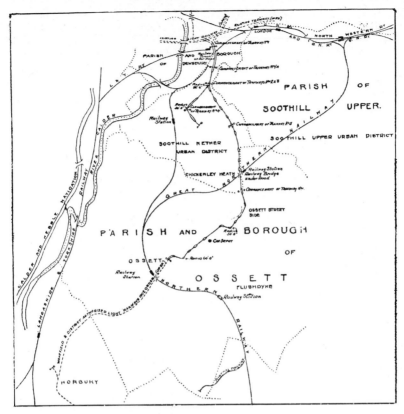

The Dewsbury and Ossett Tramways, showing local authority boundaries and railways. Soothill Nether Urban District became part of the Borough of Dewsbury in 1912. The tramway junctions shown in Dewsbury were never constructed. (*The Light Railway and Tramway Journal*

Heath with only four trains a day stopping there would hardly be called a service, and the parcel traffic was not catered for at all. A great number of people residing in Church Street, Street Side, Gawthorpe and Chickenley Heath came to Ossett to shop, and their goods were then delivered by errand boys. Ossett Corporation also proposed erecting a refuse destructor, adjoining the route of the tramways in Church Street, and the corporation wished to use the tramways for hauling different kinds of goods and materials to and from the destructor. Furthermore, the Corporation obtained the greater part of the coal used at their gas works from a colliery at Gawthorpe. The coal was conveyed from the pit to the gasworks by horse and cart, and at some time in the future the Corporation might wish to use the tramways for carrying it. Ossett also maintained that in some towns tramways were used even for sending workmen their dinners.

By 31 March 1904 the Board of Trade had over-ruled the objections of the Great Northern Railway Company, and the proposed tramways were authorised in the Dewsbury Corporation Tramways Order 1904, the Soothill Nether Urban District Tramways Act 1904, and the Ossett Corporation Tramways Order 1904. The Dewsbury and Ossett Orders were to be confirmed by the next subsequent Tramways Order Confirmation Act.

The proportions of the tramways to be owned by the three local authorities differed greatly. Dewsbury, which was the largest authority, owned the shortest length of tramway, whilst the greatest length was owned by the smaller authority, Soothill Nether U.D.C. Ossett owned about a mile of track. Soothill Nether's share of the contract was £39,945 which included new streets and street widenings; Ossett's share for building its mile or so of tramway was £17,284, and Dewsbury Borough Council authorised the Town Clerk on 16 January 1908 to apply for borrowing powers for the sum of £4,098 2s. 1d. The Ossett proposals differed from the earlier Wakefield District scheme in that it would reach Ossett from the main Dewsbury—Wakefield road via Church Street instead of Dale Street. Ossett also built the car sheds in Church Street, which brought its outlay up to £22,856.

The three tramways were to be worked as one system by the National Electric Construction Company Ltd. When the powers obtained by the Wakefield & District Light Railway Company lapsed, Ossett Town Council had approached the National Electric Construction Company offering to construct tramways and then lease them to the company, as an alternative to making terms with either of the companies already established in the area. An agreement was reached, and similar arrangements were then made by the Company with the Dewsbury Corporation and the Soothill Nether Urban District Council. It was subsequently agreed that the company would build the lines as one joint contract and hand them over to the three local authorities on completion, taking a lease at a rental calculated on the amount required by each authority to pay interest and Sinking Fund charges. The agreements with Ossett and with Soothill Nether would run until 1950.

The National Electric Construction Company which was formed in 1897 and took the N.E.C. title in 1903 was the second largest syndicate in the British electric tramway industry, though much smaller than the B.E.T. Unlike the working arrangements of the Yorkshire (W.D.) Electric Tramways with the B.E.T., the N.E.C. worked the Dewsbury & Ossett Tramways directly and not through a subsidiary company. All the track was owned by the three local authorities, the Company owning no length of track at all on the Dewsbury & Ossett system, unlike many other large tramway companies up and down the country which owned certain tracks while also leasing others.

As mentioned previously, the National Electric Construction Company also owned the Mexborough and Swinton Tramways system, separated from the Dewsbury & Ossett system by many miles; there was however a closer working between the N.E.C. systems than between the Yorkshire (W.D.) Electric Tramways and the Barnsley & District Tramways, the two subsidiaries of the B.E.T. in the area. Certain major repairs to the Dewsbury & Ossett trams were undertaken at the Rawmarsh depot of the Mexborough & Swinton and some of the top covers for the Ossett cars were also made there, and from 1919 onwards, the two companies shared the same manager (Mr. W. McGibbon) and the same accountant.

Construction of the Tramway

The construction of the tramway was carried out by the National Electric Construction Company, and this included the overhead equipment, which was of both span wire and side pole type in different parts of the system. There was considerable delay even after agreements had been signed, and this caused much irritation to the public who were by this time keen to have the tramways. In February 1908, one of the resident engineers came to live at Ossett and hopes of an early start were raised. By this time the widening of the road in Earlsheaton had commenced, and this was also a good sign that things were moving at last. By 18 April 1908 a start had been made in laying the tramlines near the Earlsheaton Cemetery, and the car sheds were also under erection in Church Street, Ossett. By May 1908 really rapid progress was being made; some parts of the system were built much quicker than others, but the part near the Town Hall in Ossett made very slow progress.

The permanent way was of standard gauge 4 ft. 8½ ins.; 90 lbs. per yard rail was used and the point work was by Edgar Allen & Co. Ltd. of Sheffield. The total length of the system was 3.125 route miles and 4.45 track miles. The track drains were also manufactured by Messrs. Edgar Allen. The rails, of B.S. sections No. 1 and 1C, were supplied by the North Eastern Steel Co. Ltd., and the poles by the British Mannesmann Tube Co. Ltd.

In September 1908 there was considerable excitement that the date of the opening of the tramway could not be far off, as by then all the track had been laid completely for several weeks and it was expected that the overhead wiring would be started the following week. The tramcars were already constructed and were awaiting delivery from the Brush Works. These were transported by rail from Loughborough to Ossett station and from there on low bogies to the car sheds in Church Street. The carsheds were now almost complete and the adjacent Yorkshire Electric Power Company's sub-station only awaited its roof. Ossett Town Council's own plan for setting up an incinerator-cum-electricity generating plant had fallen through when it was found that it would be more economical to buy power from the Yorkshire Electric Power Company than to generate their own.

In Ossett Market Place, a junction between the newly constructed Dewsbury & Ossett Tramways and the lines of the Wakefield & District Light Railway was made, and the hope was that there would be eventually through-running of cars from Wakefield to Dewsbury via Ossett and the D. & O. This junction in the Ossett Market Place was made at the expense of the Wakefield & District Light Railway Company who were to maintain it for forty-two years, at the expiration of which period (1950) it would become the property of the Ossett Corporation. This loop in Ossett Market Place was used by both the Dewsbury & Ossett trams and the West Riding trams for reversing purposes, and replaced the former Wakefield & District stub-end terminus in Bank Street. In September 1906, Wakefield & District had claimed that they had rights to run over the Ossett lines; N.E.C. disputed this, but agreed in December 1906 to lay a junction between the two systems.

The *Ossett Observer* for Saturday 31 October 1908 reported that trials had been made during that week over the lines by running a car over short distances. A semi-official trial was made, which the surveyors of the three local authorities

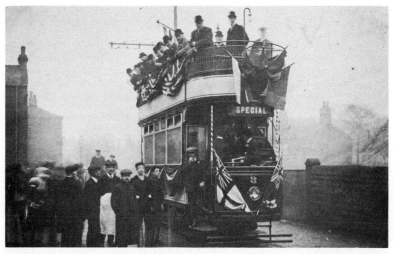

Opening day on the Dewsbury and Ossett Tramways, 12 November 1908, with car No. 3 at Earlsheaton terminus.   (Courtesy R. Brook

Another Dewsbury and Ossett opening day scene, 12 November 1908; No. 3 arriving at Dewsbury terminus, with the Town Clerk of Dewsbury acting as motorman. (F. Hartley

concerned were invited to attend. The cars started from the car sheds in Church Street, Ossett, and the whole of the lines were traversed twice. The proceedings were supervised by Mr. Primavesi, the NEC electrical engineer, who was responsible for the overhead equipment and by Mr. Wray, the local engineer. Everything was found to be satisfactory. Apart from a short delay whilst the car was at Dewsbury due to a derrick fouling the wires at the Ossett sub-station and cutting off the current, everything went well, and it was decided to apply immediately for inspection of the tramways by the Board of Trade Inspector.

The official Board of Trade inspection by Lt. Col. E. Druitt R.E., took place on 11 November 1908. The Inspector boarded the special car at 10 a.m. which left Dewsbury Market Place and ran over the whole of the system. Everything was found to be satisfactory, and sanction was given for the running of the cars for the public at once.

The following afternoon (Thursday 12 November 1908) the lines were given a formal opening. No elaborate ceremony had been arranged, but two gaily decorated cars were waiting to take the members of the three local authorities on a tour of the tramways. The Mayor of Ossett drove one car to the Chickenley Heath boundary of the borough, where the Chairman of the Soothill Nether Urban District Council took over the controls and drove the car until it reached the boundary with the Borough of Dewsbury, whose Town Clerk then became the motorman. A formal dinner was held in the evening, and public service commenced next day, Friday 13 November.

As the Dewsbury & Ossett Tramways ran on several steep gradients, Lt. Col. Druitt had made a number of recommendations in his report, and there were several compulsory stops before descending some of the steeper parts of the system. A general speed of 10 miles/hr. was prescribed, with the following exceptions: 12 miles/hr. in Dewsbury Road, Ossett, and 4 miles/hr. in Wakefield Road, Dewsbury on the downward journey from the top of the Cutting to Dewsbury Market Place; in High Street, Earlsheaton, passing Highfield Congregational Chapel and round the corners between High Street and Town Street, Earlsheaton; and between Dewsbury Road and Church Street and between Church Street and Dale Street in Ossett.

98

Compulsory stops were required in Wakefield Road, Dewsbury, before passing Leeds Road on the downward journey; in Wakefield Road, Soothill Nether (a) before crossing High Road on the downward journey and (b) before leaving the top of Wakefield Cutting, where the slipper brake should be applied before coming down the steep gradient; in High Road, Earlsheaton, before coming out into Wakefield Road on the downward journey where the slipper brake should be applied before leaving; in Wakefield Road, Chickenley Heath at Chickenley Lane and again at Syke Lane both on the downward journey.

The Inspector in commenting on the steepness of the gradient made certain other recommendations. He wrote, "There is a very steep gradient for the first half-mile out of Dewsbury in Wakefield Road varying from 1 in 12.9 to 1 in 16 and great care must be exercised in working the traffic up and down it. Before the first car goes over this part of the track in the morning, the rails should be cleaned by hand and sanded and attention be paid to them at other times if they are in a greasy condition. There are four curves with a central radius varying from 50 feet to 60 feet but none on the steep gradient". The Inspector concluded his report by stating that he had been informed by the Tramway Company that the drivers were all men with previous experience of driving on steep gradients and had had considerable practice over the steep gradients on these tramways, and so he could recommend the Board of Trade to sanction them for public running.

Operating the Tramways

Two separate services were operated, the principal one from Dewsbury Market Place to Ossett Market Place, and a branch service from Dewsbury Market Place to Earlsheaton. Before the opening, the *Ossett Observer* stated that both would be run at ten minute intervals, with additional cars on special occasions, but this level of service did not materialise for some years.

The fares were fixed at 2d. from Dewsbury to Ossett, (1d. for bona fide workmen on cars running before 7.30 a.m. and between 5 p.m. and 6 p.m. and between noon and 1 p.m. on Saturdays). Dewsbury to Earlsheaton being one penny. Children under 14 were charged half-fare. Unfortunately the Company charged 2d. for the journey from Dewsbury to Chickenley Heath station which was little more

Two Dewsbury and Ossett cars at the Dewsbury terminus in the summer of 1915, at the foot of the half-mile gradient in Wakefield Road. Alternate departures consisted of two cars, one for Earlsheaton and one for Ossett. In the 1920s the terminus was moved to the left-hand kerb.
(F. Hartley

than half-way between Dewsbury and Ossett. This cause great annoyance, and was argued about in the local council chambers and by the Dewsbury Tradesmen's Association.

By February 1909 there were complaints from Soothill Nether Urban District Council concerning the open tops of the cars and suggesting that they should be top-covered, as in bad weather there was considerable overcrowding in the lower deck by people wishing to avoid the discomfort of the upper deck. Soothill Nether Council was backed up in this suggestion for covering the upper decks, by Ossett Town Council. Mr. McGibbon, the tramways manager at Ossett, said that the covering of the upper decks was under consideration, but it took many years of deliberations before all the cars were fitted with top-covers. Even as late as 1922 complaints were still being made by the Dewsbury Town Council to the management regarding the lack of top-covers.

It was the rule on this system that people holding workmen's tickets were allowed either inside or outside (i.e. on the open top deck) when travelling to and from work in the mornings, (when most of the people travelling would be workmen), but at tea-time, people having workmen's tickets were not allowed in the lower deck. They had to travel on the outside whatever the weather, and it was no joke trying to get some sort of shelter from the wintry storms behind the trolley standard!

The tram service between Dewsbury and Ossett was improved considerably during September 1910. Instead of the half-hour service which had been run up to 10 a.m. and the 20 minute service afterwards, the half hour service now ended at 7.45 a.m., after which time cars ran every twenty minutes up to 10 a.m. and then every ten minutes for the rest of the day. On Sundays commencing at 9.30 a.m. there was a 20 minute service for the rest of the day. Service between Dewsbury and Earlsheaton was every 20 minutes, increased to 10 minutes on Wednesdays and Saturdays. It was the custom for a Dewsbury car and the one to Earlsheaton to leave the Dewsbury terminus at the same time and run together as far as the junction.

During the years 1912 and 1913 the question of the Dewsbury Corporation Tramways to Shaw Cross and Westborough was very much in the news (details of these proposed tramways are given elsewhere). For this proposed line, down Leeds Road from Shaw Cross to connect with the lines of the Yorkshire Woollen District Tramways across the Dewsbury Market Place, running powers over the D. & O. lines by the side of Dewsbury Town Hall to the terminus would have to be obtained. In one of the later schemes it was intended to lease the Shaw Cross to Westborough Tramways to the Dewsbury & Ossett Tramways, and these running powers would not then have been necessary. The D. & O. terminus at Dewsbury was a double line in the middle of the roadway, and here the cars waited after they had disgorged their loads. This layout was retained long after it had become a danger due to the increase in motor traffic, and only in the 1920s when all hopes of the Dewsbury to Westborough tramways had been abandoned was the terminus altered to end in a length of single line at the roadside. The cars were then able to stand by the side of the kerb instead of being in the line of the through traffic.

There were no proposed extensions to the Dewsbury & Ossett Tramways at any time, in fact the whole of the system as proposed in the original Bill was never constructed, the portion omitted being the loop through the village of Earlsheaton and rejoining the main Wakefield Road at Earlsheaton Cemetery. The system remained almost unaltered from the time of its construction to the time of its demise, except for the doubling of the line at one or two points and the alteration to the terminus in Dewsbury Market Place. There was a suggestion to double the line in Church Street, Ossett in 1913 but possibly due to the war it was never accomplished. Some of the passing places were replaced by track doubling on the Wakefield Road section. There were originally eight passing places between the bottom of Wakefield Cutting and the railway bridge at Chickenley Heath station. These were reduced to two passing places and a long stretch of double track alongside Earlsheaton Cemetery (on either side of Syke Lane) and the passing place at Chickenley Heath station was lengthened.

Dewsbury and Ossett No. 6 arriving at Earlsheaton terminus. An extension was authorised from this point through Earlsheaton village to rejoin the main Wakefield Road, but the necessary road widening was never carried out. (F. Hartley

There were high hopes of regular through running of cars from Wakefield to Dewsbury, using the connection in Ossett Market Place with the Wakefield & District Light Railway. In practice, the through running was limited to very infrequent occasions. These included certain Saturdays when Wakefield Trinity rugby football team played Dewsbury at Crown Flatt. The ground was on top of the hill on the eastern side of Dewsbury, near the Dewsbury to Wakefield main road, before this road descended through the Cutting and so to the Dewsbury terminus. On these occasions through cars from Wakefield did run over the Dewsbury & Ossett tracks from Ossett Market Place as far as the top of the Wakefield Cutting in Dewsbury. As the Yorkshire (West Riding) trams were not fitted with mechanical track brakes, they were not allowed to go down the steep Wakefield Road to the Dewsbury terminus, and reversed at the loop at the top of the Cutting, where they disgorged their loads of supporters. It does not seem that when Dewsbury played Wakefield there was through running from Dewsbury to Wakefield through Horbury. Usually the D.&O. services were stretched to capacity on Saturdays, and there would not be spare cars to run such a service unless cars were borrowed from the West Riding Tramways.

Some other occasional instances of through running were noted by the local press. One such instance was through running by D.&O. cars over the West Riding and Leeds systems from Ossett to Roundhay Park in Leeds on 22 July 1916. To quote the *Ossett Observer,* "The scholars and teachers of the Dewsbury Road Wesleyan Sunday School, Ossett had an enjoyable outing to Roundhay Park, Leeds; the cost being defrayed by the Mayor's father, ex-Alderman G. H. Wilson of Heath House. The adult members made the journey by charabanc and wagonette and the scholars went all the way by tramcar, the specially reserved vehicles going through the distance over three separate tramway systems, via Ossett, Horbury, Wakefield, Lofthouse and Leeds". The cars loaded up on their own system at the chapel in Ossett-Street-Side.

In 1911 it was proposed to run a motor bus service from the Bull Ring in Wakefield to the "Flying Horse Inn" at Ossett along the main Dewsbury to

101

Commercial Car Hirers' omnibus at the Old Flying Horse Inn, Ossett, about to leave for Wakefield. This service was begun in July, 1911 as a personal venture by the Dewsbury and Ossett tramway manager, Mr. McGibbon, but was later discontinued.

Wakefield Road, in connection with the trams. Mr. McGibbon, the Manager of the Dewsbury & Ossett Tramway ran this bus service, as a personal venture. The bus was a "Commer" and the owners were Commercial Car Hirers Ltd. It was not an unqualified success, and frequent breakdowns which occurred on the service caused it to be abandoned.

The 1914-18 War period was a very critical time for the Dewsbury & Ossett Tramways. For its size the Company had a greater percentage of men called to the colours than any other system in the country. This caused drastic curtailing of services, and in October 1917 the morning service between Dewsbury and Earlsheaton was discontinued altogether. During the early months of 1918 there were several arguments between the Dewsbury Town Council and the Dewsbury & Ossett Tramways because the latter could not maintain the statutory twenty minute car service specified in the lease. This was somewhat unfair to the Company, as the Town Council knew the position of the Company with regard to its shortage of man-power. By September 1918 Mr. McGibbon informed the Dewsbury Town Council that his men had been called up to the colours to such an extent that unless time was allowed to train other men as drivers, then the service between Dewsbury and Earlsheaton would have to be suspended altogether. The ending of the War two months later in November 1918 prevented this from happening. Even so, the Dewsbury Town Council still pestered the Company about their services and Mr. McGibbon wrote that as soon as possible an increased service of cars would be made available. The service was restored by March 1920.

Overcrowding of the trams was another source of concern to the various local authorities. This was not due to the War period alone, but was a constant irritation. Time and time again there are references in the various Council minutes to overcrowding. Stress was laid by the councils on the fact that the Dewsbury & Ossett Tramways were constructed under the Tramways Act 1870 and not the Light Railways Act of 1896, and as such they were not allowed to carry additional passengers above the seating capacity. These conditions were not adhered to by the Company, particularly in wet weather and during the period when the cars were open-topped. In spite of everything the overcrowding went on.

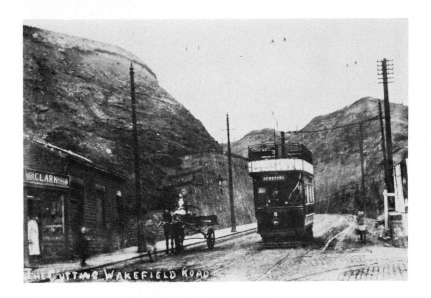

The principal gradient on the Dewsbury and Ossett tramways was the half mile section from the Dewsbury terminus to the top of Wakefield Road cutting. These two views of the cutting show car No. 5 before 1914 at the junction with the Earlsheaton branch, and top covered car No. 7 near the top of the cutting in the early 1930s.   (F. Smith and Dr. Hugh Nicol

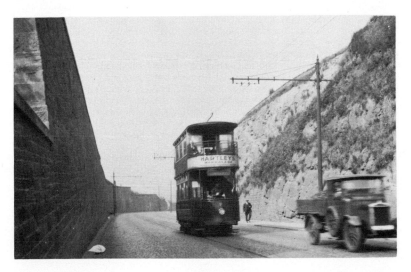

Church Street tram depot, Ossett, after the Dewsbury and Ossett tram fleet had been top-covered (the last open top cars received covers in 1925). No. 2 was one of two cars which carried rocker-panel advertisements by the Dewsbury painter and decorator Mr. Ruddlesden. The building survives as an electricity board depot, complete with track fan.   (Dr. Hugh Nicol

In common with the other tramways in this book, the number of passengers carried reached a peak in 1920 (2,959,170) but declined only slightly thereafter, rising again in 1929 to surpass the 1920 figure. This reflected the virtual absence of motor bus competition on this route until an Ossett—Halifax service was introduced about 1931. Top covering of the tram fleet extended over ten years, from 1915 to 1925, six covers being made at Preston and the other four at Rawmarsh after the Mexborough and Swinton and Dewsbury and Ossett had come under common management.

In 1928 the Company again thought of running motor buses in connection with the trams. In March of that year it applied to the Ossett Corporation for the right to run a bus service from Dewsbury along the new road which the Ossett Council had constructed linking Ossett Market Place with the Wakefield Road at the point where that road is joined by the road from Leeds. It was hoped that as time elapsed houses would be built along this new road, which was named Kingsway. This bus service was intended to augment the tram service between Dewsbury and Ossett, and also to provide an alternative route into Ossett. Mr. McGibbon proposed putting on six new buses. This would give a five minute service between Dewsbury and Ossett, alternately by bus via Kingsway and by tram via Church Street. It would have lessened the overcrowding, but the civic fathers thought that such a service would create congestion on the roads. Little did they realise the congestion which was to come! There was also considerable discussion in the local council chambers concerning the word used by the Dewsbury & Ossett Company in asking for the "right" to run buses in Kingsway, and Ossett Council feared that this meant they wanted the sole right to run buses along this road. Discussions continued without result for a considerable time.

In 1930, during discussions which were taking place on a possible amalgamation of Dewsbury and Ossett, the question of the tram service was again raised. The National Electric Construction Company had put forward a suggestion that motor buses or trackless trams should be substituted for the trams. Both Dewsbury and Ossett Town Councils accepted an invitation to inspect the

Company's new trackless trolley buses which were in operation in the Mexborough area. The following week representatives from both Ossett and Dewsbury Councils visited Mexborough, Doncaster and Rotherham to see the new trackless trams in action. The representatives were greatly impressed by what they saw, especially by the double-deck Doncaster ones. Single-deck trackless trams had been running for a long period from Guiseley to Otley, operated by the Leeds Corporation Tramways. Earlier when it had been suggested that trackless cars be used in the Dewsbury district, the Leeds manager said they were unsuitable for such a hilly area. Now there appeared to be considerable enthusiasm due to the improved features of trolley buses.

The National Electric Construction Company held discussions with all the local councils as to the future of the trams. The N.E.C. wished to run a trolley bus service between Dewsbury and Ossett to replace the trams. As late as June 1932, rather more than a year before the trams were actually replaced, a detailed scheme was put forward covering the possibility of replacing the tram by trackless cars, to the effect that the tramway company would pull up the tramlines and reinstate the roadways. They would make a cash contribution in respect of the relief of the liability for the future maintenance of the roadway for the remainder of the unexpired portion of the lease (i.e. for 20 years). They were to settle the value of the tramlines, overhead equipment, car sheds etc., which on the expiration of the lease would become the property of the Ossett Corporation. The trackless trolley buses were to be garaged in the existing car sheds or extensions of them in Ossett. They were to make a contribution in respect of the loss of rates, if any, which the Corporation might suffer by the trams being discontinued. They were to pay the Corporation the sum of £100 per annum on the expiration of 30 years from the date of the original lease for a period of 12 years. They were also to bear the costs of the Corporation in supporting the Bill or Order applied for by the Company to obtain the necessary Parliamentary or other powers. The Corporation were to have the option at the expiration of 21 years of taking over the Company's undertaking in such terms as would be exercisable at intervals of seven years.

In the 1920s the Dewsbury terminus of the Dewsbury and Ossett tramways was moved to the roadside, but was still in the direct line of any runaway traffic down the steep hill. The building opposite tram No. 4 is Dewsbury Town Hall. (R. B. Parr

However, the proposed trolley bus system never saw the light of day. The National Electric Construction Company, with all its subsidiaries, was bought out in 1931 by the British Electric Traction Co. Ltd., and while the local N.E.C. subsidiary companies elsewhere were allowed to continue in existence, there was no subsidiary company to operate the Dewsbury and Ossett. The B.E.T. therefore decided to transfer operations to its own local subsidiary, the Yorkshire (Woollen District) Electric Tramways Co. Ltd., which in 1935 was renamed Yorkshire Woollen District Transport Company. The Y.W.D. could serve the district economically from its own motor bus depot at Savile Town, Dewsbury, and there was no more mention of trolleybuses.

The Last Trams

The Dewsbury & Ossett Passenger Transport Act of 1933 was the means by which the D.&O. Tramways were taken over by the Yorkshire (W.D.) Electric Tramways Company, and this authorised the substitution of buses for the trams which took place later that year. Nine double-deck buses were ordered in April 1933 to replace the trams. The actual date of the last trams on the Dewsbury & Ossett system was Sunday 19 October 1933, a year before the ending of the trams on the Y.W.D. system.

On this Sunday, the last car left Ossett for Dewsbury at 10.15 p.m. and returned to Ossett tramsheds from Dewsbury at 10.40 p.m. The last Earlsheaton car left Dewsbury at 10.10 p.m. and returned from Earlsheaton at 10.20 p.m. A gentleman named John Scott was a passenger on this last car and he was also a passenger on the first car in 1908.

As if to be in sympathy with the proceedings, a few minutes before the car from Ossett arrived at the Dewsbury terminus, there was a power failure temporarily and for a few yards the tram travelled in total darkness. This power failure delayed the departure of the last cars which eventually left Dewsbury nearer eleven o'clock than 10.40 p.m., the scheduled time. Driver Fothergill was in charge of the last tram and it left Dewsbury terminus to the strains of "Auld Lang Syne".

A crowd of people had assembled in Ossett Market Place to greet the tram on arrival there. The car was crowded for the very last journey of all from the Market Place to the car sheds in Church Street. The car left Ossett Market Place at 11.24 p.m. and many of the passengers remained on the car right into the depot yard and until it actually "docked" and the lights were turned out.

The *Ossett Observer* for 26 October 1933 gave some interesting figures for the passengers carried throughout the whole period of the system's existence.

"The usefulness of the system is evidenced by the large number of passengers carried throughout the whole period. There has naturally been a falling-off since the Wakefield to Dewsbury and the Ossett to Halifax bus services were instituted, but it will surprise many to learn that no fewer than 2,571,064 fares were taken last year as against 2,917,490 in 1931, and 2,811,204 in 1930".

So we come to the end of a small but very interesting and efficient little tramway system with a total mileage of under five miles and with a fleet of only twelve cars. That good relations existed between management and work people is borne out by the fact that six members of the staff had the satisfaction of serving throughout the whole of the twenty five years of the existence of the tramway; these were the general manager, W. McGibbon; the general engineer, A. Davies; motorman and later inspector A. Draper; inspector S. Gledhill; shedman (later in charge of the depot) W. Stubbs, and conductor G. Lodge.

As soon as buses replaced the trams, a loop service was instituted through Earlsheaton, over the route of the proposed tramway that was never built. A proportion of the profits earned by the replacing buses was paid to the local authorities, and this was still the case in 1979.

106

D.&O. No. 3 standing at Ossett Market Place terminus, on the loop shared by cars of the Dewsbury & Ossett and Yorkshire (West Riding) tramways. (Dr. Hugh Nicol

Accidents

Considering that the Dewsbury & Ossett Tramways traversed such steep hilly country, with its Dewsbury terminus at the bottom of a half mile 1 in 12 gradient, remarkably few accidents occurred due to runaway cars. This is greatly to the credit of the Company and to the efficiency of its drivers.

There were several minor accidents during the early years of the tramway typical of those which occurred on other systems, such as collisions with horses and carts, many due partly to the stubborness of the carters in opposing the new form of transport. There were also a few minor accidents at the Dewsbury terminus due to cars overshooting the metals and running on to the setts and which, but for the prompt action of the motormen concerned could have had very serious consequences. On 22 September 1913 car No. 8 ran on to the setts at the Dewsbury terminus, after being unable to stop at the Board of Trade compulsory stop at Fishworth Street, at the top side of the Town Hall. This compulsory stop was instituted to ensure that cars would be able to stop at the terminus, or at worst the driver would know that something was wrong and would be able to do something about it. In this case the car was unable to stop due to greasy rails and it therefore overshot the terminus, but the motorman was alert to his duties and so prevented a far worse accident occurring.

On 27 December 1913 there was an accident which caused a fatality. This occurred to the 3.30 p.m. car from Dewsbury to Ossett which after travelling for about 250 yards up Wakefield Road was brought to a standstill owing to a brewer's dray being in the way. The car had six passengers in it. The driver eased the car backwards a few yards in order to allow the wagon to be moved, but he was unable to stop the car again. It ran backwards down Wakefield Road right to the terminus where it left the metals and came to a standstill on the setts. One woman passenger was apparently thrown from the car, or jumped from it (it is not clear which) and received fatal injuries. Before leaving the metals at the bottom of the hill, the car also collided with a furniture van, spinning the horse round as it careered in its mad rush. The tram driver, as it would appear from the enquiry "lost his head" and failed to apply the slipper brake which would have brought the car to a standstill. From subsequent happenings, it would seem that it was the furniture van which prevented the car from charging across the setts and into the boot shop which faced the terminus.

In the following year on 21 March 1914 another car over-ran the Dewsbury terminus. This was a car from Earlsheaton which had discharged its load of passengers at the terminus and then had taken on a new load and was standing awaiting the time for departure. The conductor, unaware that the driver had left the car, released the brake and went upstairs to fasten the trolley rope round the trolley boom as was the custom at the terminus. The result was that the car ran down the slight incline at that spot and across the street on the setts and finally came to rest in front of a couple of market stalls, it being Saturday night.

The most serious of all the accidents on this system occurred on 12 October 1915. Car No. 3 was the 4.15 p.m. tram from Earlsheaton to Dewsbury and was driven by John James Callaghan. Fortunately there were only three passengers on board at the time, a woman and two girls, otherwise the results would have been far more serious than they were. Exactly where the car got out of control is difficult to say, but there had been a slight shower of rain during the afternoon and it has been suggested that this made the rails greasy and so caused the wheels of the car to skid. A pony and flat cart with its owner, Mr. B. Buckley sitting on its edge, was in the direct line of the oncoming car and when Mr. Buckley saw it he turned the cart into Rishworth Street. Unfortunately he was too late; the tram struck the cart and overturned it and threw the pony down on the ground. Mr. Buckley had a very narrow escape. It was here, opposite the Town Hall, that the conductress jumped off the car. She was later taken to the Infirmary to be treated. The pony and cart also knocked down two women. The tram then collided with a horse and cart, spinning the rear end of the cart round and in doing so injured another man. The car over-ran the terminus, and careered across the setts straight into Hilton's boot shop, coming to rest embedded in the shop's lower structure. A fire broke out but though the fire brigade was sent for, a few buckets of water soon quenched the outbreak. At 5.30 p.m. the upper storeys of the building (which were used by the adjoining Scarboro Hotel) crashed down on the unfortunate tram. The whole event attracted a large crowd of people.

In November a Board of Trade enquiry was opened by Lt. Col. Druitt, into the accident, and the conclusion was reached that the greasy state of the rails after the shower of rain was the main contributing factor. It was suggested that the rain and coal dust on the lines from a colliery almost adjacent to the Wakefield Road (the Ridings Colliery of Messrs. Crawshaw & Warburton Ltd.) helped to make the lines

Dewsbury & Ossett No. 3 embedded in Hilton's boot shop in Dewsbury Market Place on 12 October 1915. Shortly after this photograph was taken, the building collapsed on to the tram, as shown opposite. (both pictures F. Hartley

greasy. The driver had applied sand when he found that he was unable to stop the tram; the wheels locked, and then skidded on the greasy rails. There was considerable discussion at the enquiry between Mr. A. Davies (engineer to the Company) and the driver (Mr. Callaghan) on this point of the skidding and how it should have been prevented by the alternate application of the brakes and then releasing them, until the car held the road. Mr. Davies said the car (No. 3) had been overhauled the previous day. Other drivers testified to the good working condition of the tram. Mr. Davies said that the procedure of sanding and applying the brakes and then releasing alternately and re-applying them and repeating this until the car was got under control was unfortunately not applied due to the "human element".

After the accident car No. 3 was taken back to the depot at Ossett and remained there for the rest of the War years. The body was raised on to some barrels and it was used as a "quarry" for spares. Not until the Company began to re-organise itself after the war years was No. 3 re-conditioned, and it was then fitted with a top cover and eventually re-entered service. Unlike the Yorkshire (W.D.) Electric Tramway Company, the Dewsbury & Ossett did not re-number this car after its accident; it carried its original number until it was scrapped when the trams were abandoned. The accident cost the Company £2,000, half of which was charged to the current year and the remainder carried forward. But for this, the company's profit for 1915/16 would have been a record.

Meanwhile, the general purposes committee of Dewsbury Borough Council had inspected the ruins of the boot shop and hotel, and wished to discuss with the owners of the hotel (Messrs. Ramsden, brewers of Halifax), a plan to set back the building line on that side of the Market Place. This would have widened the Market Place considerably, and would have removed the objection to a possible joint terminus and connection with the Yorkshire (W.D.) Electric Tramways. A letter was read from Messrs. Ramsdens' solicitor on 10 January 1916, but it was resolved that the terms offered by the brewery company be considered no further.

Another Dewsbury & Ossett incident involved No. 9, an ex-Mexborough car shown in the right hand picture. These cars had single (instead of twin leaf) saloon doors and ran on Mountain & Gibson radial trucks, just visible in this picture. These were later replaced by rigid trucks.

(R. Brook

A car of Dewsbury & Ossett series 1 to 8 on the traverser at the Brush Electrical Engineering Company's works at Loughborough in 1908, showing the half-turn stairs, twin-leaf saloon doors, and mechanical track brake. The livery was dark red and broken white.
(Brush Electrical Engineering Co. Ltd.

DEWSBURY & OSSETT ROLLING STOCK

This tramway, a late starter, had no need to experiment and was able to adopt proven types of cars and equipment already in use elsewhere. Its cars gave good service with little modification other than the fitting of top covers, which took place rather later than elsewhere, perhaps because the presence of steep gradients made it seem inadvisable to add to the weight of the cars. Common ownership with the Mexborough and Swinton Tramways enabled some of the heavier repair work to be carried out at the latter's Dale Road depot in Rawmarsh, and four of the top covers needed by the Dewsbury and Ossett Tramways were made there. On two occasions, Mexborough and Swinton released cars permanently to form additions to the Dewsbury and Ossett fleet.

Nos. 1-8   Double deck open top four wheel cars with three windows per side, built 1908.
Bodies built by Brush Electrical Engineering Co. Ltd., Loughborough.
Dimensions: 16 ft. 0 in. long over corner pillars, length over fenders 28 ft. 0 in., width 7 ft. 1 in., interior height 6 ft. 9 in., height to trolley plank 9 ft. 6 in.
Seating for 22 passengers inside and 32 outside, total 54.
Electrical equipment supplied by the Brush Electrical Engineering Co. Ltd., Loughborough. Two Brush motors of 35 horse power each. Two Brush controllers, probably of type H2.
Truck: Brush 21E of 6 ft. 6 in. wheelbase.
Braking: Hand wheel brake, mechanical track brake, rheostatic brake.

These cars, which formed the entire Dewsbury & Ossett fleet until 1911, were of a standard Brush design already supplied to the other subsidiaries of the National Electric Construction Company at Rhondda and Torquay though differing from

110

One of the two top covers delivered to the Dewsbury & Ossett tramways by English Electric (Preston) in 1921.　　　　　　　　　　　　　　　　　　　　　(Courtesy GEC Traction Ltd.

some of these in their trucks and equipment and in some other details such as saloon doors and interior height. The most evident differences between these cars and the earlier Brush vehicles on the Y.W.D. system were their half-turn direct spiral stairs, air-scoop ventilators, destination boxes hung immediately beneath the canopy (above the driver's head) and the provision of two swan-neck lighting standards on the top deck. All cars had hand slipper brakes operated by the usual hand wheel mounted around the handbrake column, and Peacock geared hand wheel brakes. The cars were supplied with extending platform gates, but these were soon removed.

The decision to fit the cars with three-window open balcony top covers was evidently taken in 1914 or early 1915, but the process took nine years to complete. Board of Trade approval was given on 28 October 1915, and the work was evidently paid for out of revenue. The first two covers were made by the United Electric Car Company Ltd. of Preston in 1915. Two more were ordered from the Preston works (by this time English Electric Co. Ltd.) in August 1921, the second of which differed in that the trolley cable was run under the roof, and this feature was repeated in two more covers supplied by English Electric in 1925. All these orders were placed by the parent company, National Electric Construction, and all six covers were made from the same drawings. The former D.&O. engineer, Mr. Davies, stated that the top covers came by rail to Ossett station and were towed from there to the car sheds on low bogies.

The 1925 covers completed the top covering of the D.&O. fleet (which then numbered ten cars) because four covers of the same pattern had meanwhile been made for the D.&O. by the Mexborough & Swinton Tramways at Dale Road, Rawmarsh, between January and September 1922, at a cost of £1293 17s. Since all ten covers were outwardly identical, it is not possible to say in what order the ten cars were dealt with. On being top-covered the cars retained their shallow upper deck end panels and wire mesh, contrasting with the deep waist-high valances which were a distinctive feature of the Y.W.D. fleet after its final rebuilding in Major Chapple's day.

Nos. 9-10   Double deck open top four wheel cars with three windows per side, acquired in 1911.

Bodies built in 1906 by Brush Electrical Engineering Co. Ltd., Loughborough.

Dimensions and seating as for cars 1 to 8, but with slightly lower saloons.

Electrical equipment supplied by British Thomson-Houston Co. Ltd.

Two GE 58 motors of 35 horse power each, two BTH B18 controllers.

Truck: Mountain & Gibson radial of 8 ft. 6 in. wheelbase, replaced by Brush 21E type after a few years with Dewsbury & Ossett.

Braking: Hand wheel brake, mechanical track brake, rheostatic brake.

When the Mexborough & Swinton Tramways completed their system in 1908 they had twenty trams, which they soon found were more than they needed. In 1911, they sold two of them to the Dewsbury & Ossett Tramways for £860. These two cars had been Nos. 10 and 14 in the M.&S. fleet; they became 9 and 10 in the D.&O. fleet, and it is more than likely that M.&S. No. 10 kept its old number and became D.&O. 10, and M.&S. No. 14 became No. 9. No. 10 had remained open topped, but No. 14 had been fitted in 1907 with a low-height Brush top cover, only to lose it as the result of a runaway accident on Warren Vale Hill on 30 July 1908, when the car ran away and ended up on its side in a field. The top cover was quickly repaired and fitted to another car, but No. 14 did not run again for nearly two years, and was then returned to open top condition and soon sold to the Dewsbury & Ossett.

Cars 1 to 16 on the Mexborough and Swinton Tramways had originally been fitted with Mountain & Gibson radial trucks, and the two cars came to Ossett still on these trucks. They were replaced by the 21E type after a few years' D.&O. service. Although similar in most respects to the original Dewsbury & Ossett cars, Nos. 9 and 10 could be readily distinguished by the fact that the destination indicator boxes were mounted above the balcony handrails and that the stair rails ended by being jointed into the upright stanchion at the foot of the stairs instead of continuing in the form of a loop. In open top days, these two cars could also be distinguished from Nos. 1 to 8 by their lower trolley standards, and after being top covered, by their reduced overall height compared with that of Nos. 1 to 8.

D.&O. ex-Mexborough cars 9 and 10 in Ossett depot. These two cars were slightly lower than the original D.&O. vehicles. The motor tower wagon is just visible behind No. 9.

(Dr. Hugh Nicol

112

Dewsbury & Ossett 7 and 11 at Dewsbury terminus. No. 11 (right) was one of two low-height cars acquired in 1928 from the Mexborough and Swinton tramways. An end view of this car showing the side-mounted trolley and lowered roof appears on page 165. No. 12 was similar but had a three-window lower saloon. (Dr. Hugh Nicol)

Nos. 11-12 Double deck cars with open balcony top covers, acquired in 1928. Bodies built in 1906 by Brush Electrical Engineering Co. Ltd., Loughborough and subsequently top covered and reconstructed.
Original dimensions and seating as for cars 9 and 10.
Electrical equipment supplied by British Thomson-Houston Co. Ltd. Two GE 58 motors of 35 horse power each, two B18 controllers.
Truck: Brush 21E type of 6 ft. 6 in. wheelbase.
Braking: Hand wheel brake, mechanical track brake, rheostatic brake.

The conversion of the Mexborough and Swinton Tramways to trolleybus operation between November 1928 and 9 March 1929 rendered the remaining 16 M.&S. cars surplus to requirements, and two cars (Nos. 7 and 15) were sold in 1928 to the Dewsbury and Ossett for £50 each, becoming D.&O. 11 and 12 respectively. Both cars had been fitted in 1907 with low-height Brush top covers designed to pass beneath the low railway bridge at Swinton station, having a domed roof profile and side-mounted trolley base. No. 7 (D.&O. 11) had been rebuilt at Rawmarsh in 1923 with a six-window lower saloon. A spare truck was bought from Mexborough at the same time.

For details of the Mexborough cars, the author is indebted to Mr. C. C. Hall's study of the Mexborough and Swinton Tramways published in issues 51 to 58 of *Tramway Review* in 1967-69.

Mention must also be made of the current collectors on Dewsbury & Ossett cars. In open top days, a rope was fitted for turning the trolley, but the rope was not allowed to trail and there was no fitting by which to secure it. Instead, the rope was wound around the trolley boom when not in use, and knotted near the trolley standard. At each terminus, the conductor ran upstairs, unfastened the rope, and threw it over the side of the car. He ran down to the street, grabbed the rope, turned the trolley round, and then flung the rope up on to the top deck. He ran upstairs again, wound the rope around the trolley boom, and knotted it at the junction of the boom and the standard. This trolley rope ritual was once the cause of an accident, but the company never rose to the heights of having any automatic trolley reversers. When the advent of top covers required a change in procedure, the cars were fitted

113

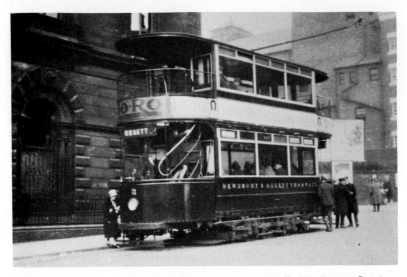

Dewsbury & Ossett No. 3 in final condition and maroon and off-white livery at Dewsbury terminus. This was the car involved in the runaway illustrated on page 108, and later rebuilt.
(Science Museum, Whitcombe Collection

with a bamboo pole carried on hooks below the underframe. One car, believed to be No. 7, was fitted in the 1920s with an experimental trolley skid.

Liveries

The original livery of the Dewsbury and Ossett Tramways was dark red and off-white, both lined out. As delivered, the waist panels were divided in lined-out rectangular panels coinciding with the three saloon windows, the centre panel carrying a belt or garter with the full title of Dewsbury, Ossett and Soothill Nether Tramways. The lining out on the red waist panel had ornamental corners, and the upper deck panels were edged in brown. Unfortunately the undertaking soon covered nearly every available space on the cars with enamelled iron advertisement sheets screwed on to the panels, completely obscuring the lining-out except when a vacancy occurred. The D.&O. did not imitate the Y.W.D. by painting the advertisements directly on to the car panels, except for two cars whose rocker panels advertised Ruddlesden, the Dewsbury painter and decorator; this was painted by one of Ruddlesden's own men.

The D.&O. did not normally employ a full time coach painter, preferring to put this work out to contract. For some years the regular painter was a Mr. Salisbury, who had a small coach-building business near the "Flying Horse Inn" in Ossett, not far from Ossett car sheds. Details of the repainting procedure were described to the author as follows: (1) rubbing down (2) stopping with white lead paste (3) undercoat (4) main top coat and (5) varnishing. Although the cars got into disrepair during the 1914-18 war, none were ever painted battleship grey. They were "touched up" as necessary, using the paint which the company had in stock.

The top covers arrived from Preston ready painted in off-white to match the cars, but after the 1914-18 war a change was made to the livery, which became maroon and off-white, the maroon being applied to all areas below the waist rail and to the ventilator strip above the lower saloon windows. The window surrounds on both decks were painted off-white, as were the upper deck panels, with a maroon strip below the upper deck windows. In this livery, the words "Dewsbury and Ossett Tramways" were spelt out in full along the maroon waist panel, and were in gold leaf, blocked blue and shaded black. The fleet numbers, which were always placed above the headlamp, were similarly in gold, blocked blue and shaded black. In the final years of operation the main upper deck side panels were changed to maroon, leaving the balcony valances and window pillars as the only areas still in the lighter colour. All maroon panels were by now unlined, but the remaining cream panels were edged in brown.

Extracts from Board of Trade Returns, 1910-14 and 1919-32
Dewsbury & Ossett Tramways

	Capital expenditure to date	Net surplus on year	Miles open	Number of cars	Passengers carried
1910	£4587	£2732	3.11	8	1,303,244
1911	£4758	£3595	3.11	8	1,332,669
1912	£4781	£4481	3.11	10	1,490,926
1913	£5457	£4509	3.11	10	1,540,194
1914	£5471	£4569	3.11	10	1,743,354
1919	£5471	£7868	3.11	10	2,390,543
1920	£5471	£6573	3.11	10	2,659,513
1921	£5471	£5294	3.11	10	2,959,170
1922	£5471	£4471	3.11	10	2,675,482
1923	£5471	£4600	3.11	10	2,718,316
1924	£5471	£4623	3.14	10	2,762,165
1925		£4670	3.14	10	2,780,240
1926		£4217	3.14	10	2,713,045
1927		£2089	3.14	10	2,621,539
1928		£2428	3.14	10	2,905,646
1929		£2698	3.14	10	3,040,374
1930		£2657	3.14	12	2,917,490
1931		£1924	3.14	12	2,811,204
1932		£817	3.09	12	2,571,064

Dewsbury, Ossett & Soothill Nether Electric Tramways

Owned by the parent company (the National Electric Construction Company)	0.00 miles
Owned by Dewsbury Corporation (having taken over Soothill Nether U.D.C.'s portion at the amalgamation of 1910) plus its own portion	2.00 miles
Ossett Corporation	1.14 miles
	3.14 miles

115

CHAPTER SIX

THE WAKEFIELD AND DISTRICT LIGHT RAILWAYS

The city of Wakefield is situated on the river Calder some eight miles south of Leeds, five miles east of Dewsbury and six miles west of Castleford. New Stone Age and Roman remains have been found in the area, and when the Romans withdrew in 410 AD the area was settled first by the Angles and Saxons, who gave us the place-names ending in ton (e.g. Normanton) and then by the Norsemen or Vikings who gave us the many village names ending in thorpe. Sandal Castle, some two miles south of Wakefield, was the dominant military fortress in the district, built by the Earl of Warenne soon after the Norman Conquest. It witnessed the Battle of Wakefield in 1460, and after a siege by the Parliamentary army in 1645 was demolished by the victors so that it could not be used again.

Wakefield Bridge, of nine arches, was built in 1342 and has been twice widened. The chantry chapel of St. Mary was built at the same time as the bridge, and is the largest and most beautiful of the four such bridge chapels in England. It has been renovated and rebuilt several times since 1797, but the lower structure and crypt is original. The west front was last rebuilt in 1940.

A cattle market was established in 1756, and later a corn market. There is good farming land around the town, and the area later became the chief centre of the forced rhubarb industry. Coal and iron were mined in the vicinity from shallow pits by some of the abbeys. With the coming of the Industrial Revolution, textile manufacture came to Wakefield, with several woollen mills in the town, and the coming of the canal (Aire and Calder Navigation) and the railways (Great Northern, and Lancashire and Yorkshire) helped the growth of industry. Modern deep mining took the place of the shallow workings, and stone quarrying also became important in the area, as did the making of bricks. But the towns and villages kept their identities, and were separated from one another and from Wakefield by stretches of semi-rural countryside.

With the establishment of county councils under the Local Government Act 1888, Wakefield became the seat of the West Riding County Council. A fine county hall was built in Wood Street, and is now the headquarters of the West Yorkshire Metropolitan County Council. Next to it is the Crown Court and beyond it the Town Hall. In the same year, 1888, the Diocese of Wakefield was created out of that of Ripon and the parish church of All Saints became the cathedral of the new diocese, the town's status being raised to that of a city.

Wakefield had privately operated horse buses and wagonettes from the 1840s. The earliest mention of tramways appears to date from 1862, when a circular letter from Mr. George Francis Train was read on February 5 at a meeting of Wakefield town council, evoking no response. Nothing more seems to have happened until 1878, when a London engineer, E. E. Allen of Victoria Chambers, Westminster, proposed a tramway from Alverthorpe through Wakefield to Agbrigg. Correspondence with the Town Clerk through local solicitors Marsden, Williams & Co. continued until 1880, but the parties concluded that the tramway would be unremunerative.

A fresh attempt was made in 1882 by the Wakefield Tramway Company Ltd., which hoped to run trams from Wakefield to Sandal and Agbrigg. The promoter was Mr. John Belton of 81 Hatton Garden, London, and the engineers Messrs.

Newton & Vawser of Manchester. After Wakefield Council had given their approval on 10 October 1882, application was made for a Provisional Order. The proposal was to lay a single line tramway of 3 ft. 6 in. gauge, with passing places, to be worked by cable or steam traction, from St. Michael's Church in Westgate, Wakefield, through Westgate, Little Westgate, Kirkgate, over the Chantry Bridge across the river Calder and then along the two roads to Sandal and Agbrigg.

Some of the owners of properties in Little Westgate immediately objected, owing to the narrowness of the road and because they frequently kept their carts standing in front of the shops. The promoters offered a choice of three solutions; to run no cars through Little Westgate on market days, to construct crossovers so that their cars could pass the parked vehicles, to run "cars without rails" through Little Westgate (presumably horse buses), or to apply for fresh powers to avoid Little Westgate altogether and route their lines through the Bull Ring and into Kirkgate by the side of the Parish Church (from 1888 the Cathedral). The third alternative was adopted, and the company then proceeded with a Parliamentary Bill. Steam traction was now specified.

Objections now arose from another quarter, because the tramways were to pass over the Chantry Bridge. They were based not on any respect for the antiquity of the bridge and chantry, which dated from A.D. 1342, but on the damage and extra maintenance which the tramway would entail. The chief objectors were the Justices of the Peace for the West Riding, who were responsible at that time for the maintenance of the bridge, and were worried whether the bridge would stand the weight of tramcars, particularly if steam traction were used. A count taken from 6 to 27 May 1883 showed that about 1000 vehicles a day used the bridge, excluding handcarts, the busiest days being Fridays, which were the corn markets. The trams would have added perhaps 70 or 80 to this figure, giving an average of about one vehicle per minute.

A three-horse omnibus of the Wakefield City and District Omnibus Company Ltd. in front of the Corn Exchange at the top of Westgate in Wakefield. The tram track visible in the foreground shows that this photograph was taken shortly before horse bus services ceased in July 1904.
(Courtesy West Riding Automobile Co. Ltd.)

The objectors were also worried that tramcars might meet traction engines on the bridge and be unable to pass them. These vehicles were eight feet wide, with bales of wool often overlapping. The width of the bridge was only 20 ft. 7½ in. at one end and 21 ft. 9 in. at the other, with a footpath on either side of the roadway, and there was a sharp bend on the northern side where the road went round the King's Mill. The gauge of the tramways was to be 3 ft. 6 in., with a double track across the bridge, and the Board of Trade required a clearance of 18 inches between passing cars, which would limit the promoters to cars five feet wide, rather narrow even on a 3 ft. 6 in. gauge. The alternatives were to lay a single track, or a closely-spaced double track worked as single line, with only one tram allowed on the bridge at any time. No solution was found, and the result was that when the company's Bill came before the House of Lords committee on 14 June 1883 it was thrown out. This was the last serious attempt to provide tramways in Wakefield in the pre-electric era.

Instead, Wakefield was served from 1890 by a service of three-horse double deck omnibuses, which had a stand in front of the Cathedral and another at the Corn Exchange. The Wakefield City and District Omnibus Company Ltd. was incorporated on 3 July 1890 with a capital of £6000 in £1 shares, and had its registered office at 36 Wood Street, Wakefield. It provided from eight to eleven journeys per day from Wakefield to Agbrigg and Sandal in 25 minutes and to Lofthouse and Horbury in 35 minutes, with two journeys four times weekly to Thornes and Calder Grove. Two of the Sandal buses continued to Newmillerdam, and all routes had extra buses on Saturdays. From October 1894 to May 1895 there was also a service to Ardsley, but it was withdrawn for lack of support. From 1 May 1895 the company provided horses for Wakefield City Fire Brigade, and in 1903 the company had 46 horses, seven 26-seat three-horse omnibuses with garden seats on the top deck, and five 12-seat chars-à-banc. The company withdrew their services in July 1904 in anticipation of the opening of the tramways, and the 38 remaining horses and the 12 omnibuses were sold on 11 July. One of their best known drivers was Jimmy Hesling, who became a driver on the electric trams in 1904 and continued until they closed down in 1932.

In the closing years of the last century, following the success of electric tramway systems at Bristol and elsewhere, there took place a "tramway mania" as rival groups of promoters sought to obtain concessions for those urban areas not already provided with tramways. The Wakefield district was an obvious target, and during the five years from 1900 to 1904 no fewer than eight companies became involved in the promotion of electric tramways in the area. Only two of these actually operated any trams, the role of the others being to promote schemes and (when authorised) sell them to others, or to buy the powers thus granted, form a construction company to build the lines, and sell them to an operating company when built. This procedure, more common in North America than in Britain, renders the historian's task especially difficult in this case.

The first company active in the area appears to have been The Electric Tramways Construction and Maintenance Company Limited, founded by electrical engineer Michael Holroyd Smith of Halifax in 1886. Although Holroyd Smith was actively promoting electric railways and tramways at this time, the company he registered remained dormant until it changed hands in the 1890s, when its new owners drew up plans for light railways which would have formed extensions to the Leeds municipal tramway system. The promoters had grandiose ideas; a report of their annual general meeting stated that in Yorkshire there was great scope for development of electric tramways, and that one day there would be a network of electric tramways through Lancashire and Yorkshire which would connect every town of importance and would cost only one tenth of the capital cost of the Lancashire and Yorkshire Railway. One line for which Board of Trade sanction was sought in 1900 was for one and a half miles from the Thwaite Gate terminus of the Leeds tramways to the township of Stourton, but although the company changed hands again in 1901 and increased its nominal capital in readiness for the start of construction, the powers obtained were then sold to the promoters of Wakefield and

District and the company left the stage. In 1904 its affairs were in the hands of Treasury officials, and it was later compulsorily wound up.

Meanwhile, two rival groups announced plans to build electric tramways to serve the city of Wakefield. Leading the field was the engineering firm of Pritchard, Green and Company of Birmingham, a partnership of chartered engineers Edward Pritchard and Robert Green, who were involved in many tramway and electric supply schemes from 1883 onwards. They drew up plans in 1899 for the construction of a tramway or light railway linking Wakefield with Horbury, Outwood, Sandal Magna, Agbrigg and Alverthorpe, and submitted an application to the Light Railway Commissioners, quoting the gauge as 4 ft. 0 in. There then followed the usual period for the submission of objections, and the directors of the Wakefield City and District Omnibus Co. considered the question at a special meeting on 3 October 1899.

Shortly afterwards, the directors of the Wakefield City and District Omnibus company were approached by a rival promoter, the Drake & Gorham Electric Power and Traction (Pioneer) Syndicate Ltd., who, it seems, offered to buy the shares of the omnibus company at a favourable price of more than £1 per share if the latter company could, by objecting, defeat the Pritchard Green scheme and leave the way clear for Drake & Gorham. An agreement was reached in 1900 and the directors resolved to oppose the other tramway scheme, but unfortunately, when it came to paying money to oppose the Order, the omnibus company could not afford to be represented, presumably because Drake & Gorham had withdrawn. The company's case thus went by default, and their 'buses would have to bow to the march of progress.

On 8 June 1900 an enquiry was held at Wakefield by the Light Railway Commissioners into the application by the Pritchard, Green group. The promoters were John Fell, Joseph James Gittings, Enoch Horton, and Walter James Kershaw; Fell was a contractor who had built tramways in the Potteries and elsewhere. Robert Green, the engineer, said that the length of the lines was a little over ten miles, to be worked by electricity, and the gauge proposed was now 3 ft. 6 in., though they would use 4 ft. 8½ in. (costing an extra £10,000) if the Commissioners preferred. The Commissioners did prefer, and specified 4 ft. 8½ in. gauge, so as to facilitate eventual connection with Leeds. Various other points were satisfactorily resolved, except for the Chantry Bridge in Wakefield. The Commissioners said they would defer their decision until a satisfactory arrangement was made between the promoters and the local authorities for the widening of the bridge. If a settlement could not be reached, the application would be considered afresh and provision made in the Order for the protection of the Corporation and the West Riding County Council.

Discussions about the bridge went on for many months. The West Riding County Council, who were now responsible for it, could not see their way to widening the structure, much less to building a new one nearby, an alternative discussed in January 1901. A complication was that the Aire & Calder Navigation insisted that any widening should take place on the east side, which would have meant pulling down the Chantry Chapel, widening the bridge, and then re-erecting the Chapel on the new alignment. Even a cheaper scheme, to erect a 3 ft. wide footway on the outside of the west parapet, was rejected, unless the tramway paid for it. But the tramway promoters were sufficiently confident to resubmit their application in broadly its original form, hoping for authorisation. Their opponents again prepared details to show that the bridge was inadequate to carry a tramway in addition to the existing traffic; a census taken during the first four days of May 1901 showed a daily average of 1000 vehicles and 1000 bicycles, and it was estimated that when there was a football match 25,000 people passed over the bridge on foot in less than an hour. Against this, it was pointed out that if trams were used the number crossing on foot would be lower.

119

The Chantry Bridge, Wakefield, shortly before tramway operation ceased in 1932, with car 28 en route from Agbrigg to Ossett. A hoarding on the left announces the construction of the new Wakefield Bridge, which was inaugurated on 1 June 1933. An earlier view of the bridge appears on page 151. (Dr. Hugh Nicol

The renewed application was considered in June 1901, and Col. Von Donop inspected the bridge and reported to the Board of Trade and the Commissioners. He considered it strong enough to carry the tramway, and recommended that the application be granted, saying "I am therefore inclined to recommend that the difficulties of widening the bridge are not insuperable" (it had already twice been widened) "or if the widening cannot be carried out for the present, the narrowness should not be considered fatal to the light railway being allowed to run over it. Even with two lines of 4 ft. 8½ in. gauge laid at 3 ft. 6 in. apart, there will still be a space of 2 ft. 6 in. between the kerb and the nearest light railway carriage". The powers were granted in the Wakefield and District Light Railway Order issued on 13 September 1901, for ten miles of 4 ft. 8½ in. gauge line, and the bridge had to serve until a new one was built alongside in 1933. Meanwhile, the Order required the company to pay £2000 towards its repair.

The promotion of the tramways under the legislation applicable to light railways did not deprive the local councils of their powers of compulsory purchase. A clause was inserted to the effect that if each local authority resolved to purchase within six months after a period of 25 years or each subsequent period of seven years, the company must sell the undertaking to them at the fair market value as a going concern, to be assessed if necessary by an arbitrator to be appointed by the Board of Trade. This gave the company rather more protection than it would have obtained under the Tramways Act 1870, for not only would all the local authorities have to act in harmony, but the value of a profitable undertaking as a going concern would be higher than the written-down value assessed under the provisions of the Tramways Act. A similar situation existed at Grimsby, and proved greatly to that company's advantage.

Meanwhile, the promoters had applied for 5½ miles of extensions, which necessitated a further inquiry. Of this figure, 1½ miles would extend the Horbury tramway to Ossett, one mile of this being in the borough of Ossett, and the rest would extend the Outwood route northwards through Lofthouse, Rothwell Haigh and Stourton to the terminus of the Leeds tramways at Thwaite Gate, incorporating and replacing the unbuilt line previously authorised to The Electric Tramways Construction and Maintenance Co. Ltd., who later received a cash settlement. The application also included a short extension up Agbrigg Road to its junction with Belle Vue Road. These lines would serve an additional population of 31,700, bringing the population served by the whole scheme to about 91,000. Ossett had a population of 12,903 and Horbury 6,700 at the last census. The road between them was wide enough for tramlines, except at one very narrow place in Horbury which the company would widen.

The enquiry into the extensions was held at Ossett Town Hall on 5 October 1901. The consulting engineer, Robert Green, estimated the cost of the enlarged system as £118,500, made up of £43,000 for laying the tracks, £20,000 for the electrical equipment, £14,000 for car sheds, repair shops, offices and land, £14,000 for 20 cars at £700 each, £12,500 for road widenings, and £15,000 for legal costs and the cost of obtaining the Board of Trade Order. To run a ten minute service would require 15 cars, but a five minute service would need 24 cars, so a ten minute headway was evidently assumed. The only objections to the extensions came from the two railway companies (G.N.R. and L.&Y.R.) who were afraid that the tramways and light railways would affect their revenue. In this case their opposition was unsuccessful, and the powers requested were granted in The Wakefield and District Light Railways (Extensions) Order 1902. The only other difficulty was the need for a level crossing on the Leeds route at Robin Hood with a mineral railway, where provision was made for a man with a red flag to control the traffic.

As soon as the first Order was granted, the promoters formed themselves into the Wakefield and District Light Railway Company Limited, with a capital of £120,000 in £1 shares, of which £40,000 could be preference shares. There were to be five directors, each of whom had to hold in his own right at least £250 in shares. A draft agreement had already been drawn up with the Leeds Corporation for mutual through running, and this was signed on 26 November 1901. The Corporation was to extend its lines to the boundary to meet those of the company, and could purchase within 25 years any part of the company's lines which subsequent boundary extensions might bring within the city of Leeds.

In the same month of November 1901, the Wakefield and District Light Railway Company applied to the Board of Trade for a further seven miles of extensions, which would bring its authorised total to just over 22 miles. The Extensions Order was held back to include them, and when finally issued on 19 August 1902 it authorised additional lines from Wakefield to Alverthorpe, from Wakefield to East Ardsley, and from Rothwell Haigh to Rothwell and Oulton. The company meanwhile continued in the task of raising its capital so that construction could begin, and also began work on plans for further extensions from East Ardsley to Tingley, from Oulton to Castleford, and from Wakefield to Normanton and South Featherstone. These lines would connect its own authorised system with various other proposed tramways, but before anything more could be done, the Light Railway company itself became the subject of a take-over bid, which it accepted. To trace this, it is first necessary to trace the origin of the tramways being promoted some five miles further east.

During the setting-up period of the Wakefield and District Light Railway, a separate tramway was being promoted not far away in the Urban Districts of Castleford, Pontefract, Whitwood, Normanton and Featherstone. Its story begins on 1 June 1899 with the registration of The United Kingdom Tramway, Light Railway and Electrical Syndicate Ltd., a London-based group whose directors were Major Hector Tulloch (civil engineer), John Parnell and Frederick H. Tulloch and the secretary Captain George E. S. Venner, with offices at 28 Victoria Street, Westminster. The Syndicate was involved in tramway schemes at Castleford, Sunderland District, Bishop Auckland and Northwich, but the death of Hector Tulloch in 1903 caused the withdrawal of a large amount of money, and only the Sunderland District interest was retained, the Syndicate being wound up in 1909.

On 9 August 1901, the UK Syndicate obtained a tramway provisional Order with the title The West Riding Tramways Order 1901, authorising twelve miles of tramway from Normanton through Castleford and Pontefract to South Featherstone. This done, they registered on 28 June 1901 a local company, The West Riding Tramways and Electricity Company Ltd. with offices at Greek Street Chambers, Leeds, to build the lines and run them. Venner was secretary, but the directors were local businessmen and civil engineers from Leeds and Pontefract. A further Tramway Order was obtained on 8 August 1902 for 2½ miles of tramway from Pontefract to Knottingley, but there followed a take-over bid from the same interests that were negotiating for Wakefield and District. This was accepted, and instead of trying to raise its authorised capital, the local company took its profit and disappeared. Its tramway scheme had been estimated to cost £50,000, with 25 cars, but the shares were never allotted and after 1903 it submitted no returns. It was struck off the register in February 1906.

There next appeared a company with the strangest name and briefest existence so far, the Ito Syndicate Limited, registered on 9 January 1902 to acquire the benefit of divers Acts and Orders relating to tramways. Its nominal promoters were G. H. Chamberlain, J. Crowther and F. Nash, all based in London. No prospectus has been traced, but the company appears to have been a speculative venture formed to buy up all the tramway powers obtained in the Wakefield and Castleford areas and combine them in one unified scheme that could be resold at a profit. In this it succeeded, for its authorised capital of £42,450 was used to buy tramway powers which it soon afterwards resold for £60,000. Having achieved this, the Ito Syndicate wound itself up on 1 April 1904, leaving the future tramway system over-capitalised to the extent of a further £17,550. It still appears in the Handbook of Defunct Companies, with no inkling of the purpose for which it was formed, so well did its promoters cover their tracks.

The purchaser of the tramway powers, under an agreement concluded with the Ito Syndicate Limited on 27 November 1902, was Ernest Schenk of 69 Curzon Street, London W, and later of Ingoldsby, Birchington-on-Sea. Schenk, whose associates included merchant banker J. B. Schroeder, was a director of many companies including the Crystal Palace Company and the Manx Electric Railway Company, and had engineered the purchase of the Manx Electric system after its original operators had gone into liquidation. From this point, the financial history of the Wakefield and Castleford tramways resembles to some extent that of the Manx Electric, with a construction syndicate which would make a profit from building the lines and selling them to another company formed to operate them.

This new syndicate took shape as the Yorkshire Electric Tramways Construction Syndicate Limited, registered on 25 April 1903 with a capital of £280,000, of which 180 preference shares of £1000 each were to be allotted by subscription and 10,000 ordinary shares of £10 were to be allotted to the vendor, Ernest Schenk. The chairman was Herbert S. Leon of Leon Bros., Throgmorton Street and the Stock Exchange, director of the Anglo-American Telegraph Company, and the other directors were Albert G. Kitching J.P., of Chase Court, Enfield, director of the Metropolitan Railway Company and the Manx Electric Railway Company, and Ernest Schenk. The secretary was W. H. Andrews of 20 Victoria Street, Westminster, the consulting engineer was V. D. B. Cooper, and the solicitors were Messrs. Ashurst, Morris, Crisp & Co. of Throgmorton Avenue, London EC. The Syndicate gave itself very wide powers, including the acquisition of tramways (municipal and other) in the UK and elsewhere, generating electric power, operating tramways and light railways, and building rolling stock. Three days later, on 28 April, it undertook to pay Ernest Schenk the sum of £64,193. 14s., out of which he would pay all the various parties the sums due to them under the November 1902 agreements. The Syndicate would also pay the contractor for all work done after 25 November 1902.

All the companies previously involved now retired from the scene save for the Wakefield and District Light Railway Company Ltd., which had placed the contracts for the Wakefield lines and was soon to operate them, on behalf of the Syndicate. The Syndicate issued a prospectus, stating that it had been formed to acquire four Orders and to construct tramways in the Leeds, Wakefield and West

Riding districts in continuation of the Leeds Corporation system and connecting it with tramways already authorised, and by proposed extensions, with the towns of Wakefield, Pontefract, Knottingley, Dewsbury, Castleford, Normanton, Featherstone, Horbury, Ossett, Alverthorpe and Rothwell. The length of route already authorised was about 38 miles, and the entire system with the proposed extensions would cover about 55 miles, serving a population of about 750,000. A contract had been signed with Dick, Kerr & Co. Ltd. for the construction and equipment of the lines, which included completion of the Leeds to Wakefield section within twelve months. Upon completion of the first sections, it was proposed to form a Tramway Company to take over the lines and operate them, and to finance the proposed extensions the Syndicate's capital was to be increased to £450,000.

The methods by which the Construction Syndicate hoped to join the Wakefield tramways with those of Castleford and Pontefract will be described in the next chapter, but it is convenient to deal here with the tramway company that was formed to operate the lines, and which (alone of those mentioned) still exists today, with change of name. This was the Yorkshire (West Riding) Electric Tramways Company Limited, registered on 4 April 1905 with a share capital of £700,000 (£250,000 in six per cent preference shares, £200,000 in ordinary shares and £250,000 in 4½ per cent mortgage debentures). Its objects were to construct and work the lines authorised by the Wakefield and District Light Railway Order 1901, the Wakefield and District Light Railways (Extensions) Order 1902 and the West Riding Tramways Act 1904. The first directors were Herbert S. Leon of Bletchley Park, Bucks. (chairman), George E. Leon of 5 Throgmorton Street, London EC (member of the Stock Exchange), W. B. Keen, chartered accountant, and Ernest Schenk. The Construction Syndicate would build the lines and sell them to this company at a profit to be divided equally between the Syndicate's shareholders.

In the West Riding prospectus, potential investors were told that 45½ single track miles of tramways were authorised, of which 32 miles were completed and 27 miles in operation, and that the work to date (executed by Dick, Kerr & Co. Ltd.) had cost upwards of £435,000, including a generating station. The construction and equipment of the remainder of the system was estimated to cost a further £280,000, making a total of about £715,000. Meanwhile, 9,400 shares were allotted in September 1905 to Dick, Kerr & Co. Ltd. in part-payment of the contract price of the works.

Of the tramway systems described in this book, West Riding was the only one to construct from its own resources a complete tramway system, including generating stations, and to lease nothing. By 1912, its capital outlay had amounted to the substantial sum of £750,084. This compared with £336,139 for Yorkshire Woollen District, which leased nearly half its track from five local councils, and a mere £5,457 for the Dewsbury and Ossett, whose whole plant was municipally owned and which thus only had to provide rolling stock. The difference, however, is not wholly accounted for in this way, and it is clear that from the start the Yorkshire (West Riding) Tramways Company Limited was substantially over-capitalised, the amount being the sum total of the paper profits realised by the various promotion and construction syndicates and the persons who had brought them together. The new tramway company's prospectus spoke of an estimated annual profit of £57,000, which if realised would have rendered the capital burden less important, but tramways in West Yorkshire (and elsewhere) rarely lived up to the expectations of the original promoters. As an example of the involvement of merchant bankers in the British tramway field, West Riding was to remain unique.

The remainder of this chapter will deal with the construction of the original Wakefield and District system from Sandal Magna through Wakefield towards Leeds and from Ossett to Agbrigg, plus the Rothwell branch. These lines were completed and opened before the formation of the Yorkshire (West Riding) Electric Tramways Co. Ltd. in April 1905, whereas the Castleford lines were added by West Riding and will be described in the next chapter, together with various lines that were not built.

Laying the tracks in the Bull Ring, Wakefield, early in 1904. The rails were laid on an eight-inch bed of concrete and were paved in granite setts. Track gauge was 4 ft. 8½ in.
(Commercial postcard, courtesy J. H. Price)

The main contractor for the tramways was Dick, Kerr & Co. Ltd. of Preston. The track was laid to a gauge of 4 ft. 8½ in., in the hope that there would be through running into Leeds, which used the same gauge. In constructing the track, the roadway was excavated to a depth of 12½ inches, and a bed of concrete eight inches deep was then laid to carry the track and paving, this bed being 8 ft. wide for single track and 17 ft. wide for double track. On nine miles of track the roadway between the rails and for 18 inches on either side was paved with 5 in. by 4 in. granite setts; on the remaining 16 miles the roadway between the rails was filled with tarmacadam, which the company replaced with setts at considerable expense some years later. The rails were of the girder type, weighing 95 lb per yard and laid in 45 ft. lengths; they were 6½ inches deep, with a groove 1½ in. deep. Quite long sections of track were laid at one side of the road, especially on the single line stretch between Horbury and Ossett, where the track was on the south side of the carriageway.

The overhead line was suspended from 31 ft. steel poles, of which six feet were sunk into the ground and fixed in a bed of concrete. The poles were made up of three sections of steel tube and were generally placed 40 yards apart. Side poles with bracket arms were the most common, but there were sections on which the overhead was suspended from span wires, and the stretch in Westgate, Wakefield, initially used centre poles. In the towns, the roadside poles carried ornamental scrollwork, but elsewhere they were plain. A suggestion that the poles should be connected with the sewage system and act as vents was not adopted, though a later agreement provided for some poles in Castleford to carry street lighting—not by electricity, but by gas!

The principal depot was at Belle Isle, Wakefield, on the Sandal route about half a mile south of Wakefield bridge. It contained five tracks plus one leading to the repair and paint shops, and was next to the company's generating station. Both were built on the site of a former dyeworks. The property backed on to the River Calder, and included a wharf to which coal for the generating station was brought by barge. There were two smaller depots, each containing three tracks and a substation, one at Rothwell Haigh and the other at Sowood Lane, Ossett, they were constructed mainly to reduce "dead mileage" on the two longest routes. A third substation was at Union Street, Wakefield, and a fourth was later added at Lofthouse Park.

Above: The main car shed at Belle Isle, Wakefield, shortly after the delivery of covered-top cars 31-55 in 1905. (L. Holt

Below: The remains of the tramway wharf on the River Calder at Belle Isle, Wakefield, photographed in September 1969. Here the barges unloaded their cargo of coal for the tramway power station. (W. Pickles

The steam raising plant at Belle Isle consisted of four Lancashire boilers, with "Lord" furnaces, mechanical stokers, a Green's fuel economiser, a water storage tank with a capacity of 20,000 gallons, and two feed pumps capable of delivering 24,000 lb. of water per hour against a pressure of 150 lb. per square inch. The feed water was drawn from the river Calder and the town supply, the water for condensing purposes came wholly from the river. Three Howden high-speed triple expansion condensing engines were installed, working at a pressure of 150 lb. per square inch and running at 375 revolutions per minute. They drove Dick, Kerr high-tension alternators which generated three-phase current at 6,300 volts, 25 cycles per second, each set being provided with a direct-drive exciter. They had a continuous output of 400 kW, and were designed to take an overload of 25 per cent for one hour, with a moderate rise in temperature. All three generators could be run in parallel, and means were provided for raising their output voltage to 6,600 to compensate for losses in the mains. Dick, Kerr & Co. Ltd. built the switchboard.

The substations were fed from the main station by duplicate three-core lead covered high-tension cables, and contained 200kW Dick, Kerr compound-wound rotary converters running at 750 revolutions per minute, producing direct current at 500 to 550 volts. There were two converters at Rothwell, two at Ossett, and three at Union Street, Wakefield. The new Lofthouse Park substation added in 1908 had two 200kW motor-generators.

Left: The three-track Yorkshire (West Riding) tramway depot at Sowood Lane, Ossett, on the Wakefield—Ossett section. The building and track still exist.   (Dr. Hugh Nicol

Right: On many miles of the West Riding tramways the space between the rails was originally filled with water-bound macadam, which the company replaced with granite setts from 1912 onwards. Car 29 is seen here at Sandal terminus during the first year of operation. This car was transferred in 1906 to the Castleford section.   (L. Holt

The main route, from Sandal to Leeds, started in Sandal near the Sandal Castle Inn, and was of single track with passing places until 1925, when the whole section in Barnsley Road was doubled. Since the track on Wakefield Bridge and in Kirkgate was already double, this gave continuous double track from Sandal to the Bull Ring in Wakefield. There was a triangle of tracks in the Bull Ring; Ossett to Agbrigg cars used the southern side and Sandal to Leeds cars the north-eastern side, the third (north-western) side giving a connection that enabled workings from Westgate to go on the the Leeds section without having to reverse. The exit into Northgate was by a short section of single track with a junction.

From Northgate the tramway continued for nearly seven miles along the main Wakefield—Leeds road and was largely double track, except for a length of single and loop through Newton Hill and another between Lofthouse and Robin Hood, plus a section of interlaced track in Lofthouse. Originally there was a further stretch of single track in Bell Hill leading to the end-on junction with the Leeds tramways at Thwaite Gate, Hunslet, but this was doubled in 1920. There were stretches of open country between the villages, and long sections of the route were unlit, causing the Board of Trade to insist on adequate headlamps for the cars.

The other route, from Ossett to Agbrigg, started in Bank Street, Ossett, until the Dewsbury & Ossett tramways were constructed, when the terminus was moved to a common loop in the Market Place in readiness for the D.&O. opening on 12 November 1908, and the spur in Bank Street was lifted. The line then ran along the south side of Station Road to Horbury, mostly as single line with passing loops. Later the track from Sowood Road onwards was doubled, but there was always a stretch of single line through the very narrow roadway in the centre of Horbury near Queen Street. From Horbury the line was double throughout to Wakefield, and a 1914 map shows a stub leading into Alverthorpe Road at Westgate End, in readiness for the proposed route to Alverthorpe. Similarly, a spur led off the Leeds route at

A Wakefield to Ossett car in Station Road, Ossett, showing the roadside single track.
(Courtesy H. Tolson

Wakefield and District 10 at St. Catherine's Church, Belle Vue, on a pre-opening trial run over the Agbrigg route in July 1904. The original photograph is captioned "First tram up Belle Vue".
(R. A. Mills, courtesy A. K. Kirby

Wentworth Street, Wakefield, ready for the proposed line to Ardsley. Entering Wakefield via Westgate, the line crossed the bottom of Wood Street to enter the Bull Ring.

Here the Ossett—Agbrigg cars traversed a double-track junction leading on to a single line, which curved to the right to join the track from Kirkgate. Here the cars worked "wrong line" for a few yards before taking the crossover near the Cathedral. The two services then shared the track to the junction beyond Wakefield Bridge, and the Agbrigg cars then continued along the Doncaster Road on single track with passing loops. This section was doubled in 1925, but the final section in Agbrigg Road to the terminus at Belle Vue Road remained single.

By August 1904 all the lines except the Rothwell branch were constructed and ready for their Board of Trade inspection. This was carried out on Tuesday 9 August 1904 by Major E. Druitt, RE, and Mr. A. P. Trotter, and began at the Leeds boundary at 10.0 a.m. The car travelled to Wakefield on the down line and returned on the up line, before proceeding again to Wakefield. The inspection party then went to Ossett and back to Wakefield, continuing to Agbrigg and finally to Sandal. The lines were passed as ready for public use subject to the speed restrictions laid down by the inspector and subject to some minor works being completed by 1 September, including the display of warning notices of low trolley wires below Stourton G.N.R. bridge and at the bridges over Kirkgate and Westgate in Wakefield. Mr. Trotter was critical of the space behind certain switchboards in substations, which were too narrow to permit work to be done, and asked for them to be widened. The Board of Trade certificate was issued on 16 August 1904.

A general manager, Mr. Harry England, was chosen at the end of 1903 and took up his new appointment on 1 January 1904. He had been traffic manager (general manager from 1900) of Bolton Corporation Tramways, and moved in 1901 to be manager at Sunderland. Mr. England invited representatives of the press to ride over the new tramways on Saturday 13 August 1904, and to inspect the

generating station and tram sheds at Belle Isle. When the party reached Thwaite
Gate, they noted that tracks were being laid to connect the Wakefield & District and
Leeds City systems, an agreement for through running having been reached during
July. There were press complaints that horsemen tried to impede the special cars,
and at Lofthouse a steam lorry was straddled across the metals while the driver and
his mate watched a cricket match! After a little while they moved the steam lorry so
that the tram could pass, and then settled down to enjoy the match again.

The day of the public opening was Monday, 15 August 1904. It was quite a
festive day, and the Bull Ring was crowded for most of the day with would-be
passengers, with a scramble for seats as each car came into the square. The local
paper said that it was quite delightful for the irregularities and the general fun of
the thing; no time was kept, the cars running as and when they could. Sometimes
four cars would arrive at a terminus at the same time, and en route cars had to back
on to loops to allow other cars to pass. In the villages, the tradesmen turned out to
welcome new customers, but the passengers only wanted to stretch their legs and get
back on the cars; in fact some did not even bother to alight. The conductors, being
new to the work, were not only slow but apparently allowed pounds to slip through
their fingers, many passengers boasting that they had not even been asked for their
fares.

Unfortunately for the historian, these press reports do not say where the cars
ran to on this first day, and there is evidence that the Leeds route was only opened as
far as Newton Bar; perhaps work had still to be done beyond this point to meet the
Board of Trade's requirements. A photograph exists of car 4 at this point, dated 15
August 1904 and captioned "first car to Newton Bar", with paper stickers reading
"Sandal & Newton Bar", suggesting that Newton Bar was not included on the
destination blinds. Two days later, on the evening of 17 August, there was a power
failure at the generating station which closed the system down for two hours. Service
to Thwaite Gate started within a few days, but press references are unclear as to the
date. Eighteen cars had now been delivered, but the remainder of the first 30 did not

Car No. 4 at Newton Bar (between Wakefield and Outwood) on the first day of public service,
15 August 1904. The original photograph is captioned "First car to Newton Bar".

(Courtesy A. Thompson

Car 25 at the junction of Wood Lane, Rothwell, and the main Wakefield—Leeds road, near Rothwell Haigh depot. The original photograph is dated 30 August 1904, two weeks after the opening.
(Rothwell Public Library

arrive until the autumn. By the end of the year an average of 23 cars were in daily service, and in the 20 weeks from 15 August to 31 December 1904 the cars carried 1,605,221 passengers and earned a net surplus of £5,675.

The availability of tramway travel between Wakefield and Leeds had an immediate effect on the passenger traffic of the Great Northern Railway, to which the latter responded on 22 August 1904 by instituting cheap fares, as had already proved necessary to combat tramway competition between Leeds and Bradford. A more unfortunate victim was the little East and West Yorkshire Union Railways Company, which linked Rothwell Haigh junction on the Midland main line with the G.N.R. at Lofthouse, serving various collieries. This company had recently made arrangements with the Midland Railway Company for a service of passenger trains from Leeds via Hunslet to Rothwell, Robin Hood and Lofthouse, using Midland carriages and E.&W.Y.U.R. locomotives. After spending a considerable sum in erecting stations and equipping its mineral line for passenger operation, the company found that since the tramway opened its four or five daily trains were being used by only a dozen or so passengers per train. At the company's half-yearly meeting, reported in the *Wakefield Express* for 3 September 1904, the chairman announced the decision to withdraw the passenger service, and the last train ran on Friday 30 September. The press report of the decision to close said that the tramway service was being well patronised, especially on Sundays when large crowds made the journey from Leeds to Wakefield and back each weekend.

Meanwhile, construction continued of the branch tramway leading from Rothwell Haigh down into Rothwell village. This was mainly single track with passing places, though there was a stretch of double track from Haigh Road to Church Street in Rothwell, flanked by single track sections that were later doubled. The rest of the route in Rothwell along Ingram Road and Commercial Street was single track with loops, but the terminal stub near the Black Bull Inn was always double, in readiness for the proposed extension to Oulton and Methley, which never

130

Car 6 at Rothwell terminus during the period from December, 1904 to May, 1905 during which the branch was worked by Wakefield and District cars running only to Thwaite Gate. Leeds trams took over on this route from June 1905. (Courtesy The Wakefield Express

materialised. The first trial runs were made in the last week of November 1904, and the line was inspected on 29 November by Major J. W. Pringle, RE. He required (among other things) a compulsory stop to be instituted on either side of the railway crossing in Wood Lane. Public service began without ceremony in the second week of December; the line is mentioned as having opened in the *Rothwell Times* of 16 December, without quoting a date, but the Board of Trade certificate was issued on 19 December. The cars from Rothwell ran to Thwaite Gate, and the paper described the terminus at Stourton (Thwaite Gate) as a sea of mud.

This ceased to inconvenience tramway passengers after the following May, for on Thursday 1 June 1905 through running commenced from the Wakefield and District company's lines into the centre of Leeds, to continue without interruption for the next 27 years. The date is that quoted in the local press, though the formal agreement between company and corporation is dated 6 June. It could be terminated by either side at three months' notice, and allowed company cars to run into the centre of Leeds and Corporation cars to run out to points selected by the company. Each undertaking would receive the whole of the fares taken in its area, supplying the other party with stocks of its tickets, and paying the other's working expenses, calculated according to the charges for traffic and maintenance of cars in the Leeds Corporation Tramways Accounts. Other provisions concerned timetable altera- tions, incident reports and insurance.

From June 1905, the company's cars from Wakefield therefore continued along Hunslet Road, Hunslet Lane, Bridgend, Lower Briggate, Duncan Street and New Market Street to a terminal loop in the centre of Leeds alongside Kirkgate Market, nearly 10½ miles from their starting point at Sandal. This loop also served as the terminus of the Rothwell service, which from the same date was operated by Leeds Corporation cars on the Hunslet service running through to Rothwell to balance the mileage. This had the incidental advantage that although the Rothwell route included a gradient of 1 in 15 in Wood Lane, which would normally require the use

131

SPECIAL INSTRUCTIONS TO CONDUCTORS ON LEEDS AND SANDAL ROUTE.

Conductors on the above route are requested to give special attention to the undernoted instructions, and in all cases of difficulty to consult Officials, and as far as possible, to avoid friction when dealing with passengers.

Except in the case of return tickets, Conductors must not accept the through fare in the first instance but book passengers to our terminus at Thwaite Gate, and on arriving there, change over their sets of tickets and way-bills, and collect fares from that point for the distance to be travelled over in either direction.

RETURN TICKETS.—Return Tickets will be issued between Wakefield and Leeds at 1/-, and Conductors must be careful in punching these to clip out the number indicating the date on which the passenger is travelling. These tickets are only available for one day, and passengers returning will present same to the Conductors to be punched, and Conductors must see that they have been punched on the first journey on the same date.

In the event of there being any mistake in the punching of a Return Ticket, Conductors must exercise discretion, but if it is punched very far away from the date on which the passenger is travelling, the name and address of passenger, together with the number and letter of the ticket should be taken and the matter reported, but no further fare should in the meantime be charged.

As the fare between Newton Hill and Leeds will be 6d., passengers joining the Car anywhere between Wakefield and Newton Hill might also have Return Tickets if desired. Passengers wishing returns from the districts of Sandal, Agbrigg, etc., would book to and from Wakefield in the ordinary way, from which point a Return Ticket is available.

CHILDREN'S FARES—LEEDS.—Conductors will note the Regulation regarding Children's Fares on the Leeds Section, which provides that all children between the ages of 5 and 12 (or 15, if going to or from school) travel at half-fare. As the fare between Thwaite Gate and Corn Exchange (with three ½d. stages) is 1d., there is no distinction made between workmen and ordinary passengers.

COLLECTION OF FARES.—As the Hunslet Section is a busy Section, Conductors must be alert and collect the fares promptly, and they must call out the fare stages and names of the principal streets, and be careful to note stopping places, and to be generally civil and obliging to passengers.

BRASSWORK.—Conductors must not clean any Brasswork on the Leeds Section. All attention must be given to fares and passengers.

DESTINATION INDICATORS.—Conductors will set their Destination Indicators for "Wakefield" when leaving Corn Exchange, and will then change them for "Sandal" between Lofthouse Gate and Outwood. On the inward journey Conductors will show "Leeds" on their Indicators all the way from Sandal.

The side-slip boards showing the names of the districts en-route must be properly displayed and changed to suit the outward and inward journeys.

WORKPEOPLE'S FARES.—On and after the 1st of June, the Regulation regarding Workpeople's Fares over the whole of our system will be this :—

All passengers joining a Car before 7-30 a.m. will be entitled to travel at workmen's rates without reference to their profession. The regulation at present in force with regard to workpeople's fares in the evening still holds, namely :—Bona-fide workpeople boarding a Car any time after 5-0 p.m. up till any Car leaving a terminus at 6-0 p.m. (Thwaite Gate and not Corn Exchange to be reckoned as a terminus in this connection).

TOKENS.—On the Leeds Section Conductors will accept the ½d. and 1d. Celluloid Tokens from passengers and issue tickets for same of equivalent value.

LEEDS FARE STAGES.

TO OR FROM

THWAITE GATE AND WHITEFIELD ROAD	
WHITFIELD ROAD AND LEATHLEY ROAD	½d.
LEATHLEY ROAD AND CORN EXCHANGE	
THWAITE GATE AND CORN EXCHANGE,	1d.

29/5/05.

The instruction sheet issued to conductors in readiness for the introduction of through running into Leeds on 1 June 1905.
(Courtesy C. Wood

of cars with track brakes, the company would not have to equip their own cars since the Rothwell route was now worked by Leeds cars already fitted with this type of brake. In later years at least, one West Riding car ran on the Rothwell route on Sundays, either for legal reasons or to balance the mileage.

There were no through tickets on either route with the solitary exception of a cheap day return ticket at one shilling between Wakefield and Leeds. In all other cases, passengers were re-booked on passing the boundary at Thwaite Gate, for which purpose the company cars carried stocks of Corporation tickets for use in Leeds and the Corporation cars carried stocks of company tickets for issue outside the boundary. Company conductors were instructed that their cars must display the destination "Wakefield" when leaving Leeds Corn Exchange and change it to "Sandal" between Lofthouse Gate and Outwood, and that since the Hunslet route was a busy one, they were not to clean any brasswork while their car was running in Leeds.

From 1 June 1905 until it closed on 31 May 1932 the Rothwell branch was worked by cars of Leeds City Tramways running through to the Corn Exchange in Leeds. This 1906 picture in Wood Lane, Rothwell shows Leeds car 210 in the livery of chocolate, chrome yellow and white.
(C. Ineson, courtesy Rothwell Public Library

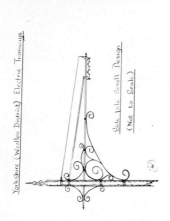

Yorkshire (Woollen District) Electric Tramways

Side pole Scroll Design
(Not to Scale.)

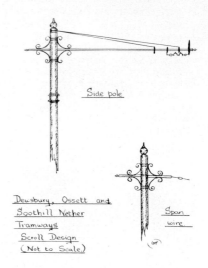

Side pole

Dewsbury, Ossett and
Soothill Nether
Tramways
Scroll Design
(Not to Scale.)

Span
wire

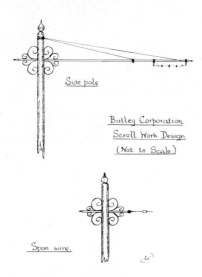

Side pole

Batley Corporation
Scroll Work Design.
(Not to Scale)

Span wire.

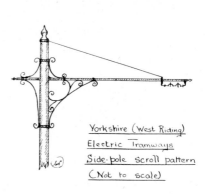

Yorkshire (West Riding)
Electric Tramways
Side-pole scroll pattern
(Not to scale)

CHAPTER SEVEN
THE YORKSHIRE (WEST RIDING) TRAMWAYS
FROM 1905 TO 1914

The Yorkshire (West Riding) Electric Tramways Company Limited was registered on 4 April 1905 to take over the working of the Wakefield and District Light Railways (Ossett—Agbrigg and Thwaite Gate—Sandal, with the Rothwell branch), and to take over on completion and operate all the various lines in the area that were to be built by the Yorkshire Electric Tramways Construction Syndicate Ltd., to give unified control of the network.

If all the proposed lines had been built, there would have been 55 miles of tramway in the areas south and southeast of Leeds, with continuous lines of tramway from Leeds, Bradford and Dewsbury to Castleford, Pontefract and Knottingley (and also from Huddersfield, had another authorised extension been constructed). In the event, unsatisfactory financial results caused the Yorkshire (West Riding) Tramways Company Ltd. to allow the powers for many of the lines to lapse, in some cases after repeated applications for extension of time, and the West Riding system remained in two separate parts, a fairly large one around Wakefield and Leeds, and a small isolated one from Normanton to Castleford and Pontefract. In this chapter we shall first examine the proposed lines that were not built, and then describe those that were actually constructed in 1905/6.

The formation of the Yorkshire Electric Tramways Construction Syndicate Ltd. in May, 1903 has already been noted, and the report of its formation revealed that it had taken over the Wakefield and District tramways (under construction) and the West Riding tramway schemes that included Pontefract and Castleford. It also inherited plans prepared by Wakefield and District for a tramway from Wakefield direct to Dewsbury, and in November 1903 the Syndicate made an application to the Light Railway Commissioners in its own name for a Wakefield—Dewsbury line. Before this could be considered, the three local councils (Ossett, Dewsbury, and Soothill Nether) resolved to construct their own tramway along much of the same route, and the Wakefield syndicate withdrew. If their light railway from Wakefield to Dewsbury via Flushdyke had been built as originally authorised, it would have been single track with 24 passing places between Wakefield (Alverthorpe Road/Horbury Road junction) and the top of Wakefield Cutting in Dewsbury, then double track down to the Dewsbury terminus in Vicarage Road.

Proceeding clockwise around Wakefield, the next extension would have been the line to Alverthorpe, branching from that to Horbury. It is rather ironic that the proposed tramway to Alverthorpe never materialised at all, since the 1882 proposals for tramways in Wakefield were for a line from Alverthorpe to Agbrigg. However, Alverthorpe had a station, and a train service.

The next line would have been a long extension from Wakefield along the Wakefield to Bradford road to Tingley Cross Roads. This would have linked up with proposed extensions to the Morley tramways, and would have provided a direct tramway route from Wakefield to Bradford via Ardsley, Tingley and the Y.W.D. tramways. This and the Alverthorpe route were quoted in a company statement of November 1907 as being the extensions next on the list, and the powers were renewed annually until they expired on 19 November 1911. During that month there were suggestions by the Wakefield City Tradesmen's Association that the Corporation and the other local authorities should construct the lines to Ardsley and

Alverthorpe and lease them to the company, as was the case on the Y.W.D. and D.&O. systems. One speaker at a tradesmen's meeting on 15 June 1912 pressed the Ardsley case before the Alverthorpe one, because Ardsley had no convenient station and stood a good chance of being linked by tram with Leeds through the Morley extensions, which would damage Wakefield's trade. The company had meanwhile declared its willingness to operate these lines if the local authorities would build and lease them, but nothing resulted and by 1914 both routes were proposed for buses.

On the east side of the main Leeds—Wakefield route were numerous proposed tramways, of which those authorised were sanctioned by the West Riding Tramways Act 1904. The application of November 1903 was for Tramways Nos. 1-32 in the districts of Normanton, Whitwood, Castleford, Glasshoughton, Pontefract, Purston Jaglin, Ferry Fryston, Knottingley, Methley, Wakefield, Stanley and Altofts, of which the most northerly line would have extended the Rothwell branch through Oulton and Methley to Castleford, giving through communication from Leeds to Castleford and Pontefract. From Rothwell terminus, this line would have run to Oulton and Methley and into Castleford along what is now the A639 road, linking up with the Normanton to Pontefract system in Church Street, Castleford. All four railway companies (Midland, Great Northern, Lancashire and Yorkshire, and North Eastern) opposed the construction of this line, which would have been a serious competitor for their Leeds-Castleford-Pontefract traffic, and the Methley-Castleford section was rejected. This left the company empowered to build only from Rothwell to Methley, which would probably offer insufficient traffic, and after a one-year extension of time from June 1906 the Oulton to Methley proposal was abandoned.

In the Castleford area, the 1904 Act authorised two branches leading to Cutsyke, one direct along the Aketon Road, and the other from Four Lane Ends at Whitwood on the proposed route to Methley, at the point where the Mining and Technical College stands today. The powers for these were allowed to expire in 1909.

Wakefield was to be linked with Normanton by two proposed routes, of which the northerly one via Stanley was authorised in the 1904 Act and the other had already been rejected. The former was to leave the Sandal to Leeds route in Northgate, Wakefield, and proceed along York Street, Pinderfields Road and Eastmoor Road to join the Aberford Road at Stanley Royds Hospital, and follow this road to a point just short of Stanley Church. Here it was to turn right, down Water Lane towards the River Calder, and cross the Aire and Calder Navigation by the canal company's Birkwood Bridge, to be paved in granite setts. Before this point, the tramway company would have had to build a new bridge over the River Calder, which involved some legal complications. There was a clause to prevent people using the bridge unless as passengers in the trams; no one else might cross the bridge except workmen of the tramway company and the canal company, Mrs. Emily Charlotte Meynell Ingram, the owner of the land thereabouts, her Agent and tenants and tenants' families. The land in the area was entirely agricultural, and there are no houses even today. The tramway would then have continued into Altofts along Church Lane and across the Midland main line to meet the Normanton—Castleford tramway in Normanton Market Place. This proposed line was the only link authorised between the company's Wakefield and Normanton tramways, and its abandonment due to the cost of the bridge and the company's financial situation left the West Riding tramways in two disconnected portions.

The other proposed link from Wakefield to Normanton, a Wakefield & District proposal of 1902, would have run from near Agbrigg terminus along the Doncaster Road across Heath Common to Sharlston Common, then northwards through Warmfield village to Normanton Market Place. From Sharlston Common, another line was to follow the Weeland road through Snydale and Purston Jaglin to Pontefract, with a branch from Purston to Featherstone Station, and after joining the Pontefract—Castleford tramway in Pontefract would have continued past the Town Hall along North Bailey Gate to Ferry Fryston and across the Great North Road to Knottingley, where it was to terminate by Knottingley Town Hall. The

Wakefield and District indicator blinds carried destinations to which tramways were not yet built; some were never even begun. Car 13 entering Wakefield Bull Ring on the first test run (22 July 1904) shows Castleford as destination, but this route from Wakefield was never constructed. (Courtesy R. Brook

section from Featherstone station through Pontefract to Knottingley was subsequently authorised in the West Riding Tramways Act 1904, but owing to railway opposition the links with Wakefield were defeated. None of these lines were built, the powers being allowed to lapse, and no other lines were applied for, though several were suggested. For those lines authorised in the 1904 Act, the powers of purchase given by section 43 of the Tramways Act 1870 were not exercisable by any of the local authorities of the Borough of Pontefract, the Urban Districts of Normanton, Whitwood, Castleford, Featherstone and Knottingley and the Rural District of Pontefract until 42 years from the date of passing of the Act. In the districts of Methley, Stanley and Altofts the purchase powers were the same as those in the Wakefield and District orders, i.e. purchase at a fair market value after 25 years provided that all the authorities acted together.

Constructing the Castleford lines

As the Wakefield tramways neared completion during 1904, the construction syndicate prepared to start work on the authorised tramway from Normanton through Castleford to Pontefract. In April 1904 the Light Railway company sent notice to Castleford Council that they intended to commence digging operations in Carlton Street and Aire Street, and work was put in hand, only to come to a near-standstill because the contractor had not been paid in full for the lines already built. There things remained for nearly a year, when early in 1905 the contractor agreed to resume work provided that £18,517 was paid in cash by 3 May. The shopkeepers in Castleford were getting tired of the delays, and had urged that the company's deposit of £1000 should be forfeited. Work was resumed, but complaints continued throughout 1905 about the delay in construction and the bad condition of the road when the contractors had finished.

Castleford Council were also concerned that so much track was needed in the town. The deposited plans dated November 1903 showed that double track was proposed along Carlton Street, Church Street, Aire Street and most of Bridge Street, and a single track in Bank Street. The Council questioned the company as to how they proposed working this part of the system, and the company replied that they would operate a one-way system with cars for Pontefract using Bank Street, Aire

137

Car 30 in Carlton Street, Castleford, en route for Normanton. Carlton Street was to have had a double track, but the plans were changed to a one-way system with single tracks in parallel streets. The paving in this photograph shows where the second track was removed without ever having been used. (H. Fawbert, Printer, Castleford

Street and Bridge Street and those for Normanton using Carlton Street. The rest of the proposed layout, including the tracks in the Western part of Carlton Street and in Church Street, would have been used by the proposed service to Methley and Leeds, which had been rejected. This meant that one of the two tracks already laid in a part of Carlton Street would not be needed, and the rest of the one-way layout was laid with single track although excavated and paved for two tracks. Even today, the buses follow the same streets and observe a one-way system in streets that have two-way traffic for other vehicles.

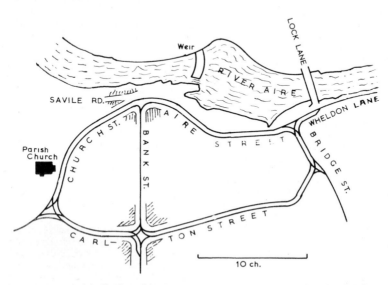

The track layout originally planned for Castleford, some of which was laid but never used.

The completed tracks in Castleford lay unused for several months, and it was January, 1906 before tenders were invited for the completion of the Normanton to Pontefract tramways. Dick, Kerr & Co's tender of £50,768 7s. 3d. was accepted, and the work was resumed in March, proceeding outwards from Castleford towards Normanton and Pontefract. The Normanton line had to pass under the North Eastern Railway's bridge in Station Road, which the railway company had agreed in 1904 could have the roadway lowered, provided that a raised footpath with handrail was provided four feet above the road. The 1 in 22 gradient was increased to 1 in 19, and a single track was laid, but it was mid-1906 before Messrs. Gallagher & Co. of Castleford completed the job. Beyond the bridge there was double track in Oxford Street, and in Oxford Road the tramway passed over a bridge which the North Eastern Railway strengthened in June 1906 ready for the trams, the tramway company paying £300 towards the cost. The remainder of the tramway to Normanton was single line with passing places, with a steep gradient (1 in 17) at Whitwood to the west of the Mining and Technical College, and a level crossing with the Whitwood colliery railway.

The depot was at Wheldon Lane on the east side of Castleford, close to the river Aire, and was approached by a short branch tramway. It had four tracks and was built to accommodate 20 cars. As the Castleford lines were isolated from the main depot at Wakefield, a paint shop was added with room for one car, and provision was made for running repairs. Next to the car shed was the tramway company's own power station, a red brick structure built by Messrs. Gallagher of Castleford containing a Herbert Morris 10-ton overhead crane, and two 310 horsepower four-cylinder diesel engines by the Diesel Engine Co. Ltd. of London, coupled to Dick, Kerr six-pole 500-550 volt 200 kW generators through a flywheel that weighed 13 tons and worked at 170 rev./min. Water for cooling the engine cylinders was pumped from the river Aire, and the engines were started by compressed air. This plant proved much cheaper than the original plan for high tension cables from the Wakefield power station with transformers, but later two rotary converters were added for standby purposes, fed from the Yorkshire Electric Power Company's supply. Diesel generation was not yet common, and fumes coming from the generating station soon caused a nuisance to Messrs. Bellamy at their nearby sweet factory; in January 1907 the tramway company agreed to build a 100 ft. chimney.

The line to Pontefract left Castleford by a length of single track under the railway arch leading to Pontefract Road, and continued as single and loop through Glass Houghton. The track construction from Castleford to Pontefract, through a mining area, differed slightly from that of the other sections in that the track was anchored down at every rail joint, and was paved wholly with setts instead of partly in macadam. A fair amount of road widening and road levelling had to be carried out on this route. The rails were the same as on the Wakefield lines, and the overhead was carried by plain side poles with bracket arms and bowstring suspension. The overhead was divided into the usual half-mile sections, with Dick, Kerr section feeder boxes.

Apart from Oxford Street in Castleford, the only long section of double track on the line was over Tanshelf railway bridge and up Tanshelf Hill (Front Street) to the terminus in Pontefract Market Place. Tanshelf Hill, with a gradient of 1 in 16 for 160 yards, was the steepest on the system and the cause of considerable discussion. Single track was proposed, but due to the gradient the Board of Trade would not agree. Then interlaced track was suggested, but again the Board would not agree, so a double track was laid, which filled the narrow road, and contained two deliberate bends laid to ensure that low speeds would be made down the hill. The Board of Trade considered that the lines were too near the footpath, and would only allow them to be used provided that the road was widened within six months of the opening.

The 1904 Act allowed the carriage of goods on the Castleford tramways, and the promoters had hopes of attracting market garden traffic. There was correspondence in October 1905 with Glass Houghton Colliery about the possibility

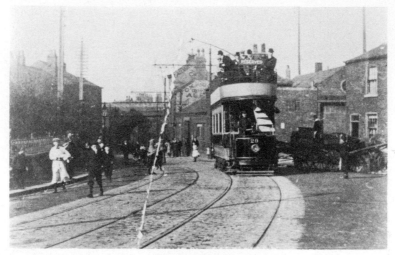

Open-topped car 29 on the Board of Trade's inspection of the Normanton—Pontefract section, 20 October 1906. The car is entering Pontefract Road, Castleford.

(Courtesy Castleford Borough Library

of conveying coal by tramway from the colliery to the Aire and Calder Navigation at Castleford, and Mr. England was asked to prepare estimates and ask the Board of Trade about the legality of such an enterprise. Subject to this, it was agreed to carry the coal if the colliery company would lay, equip and maintain the necessary tracks. The matter was discussed again in August 1911, but nothing was done.

On 8 October 1906 the first two trams arrived at Castleford depot from Rothwell Haigh depot. They were brought on low trolleys drawn by steam traction engines via Oulton and Methley, and only just cleared the Midland Railway bridge at Methley Junction. Ten more arrived during the next three days, and by the end of 1906 there were sixteen cars at Castleford, all withdrawn from the Wakefield system where they had been replaced by new cars. The first trial run, carrying officials and engineers of the company, took place from Castleford to Normanton on Tuesday afternoon, 9 October, and a trial run over the whole system was made three days later. The news spread rapidly, and there were crowds of people waiting in Pontefract to greet the car. According to the *Pontefract & Castleford Express* it was a single-decker (evidently the works car) and the driver was Mr. Burrows of Wakefield.

All was now ready for the Board of Trade inspection. This was fixed for 20 October 1906, and was carried out by Major J. W. Pringle, R.E. The inspector began at Normanton, arriving by train from London soon after 11.00, and was met by Mr. V. D. B. Cooper, consulting engineer to the company. There was some discussion about the precise position of the terminus at Normanton, and several stops were made en route to measure the distance of the line from the kerb, and at Whitwood level crossing. In Station Road, Castleford, measurements were taken to ascertain the distance of the overhead wires from the top deck under the railway bridge, which showed that clearance would be sufficient even for cars "with lids on". There was great excitement as the car proceeded through Castleford and Glass Houghton to the borough boundary with Pontefract. Here the Castleford officials left the car and the Pontefract ones joined it, accompanied by the company's solicitor. Front Street, Tanshelf came in for detailed inspection due to its narrowness, and the car went through to the terminus by Pontefract Town Hall, where a break was made for lunch.

Opening day on the Normanton—Pontefract section, 29 October 1906. A local photographer, E. J. Bloor, took several pictures at different points; this one of car 35 at Pontefract Town Hall terminus is captioned "The first car to enter and leave Pontefract for Public Traffic".
(E. J. Bloor, Castleford

Returning after lunch to Castleford, the car traversed all the tracks in the town (including Church Street and the west end of Carlton Street, the only time these metals were used), and after thus encircling the town proceeded to Normanton Market Place. Here Major Pringle left the car, having said that operating powers would be granted. Before leaving the first days of tramways in the district, it is worth repeating the story told of a miner who, seeing one of the test trams in action, boarded it and sat down. The conductor informed him that they were not accepting passengers just then, whereupon the miner retorted "Never mind. I'll make it do" and kept his seat.

On Thursday 25 October 1906, special decorated cars were run to take guests over the system to mark the formal opening. School children were lined up at the roadside at Hightown, and the cars were bedecked with flags and bunting. The official party of councillors and others was conveyed to Castleford depot, where in the speeches that followed the inspection of the site, the chairman of Castleford U.D.C., Mr. Hartley, suggested extensions to Kippax, Altofts, Featherstone and Knottingley. In reply, Mr. Beaumont, solicitor to the company, said that with bank rate at 6% they could not undertake any more extensions, and he suggested that Pontefract and Featherstone should construct the lines and lease them to the company, as in other parts of the country.

After a day's delay due to a defect at the generating station, the system was opened to the public on Monday 29 October 1906, the first cars leaving the depot soon after 5 a.m. and running every eight minutes throughout the day until the 11.08 p.m. departure from Pontefract. The last car from Normanton was the 11.36 p.m. to Castleford, connecting with the late train from Leeds. Fares were one penny for the first stage and one halfpenny for each additional stage, the stages from Normanton Market Place being Normanton Common (Atkinson Street), Wood Lane Whitwood, Aketon Road Castleford, Bank Street Castleford, Smawthorne Lane, Malt Shovel Inn Glass Houghton, Woodman Inn, Parkside Farm, Pontefract Park Gates, and Pontefract Market Place, the complete end-to-end journey thus costing sixpence for the eight miles. Workmen's fares applied before 7.30 a.m., and bona fide workmen travelling on the outside of the cars between 5 p.m. and 6 p.m. (11 a.m. to 1 p.m. on Saturdays) were charged half the normal fares with a minimum of one penny.

141

The Board of Trade certificate for Front Street, Tanshelf, was valid only for six months, after which the road had to be widened since the track was too near the frontage. There was a piece of land 5½ inches wide which the Council refused to sell to the tramway company, and this was holding up any widening of the street. The temporary permit expired in April 1907; another was issued until 3 November, but from Monday 4 November 1907 the cars turned back at the Queen's Hotel, Tanshelf and ceased running to Pontefract terminus. There was continued correspondence during 1907 and 1908 between the Board of Trade, Pontefract Council and the tramway company; the Board demanded that Front Street be widened on the south side, and the company was willing to share the cost, but the town council were adamant that as the widening was in the interest of the tramway company, it alone should foot the bill. In July 1908 the company again requested permission for single or interlaced track, but the Board of Trade again refused, insisting on double track. Eventually the footpath was set back, and the Board of Trade issued a temporary certificate on 31 July 1908 and a permanent one on 5 September, thus permitting cars to run again up Front Street to the Town Hall. During the Statute Fair each November they had a temporary terminus opposite the Court House at the top of Front Street (returning "wrong road"), the streets beyond being occupied by fairground stalls and sideshows. On 15 November 1915, car 34 disgraced itself by over-running the temporary terminus and ploughing its way through the show.

In May 1907 the North Eastern Railway Company decided to take down their bridge in Oxford Street, Castleford and rebuild it. This broke the through running from 30 June 1907, but temporary track was laid through the construction site and through running was resumed in July. The only other change in the layout was an extension at Normanton into the centre of the Market Place, completed on 3 August 1909, and on 15 October of the same year the tramway gave notice that the various authorised extensions in the area were to be abandoned. The local authorities lodged objections, but to no avail.

To improve the working, colour light signalling was installed at three points in 1912 and 1913. One of these was under the bridge at Castleford station, another by

No. 37 in Front Street, Pontefract, about to descend Tanshelf Hill with its 1 in 16 gradient. The Board of Trade insisted on double track here, despite the narrow road, and service was suspended from November 1907 to July 1908 during a disagreement over who was to pay for road widening. During the Statute Fair each November, cars ascended the hill "wrong road" and turned back at a point just beyond the car in this photograph, facing the Court House (the top of which is just visible on the left). (Courtesy West Riding Automobile Co. Ltd.

the Woodman Inn at Glass Houghton, and the third by the entrance to Castleford's Market Arcade. In addition, a very ingenious form of signalling was installed in the "White Swan" at Normanton and the "Keel Inn" at Castleford in November 1909, for which the proprietors had to pay all costs and an annual rental of £1 1s. 0d. Inside the public houses there were electric signs "Pontefract" and "Normanton" which lit up to inform customers that a tramcar was approaching for that destination. The signal was activated by the tramcar's trolley wheel striking a skate on the trolley wire some distance away, to allow ample time for people to get to the stopping place and catch the tram. There may have been another such sign in the Union Hotel.

Details of the service provided on the Castleford lines are given in a 1910 Notice to Motormen and Conductors setting out the regulations for operating during fog, when specified passing places had to be strictly observed. A 15-minute service with seven cars applied throughout the day on Monday to Friday and before 11.30 a.m. on Saturdays; after this time on Saturdays there was an eight minute service, requiring 14 cars, but if a fifteenth car was available a seven minute service could be offered. On Sundays the service ran every twenty minutes to mid-day and every ten minutes thereafter.

The great "field days" of the Castleford tramways were the race days at Pontefract. The tram track ran parallel with the race track in Pontefract Park, and from April 1912 sixpenny return tickets were issued from Castleford to Pontefract on race days. On such occasions all the tram fleet was mustered to deal with the crowds. Other special traffic was provided by the postal service, under an agreement of June 1914. From 14 September of that year, special cars were run each weekday from Castleford to Pontefract to carry mail, at £120 per annum, and from January 1915 there was a special tram at 2 a.m. from Castleford to Pontefract carrying mail and GPO staff. This tram collected mail from Baghill station, Pontefract, brought it to Castleford, and then went to and from Normanton. There was also a post box on the last tram each night from Pontefract and Normanton to Castleford.

In October 1913, it was decided to obtain estimates for doubling the whole of the track between Normanton and Pontefract. No more was heard of this, and although the outbreak of war in 1914 may have been to blame, it is unlikely that the money would have been forthcoming.

Car 42 near Sandal cricket ground in the early years of the Yorkshire (West Riding) Tramways. From the time these cars were delivered in 1905, the Leeds—Sandal through service was usually worked by covered-top cars. (T.M.S.

The Wakefield lines to 1914

The previous chapter ended with the opening of the Rothwell line on 1 June 1905, marking the completion of the Wakefield system of the Yorkshire (West Riding) Electric Tramways Company Limited, which now totalled 16.950 route miles. This section will trace the subsequent history of these lines down to 1914.

In its 1903 prospectus, the Yorkshire Electric Tramways Construction Syndicate Ltd. had included Dewsbury among its objectives. This was dropped when the three local authorities decided to promote the Ossett—Dewsbury line themselves, but in September 1905 the West Riding company offered to buy the lines as soon as they were built. This was refused, but in December the West Riding company met representatives of the Dewsbury, Ossett and Soothill Nether local authorities to discuss a lease of the line. The general manager was authorised to offer a lease of 42 years, and a draft agreement for a lease of the D.&O. tramways to the West Riding company was drawn up in January 1906, but the local authorities were evidently not satisfied with the terms offered, and, as recorded in chapter five, succeeded in obtaining better terms from the National Electric Construction Co. Ltd., which built the lines on behalf of the councils and then continued as the operator.

The Dewsbury and Ossett tramways were constructed during 1908, and West Riding relaid its track in Ossett Market Place so that through running would be possible between Wakefield and Dewsbury via Ossett. Meanwhile, West Riding's cars would no longer terminate at Bank Street, since both companies' cars would use the loop in Ossett Market Place for reversing purposes. This arrangement commenced with the opening of the Dewsbury and Ossett tramways on 12 November 1908 and proved to be permanent, since the only through running cars were football and Sunday School specials, as mentioned in chapter five. In addition, from 1910 Dewsbury and Ossett cars occasionally visited Belle Isle depot, Wakefield, to have their wheels re-tyred. In January 1915 West Riding agreed to supply power for the Dewsbury and Ossett tramways, and in the following month West Riding made a bid to take over the D.&O. system, but negotiations were soon broken off.

From mid-1905 onwards there were frequent complaints from the local authorities about the state of the roadway between the tramlines. The paving was largely macadam, with setts on each side of the rails only, and more dust was thrown up by the trams than on a track fully paved with setts. The tramway company proposed that the various local authorities should water the roads during dry weather, but they would not agree, until in August 1905 the general manager agreed that the company would share the cost. This enabled the company to transfer its Dick, Kerr water car to the Castleford system, where it remained. Estimates were prepared in July 1905 for doubling the track from Belle Isle to Sandal and also in Doncaster Road, but nothing was done for 20 years. Early in 1913, the company notified Wakefield Corporation that it intended to replace the macadam between the rails with granite setts, and hoped the Corporation would do likewise with the portion outside the 18 inch limit of the tramway paving. It also agreed to pave 80 yards of roadway outside the Clayton Hospital with wood blocks to lessen the noise.

The lines that were built in the Castleford area were tramways governed by the Tramways Act 1870, and were therefore subject to the full assessment of the General Rate for the district, plus the Poor Rate. Had they been constructed under the Light Railways Act 1896, as were the Wakefield lines, the General District Rate would have been only one-quarter of the assessment, but this was not foreseen when the West Riding Tramways Bill was prepared late in 1903. In this matter, West Riding led the way and set a precedent that had widespread effects in the tramway industry.

The point at issue was whether a tramway constructed under the Light Railways Act was a railway within the meaning of section 211 of the Public Health Act 1875, and should thus be rated at only one quarter of its annual value. The first such case had occurred in 1903, when Bradford Corporation had been summoned by Pudsey Corporation and by Calverley and Farsley U.D.C. for general district rates on the Thornbury to Stanningley route (legally a light railway) and had paid up. In May 1904 Mr. Harry England, manager of Wakefield and District, took up the challenge, and was congratulated by the *Light Railway and Tramway Journal* for his courage in being the first to have the matter raised in a clear and definite fashion. The result of the fight, said the paper, would be awaited with considerable interest throughout the country.

The first round in the "Battle of the Rates" took place before the Wakefield Justices. The company alleged that their Wakefield lines should be rated at only one quarter of the net annual value, and tendered that sum (£40 2s. 2d.). The Justices held that the rails were not exclusively used by the company as in the case of a main line railway, since they were laid in the highway which was used by the public at large. Accordingly, the company was not entitled to the exemptions given to railways. It was also stated that had the decision been otherwise, the company would have contributed less than did many individual tradesmen, or some of the occupants of larger houses, despite getting the benefits of street lighting and drainage and the regulation of traffic by the police.

In the light of this decision, the company appealed to the Divisional Court and the case of Wakefield and District Light Railways (sic) Company v. the Wakefield Corporation was heard before that court in April 1906. The three judges unanimously found in favour of the company, accepting its contention that the lines laid in the street were "land used only as a railway" within the meaning of section 211 of the Public Health Act 1875. They pointed out that although the surface of the rails might be used by other road users as well as by the trams, only the latter were entitled to use the groove with their flanged wheels and this factor brought them within the wording of the section, together with the fact that a light railway must for legal purposes at least be regarded as a species of railway however much it might resemble a traditional tramway. The Corporation then in turn appealed against this decision to the Court of Appeal, which in March 1907 decided against them. Again there were three judges and they were all in favour of the company. Nothing daunted, the Corporation took their case to the final court, the House of Lords. Once again the decision was unanimous and once again the company was victorious. The judgment of the judges (four on this occasion) was almost derisive and (most unusually) was limited to four short sentences. The Corporation were also landed with the legal costs of both sides before all four courts.*

In another case in the area of this book, Spen Valley Light Railway v. Thornhill Urban District Council, a decision had been delayed until the Wakefield case had been decided by their lordships. The Wakefield decision became a case for future reference, but local authorities were thereafter less willing to agree to the use of light railway legislation for promoting tramways to be laid in public roads (as distinct from those on private right-of-way) in view of the loss of rate income.

The foregoing decision settled the matter of the General Rate, but a further battle was necessary in the matter of the Poor Rate. This took place in July 1908, when the tramway company appealed to the Assessment Committee of the Wakefield Union, and obtained a reduction in the rateable value of the power station and car sheds, and in the gross charges in respect of the land and tramway.

The Yorkshire Electric Tramways Construction Syndicate Ltd. held its last meeting in July 1906 and was then wound up, leaving the West Riding company in sole charge, though the Wakefield and District Light Railway Company Ltd. maintained a separate legal existence until it was wound up in August 1911. West Riding notified Wakefield Corporation in July 1906 that it was applying for an extension of time for the proposed tramway extensions until August 1907. By the time this date arrived it had become clear that money to extend could not be raised,

---

* The relevant law reports are: [1906] 2 K.B. 140 (Divisional Court); [1907] 2 K.B. 256 (Court of Appeal); and [1908] A.C. 293 (House of Lords).

From *The Tramway World and Railway World*, 2 July 1908

"Midway between Wakefield and Leeds the directors of the Wakefield and District Light Railway Company have established what might be described as the first 'tramway amusement park' in Great Britain. The object of the experiment is, of course, primarily to induce traffic, but the directors have also in view the advantages which such a place of resort must confer on the workers in a district somewhat deficient in opportunities for outdoor amusement and recreation. Lofthouse Park, which has been purchased by the Lofthouse Park Company— a company subsidiary to the Light Railway Company—comprises sixty acres of land, covering the southern slope of Lofthouse Hill, and affords an extensive view of the Vale of the Calder. Already a great deal has been done to make the place attractive, and it is rapidly becoming a popular resort throughout the district. The new enterprise is being watched with much interest by those concerned in tramway management, and on June 24, at the invitation of the directors of the Park Company and the Wakefield Light Railways, a large party of managers of tramways in Yorkshire and others visited the park and inspected the progress already made. Although it was only about a year ago that the park was purchased, much has been done, as may be gathered from the illustrations of the park which accompany these notes."

"The visitor may proceed by tramcar either from the centre of Leeds or Wakefield—for mutual running powers were some time ago arranged between the Leeds Corporation Tramways and the Company—and besides the usual cost of a return ticket by tramway, no further charge is now made for admission to the park. A double siding has been constructed at the Park Gates to provide the convenient handling of the traffic. On entering the gates a view is at once obtained of a large portion of the park. In the centre of the scene is a fine pavilion containing a large concert hall, grill room, cloak rooms, etc. The hall is large enough to seat 1,000 people, and it fitted with a stage and the necessary equipment of a theatre. To the left of the stage is an alcove for the orchestra, which is thus placed between the pavilion and an outside platform which can be used for dancing. An excellent floor has been provided for dancing in the pavilion itself."

"In front of the building an attractive band stand has been constructed, and behind it is an interesting rock garden with plants of various kinds. At night both the pavilion and band stand are brilliantly illuminated by a great number of coloured lamps. A bowling green, puzzle garden and numerous side shows are provided for the entertainment of those who frequent the park, while a native village, peopled with inhabitants of the Philippines, is at present a staple attraction. An excellent beginning has been made with flower beds, which add much to the pleasant appearance of the fore-court of the pavilion. Daily concerts and firework displays on stated evenings are a part of the regular programme of the park, and the company are preparing numerous other amusements which will eventually make it possible for their patrons to indulge in any favourite sport. An athletic ground will be laid out and there will be ample space for cricket, football, etc. Later a lake will be made so that boating and skating will be possible in season."

"A novel feature is the construction in the park of a sub-station with a glass front so that visitors may see the motor generators at work. The sub-station contains also transforming plant necessary for reducing the high-pressure current which is supplied from the power-station of the Wakefield and District Light Railway Company, for the lighting and power required."

"On the occasion of the visit of the Yorkshire managers luncheon was served in the pavilion, and afterwards there was a brief toast list. Mr. G. E. Leon, Chairman of the Lofthouse Park Company, presided, and in reply to the toast of Lofthouse Park, proposed by the Lord Mayor of Leeds, gave a brief account of the enterprise which, although an experiment, would he believed be a great success. He had, he continued, been impressed with the somewhat dismal appearance of the neighbouring colliery villages and hamlets, and with the absence of any place of recreation for the people. Mr. England, the general manager of the Wakefield and District Light Railways, shared his feelings in the matter, and when the latter asked him to come down and see the Lofthouse estate and consider whether use could not be made of it as an amusement park, he readily did so. The result was the purchase and transformation of the Park. They had begun in a very modest way, but they were ambitious that the scheme should grow. He believed it would prove both a good business enterprise and a great boon to the neighbourhood."

and most of the powers were allowed to lapse. Net revenue for 1906 was £19,892 on capital expenditure to date of £438,838. Of this revenue, £11,756 was paid out in debenture interest, £5,000 reserved for depreciation and £4,443 carried over to the next account, no ordinary share interest being paid. By 1911 the capital expenditure had risen to £741, 091, and the ordinary shareholders had still had no return on their investment; the only people who had gained (apart from the various promoters) were the local inhabitants, for whom the trams were a great boon.

In an attempt to stimulate traffic, the West Riding board decided to go into the amusement park business. This was obviously influenced by the American "trolley park" idea and the Manx Electric Railway connection. A subsidiary company, Lofthouse Park Limited, was set up to run a pleasure park abutting on to the main Wakefield to Leeds road at Lofthouse. Among its shareholders were the leading personalities in the Yorkshire (West Riding) Electric Tramways Co. Ltd., such as the Leons, Keen, and the engineer, V. B. D. Cooper. Lofthouse Park was built on land sold to the company in June 1908 by a Mr. J. Horner for £8,000, and a long loop to serve as a siding and loading bay was laid on the western side of the road where cars could stand and wait for passengers leaving performances taking place in the park. A substation was added nearby, with plate glass windows so that the public could see it at work.

The grounds were laid out in flower beds, with a maze, elephant rides and other attractions to make the place a miniature Hampton Court. There were the inevitable tea rooms and conservatory, and a bandstand in which bands from far and near gave performances. A pavilion was built and used for bioscope shows and dances. An ice-skating rink also formed part of the attractions, and at one time there was an "African village". Balloon ascents and parachute descents took place there in July 1910, and in April 1910 it was agreed to provide an outside dancing platform.

A special advertising car was run in 1908 to advertise Lofthouse Park, and persons holding and producing tram tickets were allowed into the grounds at a reduced entrance fee. Eightpenny return tickets were issued from Wakefield, and in March 1910 the same concession was extended to Agbrigg, Sandal and Horbury. From March 1911, through return tickets were issued from Dewsbury to Lofthouse

The Yorkshire (West Riding) Electric Tramways' Pavilion and Conservatory at Lofthouse Park, opened in 1908.   (Courtesy Miss M. Harran

Park for one shilling. Combined tram and theatre tickets were proposed, and half-price tickets were issued to members of the Lofthouse Choral Union when travelling to and from rehearsals, and on concert nights. At times Leeds City cars ran through from Leeds to Lofthouse Park, and when traffic was particularly heavy it appears that cars were hired from the Leeds tramways to get crowds home from the Park. An earlier proposal of April 1908 had been to buy some trailers.

Having built up the business, West Riding then sought to sell the park (for not less than £21,000) to a syndicate of local showmen and others set up for the purpose. The West Riding Amusement Syndicate Ltd. was registered on 6 December 1910 to purchase Lofthouse Park "and provide an Entertainment City provided and equipped with all manner of entertainments, amusements, recreation, pleasure and other devices and ingenuities with all buildings and works convenient for the purposes thereof". The purchase price could not be raised, and instead the Syndicate took a lease of the park from 1 February 1911. The promoter and general manager was William Mottershead, a Sheffield showman, who moved into Lofthouse Park lodge (rent free) and received a salary of £250 per year plus commission, and the other shareholders (mostly from Sheffield) were four licensed victuallers, two brewers, two cigar manufacturers, a printer, a commission agent, and Harry England. Wm. Mottershead ran the park for three years, but found the going hard and gave up in October 1913. In the same year, the Park liabilities and assets were sold for £5,000 to Messrs. Whitfield, Eastwood and McHill.

A significant editorial on the subject of tramway pleasure parks appeared in *The Light Railway and Tramway Journal* for April 1913. It warned that American experience showed that the novelty wore off after a few years, and advocated that amusement parks should be not run by tramway officials but should be leased to professional amusement men. The Wakefield and Edinburgh (Portobello) examples were cited, and few other parks were created in Britain, though examples did exist at Belfast, Rothesay and in the Isle of Man. In December 1914, Lofthouse Park became a prisoner of war camp; German prisoners were marched round the village for exercise, and instead of the music of famous bands, one could hear the call of the bugle giving orders for Lights Out. Special cars were run to take prisoners to the park. Lofthouse Park Limited ceased its business on 13 October 1916 and never resumed. A few years ago, lupins still grew in the "wilderness" where the park had been, descendents of those planted there in 1908.

At Christmas 1906 there was an exceptionally heavy fall of snow, and the line was blocked for a distance of half a mile at Horbury. Mr. Davies, the company's engineer, had his men out all night to clear the tracks, and a photograph exists showing two cars at Horbury with the snow up to their waist. Mr. Davies fitted a car with a snow plough which pushed the snow to one side of the track. Later that year, a portable crossover was purchased for use during track repairs, which suggests that the permanent way laid in 1904 was proving less permanent than was hoped.

Towards the end of 1908, the Company intimated that they were hoping to re-lay the track outside the Cathedral in Wakefield, where the cathedral boundary wall had been taken back and the road widened, leaving the tram lines curving into the middle of the newly widened road. Discussion centred on how to make the layout safer for pedestrians. Before anything was done a counter-proposal was received for the removal of the tramlines in front of the cathedral, but no practical suggestion was made for an alternative route from the Bull Ring into Kirkgate. During 1912 there were more discussions about widening the Chantry Bridge; a fire at King's Mill, on the north side of the bridge, caused the Aire and Calder Navigation Company to suggest to the Corporation that now was a good time to make improvements. Nothing was done.

In February 1909, the board considered a proposal to run express cars between Leeds and Wakefield, and in September authorised the purchase of four new cars for this service, but no action was taken, despite further discussion in September 1912. The fleet remained at 67 cars from 1906 until 1919, working on 24.69 miles of route, equivalent to 40.38 miles of track. In May 1909 the company ran an

Two cars in a snowdrift near Horbury; a photograph taken in December 1906. The line was blocked for several days. (Thomas A. Green, Horbury

illuminated car in honour of the Wakefield Trinity team winning the Northern Union rugby cup, and in September 1910 an agreement was signed with Messrs. Tate to carry parcels on the trams.

On 7 February 1911 the company's solicitors wrote to the Board of Trade requesting permission to transfer the undertaking from the Wakefield & District Light Railway Company to the Yorkshire (West Riding) Electric Tramways Company Limited. The reason given was that since West Riding held the whole of the share capital of Wakefield & District, it would greatly simplify matters and save much unnecessary expense if the Wakefield company was wound up. The Board were hesitant about the transfer from a statutory company to a limited liability company, but on finding out that they had sanctioned similar transfers for Bath and for the Blackpool, St. Annes & Lytham, agreed subject to local authority approval. This was obtained, and the transfer took place in August 1911.

In December 1912 there were complaints that conductors at Sandal terminus were jumping off the tram, pulling the trolley off the wire and turning it by the momentum of the tram while standing still themselves. During the hours of darkness, this meant that the tram was plunged into darkness while on the move, and was a danger to other users of the road. The practice was rendered unnecessary four years later by fitting automatic trolley reversers. In July 1913 the first automatic signals were installed in Wakefield; a set was bought from Tramway Supplies Ltd., Leeds, for £25 and installed at the exit from the Bull Ring towards Kirkgate.

Unlike many tramway companies, the Yorkshire (West Riding) Electric Tramways Co. Ltd. was not intended by its promoters to provide public electricity supplies in its areas, since the Yorkshire Electric Power Company (incorporated in 1901) was already active in the area, supplying power from its Thornhill generating station to local authorities or local distribution companies in Wakefield, Ossett, Normanton, Castleford, Horbury, Stanley, Rothwell, Whitwood and many neighbouring districts. An opportunity did however arise at Pontefract, where the

149

town council's lighting order was about to expire. With the council's agreement, the tramway company obtained the Pontefract Electric Lighting Order 1912, serving a population of some 17,000 and buying power in bulk from the Yorkshire Electric Power Company at Castleford, aided when necessary by the company's own diesel plant. The supply commenced in April 1914, through two substations. There were also some consumers at Rothwell Haigh, supplied from the company's Rothwell substation.

The various local authorities were rather concerned at the long delay in constructing the authorised extensions, and matters came to a head in 1913 when the company sought to abandon the extensions and get its deposits back. Abandonment powers for the unbuilt lines could only be obtained if the local authorities agreed, and the company realised that the most likely way to overcome local opposition was to offer to run buses.

The first mention of buses occurs in November 1908, when a request was received from Crigglestone for a bus service between that village and Wakefield. Mr. H. England, the manager, said that a motor bus service between the two places could not possibly pay—perhaps three buses a day might pay. During the summer of 1911, Mr. England made enquiries about hiring motor buses for the Ardsley route, meeting Commercial Car Hirers Ltd. who had commenced running between Ossett and Wakefield in July, as mentioned in chapter five. However, no steps could be taken until leave to abandon the proposed light railways had been granted by the Board of Trade. A petition to the company was received in May 1913 asking that trolleybuses be run in the Thornes district of Wakefield.

In October 1913, the company announced that tramways to Alverthorpe and Ardsley could never be remunerative, and that it favoured trackless trolley or motor buses to serve these villages. In the following month the company said that it would be prepared, if cessor powers were granted, to run bus services from Wakefield to Alverthorpe and Ardsley for a sufficient length of time to test whether they would be a paying proposition. In 1914 the company prepared a very comprehensive scheme for bus services in the outlying areas around Wakefield. The routes contemplated were from Sandal terminus to Walton village, from Sandal to Newmillerdam, from Wakefield to Stanley via Eastmoor, to Alverthorpe, to Pontefract via Sharlston and Streethouse, to High Ackworth via Nostell, to Hemsworth via Nostell, to Morley via Ardsley, and to Crigglestone via Durkar. At the time war broke out in 1914, some buses were on order from the Daimler company. These were never received, and the company did not run its own buses until 1922.

New timetables were introduced in April 1914, with fewer cars in use, and caused considerable grumbling. These did not allow any standing time at the termini, as cars were timed to start the return journey as soon as they arrived. There was no time for meals either, and these had to be taken as and when possible on the road. Shifts on the Leeds—Sandal route were from eight to fourteen hours, and there was also an increase in speed, so that drivers were being worked unreasonably. This led to loss of staff, and the company eventually "saw the light" and eased the schedules.

Two narrow spots on the Yorkshire (West Riding) Tramways. The upper view is of cars 64 and 58 in Upper Kirkgate, Wakefield, and the lower one is of cars 17 and 67 passing on the Chantry Bridge, Wakefield, with the King's Mill on the left and the Chantry Chapel on the right.
(Courtesy L. Aspey

Two group photographs of West Riding tramway staff. The upper view was taken at Belle Isle depot, Wakefield, in 1904 or 1905, with manager Harry England seated fifth from right. The lower picture was taken about eight years later at Wheldon Lane depot, Castleford.

(West Riding Automobile Co. Ltd.

CHAPTER EIGHT

THE YORKSHIRE (WEST RIDING) TRAMWAYS FROM 1915

The services of the Yorkshire (West Riding) Electric Tramways Company Ltd. do not appear to have been affected too drastically during the 1914-18 war. The track and cars were in fair condition and were able to carry considerable extra traffic. The Weekly Traffic Returns show increases over each previous year of about 10% in 1916, 12% in 1917 and a further 20% in 1918, with the result that the company ended the war on a much firmer financial footing. The principal difficulties were caused by shortage of staff and rolling stock.

By May, 1915 the company was becoming short of manpower, and by November 1915 conductresses had commenced work. For these "clippies" a hinged seat was fitted to the stairs of the trams so that they could sit on it when not actually engaged in collecting fares. Women car cleaners were appointed from August 1916, and in March 1917 the board debated whether to train and appoint women drivers. There were complaints of overcrowding on the cars, particularly from workmen who in the early evening were obliged to travel upstairs. The same system prevailed on the Dewsbury and Ossett, but on the Leeds tramways they were also allowed downstairs.

In January 1916 subdued lighting was enforced in the cars, and in the following month rear lights were agreed to because of the difficulty of seeing the cars at night. In March 1916 the possibility of buying trailers was discussed, and in June the general manager was asked to obtain quotations for new cars. In October 1916 it was decided to erect trolley reversers at the termini to cut down flashing, and in February 1917 casement curtains were fitted to the cars as an anti-air-raid precaution. In June 1918 the tramways company appealed to employers to stagger working hours in the national interest so that gross overcrowding of the cars could be avoided. Later in 1918 the Yorkshire Tramway Managers Association, in which West Riding manager Harry England played a leading role, discussed the possible introduction of tramway goods services, but decided that it could not be done without special legislation.

The biggest catastrophe suffered by the Yorkshire (W.R.) Electric Tramways was a fire which broke out at Castleford tram depot early on Monday 5 March 1917. It was discovered at about 2.30 a.m. by the night watchman, who gave the alarm and summoned Castleford fire brigade.

Although recent bad weather had put some of the firemen's bells out of action, the firemen were playing their hoses on the flames within twelve minutes of receiving the call, using their steam fire pump. Leeds Fire Brigade was called and arrived at 4.25 a.m., and was quickly able to pump a bigger volume of water from the nearby river. The Castleford men had concentrated on preventing the fire from spreading to the power station which adjoined the tramshed. There were sixteen trams in the shed when the fire broke out, and eight of them were destroyed, plus the works car. One of the first men on the scene was Inspector Martin, and he with others pushed as many trams out of the depot as they could. They could not use power, and so the cars had to be manhandled. The fire was mastered by about 7.30 a.m. As often happens, the origin of the fire was not known, but it appeared to have started in some wood shavings nearby, or in a car which was being repaired. The total damage was estimated at between £10,000 and £15,000.

153

After the Castleford depot fire of 5 March 1917, in which eight cars were lost, eight others were transferred from Wakefield to Castleford, including No. 45 (left) photographed in wartime all-over brown livery at Normanton terminus, and No. 21 (centre) seen here in all-green livery at Pontefract Park, with fleet numbers on the waist panel only. In 1920 eight new cars were bought from the English Electric Company Ltd. of Preston, including No. 28 (right), and were used on the Leeds—Wakefield—Sandal service. (Courtesy N. Sagar (45,21) and M. J. O'Connor (28)

154

There was a late start to working that morning, but the eight surviving cars were able to maintain a reasonable service for the rest of the week. Eight cars were soon transferred from Belle Isle Wakefield to the Castleford section, and from 6 March eight cars were borrowed from Leeds City Tramways to replace them. The borrowed cars were purchased from Leeds in July 1919, and in 1920 eight new cars were bought from English Electric of Preston to replace those lost in the fire.

The company's results for the year to 31 December 1918 were gross revenue £140,568, net revenue £15,303, permitting a dividend of six per cent. This encouraged local councils to press once again for extensions, but in February 1919 Mr. H. England made it clear that the increase in costs due to the war had made this prohibitive. Rails which cost £6 12s. per ton in 1914 were now costing £17 10s. per ton, new single track would cost £10,000 per mile, and Sheffield Corporation was paying £3,000 each for new trams against £900 in 1914. The company was willing to run motor buses to Alverthorpe, but the condition of the road made it impracticable. In March 1919 Allerton Bywater parish council asked the company to extend its system from Castleford to their mining village, reviving a suggestion turned down in 1909.

Nevertheless, on 22 March 1920 the company stated that they intended to ask for a further extension of time, for five years, to complete the unconstructed portions of the tramways. These were granted in July 1920, but the Ministry of Transport suggested that the company should run omnibus services on these routes to test the amount of traffic likely to arise, particularly to Ardsley and Oulton. The company was prepared to do this, but in case these bus services proved a failure, a proposal was also discussed under which the surplus buses might replace the Ossett—Agbrigg trams and avoid the heavy cost of relaying the track. Nothing more was heard of this suggestion.

Passengers carried on the company's trams in 1918 were up by 50% compared with 1914, and the figure continued to increase, reaching an all-time peak of 17,599,657 in 1920. This enabled the company to pay a six per cent dividend for 1920 and put £20,347 into the reserve fund. Traffic dropped by 20% in 1921, due to industrial troubles and a coal strike, though the trams were kept running almost normally. The drop in revenue amounted to £12,722. Nevertheless, the profits earned by the trams in 1918-22 and put to reserve were the foundation of the company's motor bus business, as will be seen.

An unusual accident, with fatal consequencies, occurred near Kirkgate Station, Wakefield, on the early morning of 29 January 1920. Many overhead telegraph and telephone wires were blown down in a gale, and two of them fell on the tramway wires. A railwayman walking to work became entangled in the free end of the broken GPO wire, receiving a shock, and a colleague who tried to release him received so severe a shock that he was killed. At the subsequent inquiry, the Ministry of Transport inspector, Major G. L. Hall RE, found that the guard wires formerly provided at this point had not been replaced after dewirement damage about two years previously, owing to the wartime difficulty of obtaining supplies and the backlog of work, which the company undertook to make good.

Early in 1922, the company followed up the Ministry's suggestion by introducing experimental bus services from Wakefield to Ardsley on 6 February 1922, to Alverthorpe on 17 April 1922, and from Castleford to Lofthouse via Methley, Oulton, Rothwell and Carlton on 15 July 1922. They revealed that the traffic on these sections was insufficient to warrant the cost of laying tram tracks, and on 1 June 1923 application was made to abandon these uncompleted portions of the tramways. Before agreeing to this, the Minister of Transport said that he would have to be satisfied that the bus services would be continued, and a meeting was held at County Hall, Wakefield, on 19 September 1923 between the company and the five local councils involved, at which the company guaranteed to continue the bus services and the councils agreed not to oppose the company's application to abandon the unconstructed Alverthorpe, East Ardsley and Oulton light railways. So ended the last hopes of extensions, after twenty years of talks.

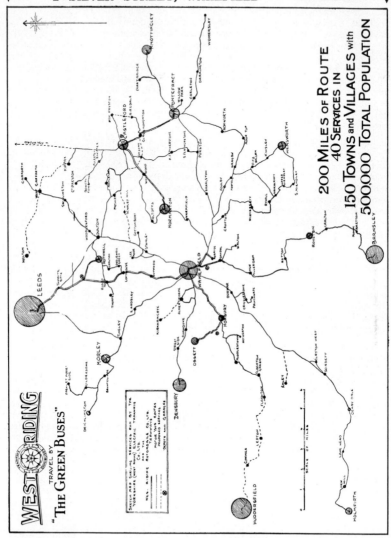

Map of West Riding tram and bus routes in the summer of 1924, reproduced from the company's Official Touring Guide. At the top left is the White Rose emblem devised by company secretary Robert England and introduced in 1924 concurrently with the new green and white tram and bus livery.

156

On 16 November 1923 a subsidiary company, West Riding Automobile Company Limited, was registered to take over the bus operations, which now covered 160 miles of route. Its capital of £80,000 in £1 shares was held wholly by the tramway company, and represented the cost of 38 Bristol single-deck buses (Nos. 101 to 138), a new 200 ft by 80 ft bus garage opened on 11 December 1922 at Belle Isle, a smaller 1922 shed at Castleford, the petrol storage tanks, pumps, tools and appliances, and a bus shelter and parcels office built in December 1922 at Cross Square, Wakefield, immediately west of the cathedral. The directors were the same as those of the tramway company, with Robert England as secretary. Of the buses, twenty-two 32-seaters had been bought in 1922 and sixteen more in 1923. A retrospective adjustment was made in the accounts back to the end of 1922.

In the Castleford area small local bus operators began to appear in 1921. One of the first was Messrs. Routledge and Son, who ran from Castleford to Leeds through Methley and Oulton, the route of one of the original tramway proposals. A number of small proprietors sprung up soon afterwards, mostly operating from a shed with no proper facilities. One firm was Newton & Ward of Rothwell, which sold out to West Riding in 1933, and another was J. Bullock and Sons of Featherstone, which expanded in competition with West Riding and was not taken over until 1950. To combat the threat to its Castleford tramway, West Riding was forced to introduce bus services parallel with its own trams.

Because of increased traffic, the second-hand cars obtained from Leeds continued in use, bringing the fleet total to 75 cars, instead of being replaced by the new vehicles bought from English Electric in 1920. An application was made to the Board of Trade in September 1922 for a revision of the maximum speeds allowed in the city of Wakefield, and Major G. L. Hall, RE, made an inspection. Some increases were allowed, the maximum becoming 14 miles/h instead of 12 miles/h, but the lowest speed limit (four miles per hour) still applied at many points in Wakefield, including all facing points, underbridges, level crossings, the Chantry bridge, the Bull Ring and all curves in or out of it, and all other sharp curves on the system. Nevertheless, the speeds on the West Riding tramways were generally higher than on the other two systems described, though this was partly because they had fewer stopping places and ran through areas that were not so densely populated. In September 1923 the company again proposed through running between Wakefield and Dewsbury, but after two months' discussion the idea was dropped.

Discussions took place in 1922-23 with the local authorities and the colliery companies about the serious effect of colliery subsidence on the track of the Normanton—Castleford—Pontefract section. The whole of this area was dependent on coalmining, and the stretch of roadway between Tanshelf station and Glass Houghton was particularly liable to subsidence, due to the nearby Prince of Wales and Glass Houghton collieries. The tramway company suggested to the local authorities that it would be desirable to remove the track from the centre of the roadway and place it at the side on wooden sleepers, a method then recently adopted by Leeds Corporation on the Roundhay route. The local authorities declined to meet the company's request, and it may have been this factor that persuaded the management that there could be no long-term future for the tramways in the Castleford and Pontefract area. The Tramways and Light Railways Association, of which Harry England was vice-chairman, had also tried to establish a right to compensation for road subsidence that damaged tramway permanent way, but in vain.

No such doubts affected the Wakefield lines, which carried four-fifths of the company's passengers, and in 1923 the company applied to Wakefield city council for permission to double the track on the Sandal route, and a year later for the Agbrigg route. Both routes had been single track with loops controlled by red and green colour light signals, except at the two canal bridges on the Agbrigg route where the tram would switch on an illuminated "STOP" sign. The Sandal route was double-tracked in 1924, and the old rails were sold at £5 10s. per ton to Hemsworth and Lofthouse collieries, probably for use as pit-props. In September 1923 a piece of

157

Harry England, general manager of the Yorkshire (West Riding) Electric Tramways from 1903 and managing director from 1922 onwards. One of Britain's best-known tramway managers, he played a leading part in the formation of the Tramways and Light Railways Association, becoming a vice-chairman in 1914 and serving for many years as a council member, frequently acting as a spokesman for the industry and as an expert witness in arbitration and similar cases. He was also active in the Association of Yorkshire Tramway Managers, which from 1918 carried out wage negotiations for the area and led the fight to obtain compensation for track damaged by colliery subsidence. His two sons, Ben and Robert, also rose to senior positions in the industry.

West Riding 71, one of eight cars acquired from Leeds City Tramways after the 1917 Castleford depot fire. These 1898-vintage cars spent their remaining years on the Agbrigg—Ossett route. No. 71 is seen here in the Bull Ring, Wakefield, after being repainted in the pre-1924 livery of two shades of green.   (R. B. Parr Collection

land was bought from Tadcaster Tower Brewery for an off-street terminus at Sandal on the east side of the road, to avoid the cars having to stand in the narrow and increasingly busy main road, and this was laid in 1924, with a tram shelter. It served long after the tramway era as the terminus of the Leeds to Sandal buses, until they were extended to Kettlethorpe. The Agbrigg route was doubled shortly afterwards, and on the rest of the system the track joints were electrically welded to give smoother running and prolong the life of the rails.

Throughout these years the running and maintenance costs were always carefully watched. In 1924, during the inquiry into the purchase of the Great Grimsby Street Tramways by Grimsby Corporation, it was suggested that the Grimsby company was skimping maintenance because they were only spending £209 per car per year. To refute this the Grimsby company invited Harry England to give evidence, and he gave £200 per car per year as the maintenance costs on the West Riding tramways. This was one of the lowest figures in Britain, and only two-thirds that of Leeds and Sheffield. Mr. England also said he was putting modern BTH box frame motors in the cars, which suggests that services were to be speeded up to forestall omnibus competition.

Harry England was by this time West Riding's managing director. He had become a director in May 1922, and managing director within three months. The other directors at that time were Sir Herbert Samuel Leon, BT. (chairman), George E. Leon, William Murray, and Ernest Remnant, formerly Ernest Schenk. Harry England's two sons were in the company, Robert England as secretary and Ben England as local manager at Castleford; local manager at Wakefield was G. H. Margrave, who also managed West Riding Automobile. There were also four engineers, D. E. Bell (electrical, Wakefield), R. Leedal (electrical, Castleford), H. Ottevant (permanent way) and A. H. Harrop (rolling stock). The company had no general manager, but this was remedied in November 1924 when Major Fred Coutts, manager of the Dearne District Light Railways and formerly at Paisley, became general manager of West Riding, being succeeded by his son Ronald on the D.D.L.R. Unfortunately, on 10 March 1925 Major Coutts died in a Sheffield nursing home following an operation for appendicitis, and G. H. Margrave who had just been offered the managership at Chesterfield remained at Wakefield, becoming general manager.

By the end of 1924, West Riding Automobile were running buses into Leeds from Ardsley, Tingley, Castleford and Ossett. Despite the agreement for through running with trams, Leeds Corporation refused permission for their buses, but the company overcame this by securing a private bus station in Leeds near the Queens Hotel. Their secretary, Robert England, said "We could not expect passengers going into Leeds to get out of omnibuses and wait in the road until a tramcar came along". Bradford were less forthcoming, and refused to allow West Riding to run into the city from Wakefield. In March 1925 the Ministry of Transport ordered Bradford to allow West Riding buses to run in from Drighlington; Bradford refused, and lodged an appeal, which the Ministry rejected in January 1926. Again Bradford refused to issue licences, until in March the Ministry of Transport applied for a writ of mandamus directed to Bradford Corporation calling on them to show why licences should not be issued. Meanwhile, Leeds in August 1925 introduced standard conditions (with protective fares) for company buses running into Leeds.

The last major alteration to the tramway system was the renewal of the track in Upper Kirkgate, Wakefield, in June 1925. It was done in two stages, first from Warrengate to Teale Street and then on to Southgate, using a temporary crossover at the bottom of Upper Kirkgate where the cars from Sandal and Agbrigg could reverse; those from Leeds and Ossett reversed on the crossover near the cathedral. Further track renewals were carried out in Doncaster Road, Wakefield, during 1927, using asphalt paving instead of the usual setts. In July, 1926, the company ceased producing its own electricity at Belle Isle, Wakefield, buying power instead from the corporation. This made possible the expansion of the facilities for motor buses at Belle Isle, and the former boiler house served until 1972 as West Riding Automobile's paint shop.

The 1923 agreement with the local authorities concerned in the Ardsley and Alverthorpe bus routes may have given the company some measure of protection against competition in this area, but no such protection existed in Castleford or Pontefract, where four of the five local authorities would grant bus licences to anyone who applied. The chairman of one authority, tackled by H. England about bus licences, said he didn't think it would affect the trams. Harry England particularly criticised councils who employed only union labour for issuing licences to bus firms with non-union staff and low wage levels. West Riding were at a decided disadvantage compared with the Yorkshire Woollen District and Dewsbury & Ossett tramways, for the latter ran on tracks either largely (Y.W.D.) or wholly (D.&O.) leased from the local authorities, who derived revenue from the leases and were much less likely to grant licences to competing buses. Major Chapple of Y.W.D. often used this argument to his company's advantage, and Y.W.D. suffered far less from competing buses than did West Riding, which owned all its track and plant and paid no rent to local authorities, though it paid full rates on the Castleford tracks, which also required constant repair owing to mining subsidence.

On 13 August 1925, the tramway company made a final plea to the urban district councils of Rothwell, Castleford, Normanton, Pontefract and Whitwood asking them to protect the tramways from unrestricted bus competition and reminding them that the company was the largest local ratepayer apart from the railways and the colliery companies. All except Rothwell refused to act, and the company then ordered twelve more Bristol buses and announced that from 31 October 1925 the tramways in the Pontefract, Castleford and Normanton areas would be closed down. It was revealed that only in two years since 1906 had this tramway not run at a loss. The local authorities, who had been indifferent or antagonistic to the trams, now professed concern at the reinstatement of the roadway and the loss of rates due to the removal of the tram track.

The *Pontefract and Castleford Express* for 30 October 1925 announced that the last car would run on Sunday night 1 November. The trams would be replaced by a five-minute bus service from Normanton to Castleford and Pontefract, augmented by a reorganised network of longer-distance services, some of which followed routes proposed for tramways at the turn of the century. These buses would run every 15 minutes from Normanton direct to Pontefract, every 30 minutes on the routes Normanton—Castleford—Fryston and Leeds—Methley—Castleford—Pontefract, and every hour on the routes Castleford—Pontefract—Ferrybridge, Normanton—Castleford—Garforth—Leeds, and Normanton—Castleford—Kippax.

West Riding trams in the new green and white livery, introduced in 1924. The upper view shows No. 9 in Westgate, Wakefield en route for Ossett, the lower one is of No. 11 at Pontefract Town Hall terminus. Nos. 11 and 13 may have been the only cars on the isolated Normanton—Pontefract tramway to receive the new livery before this section closed on 1 November 1925.   (Commercial postcards, courtesy A. K. Kirby and R. B. Parr

The last tram, No. 13, left Pontefract at 11 p.m. on Sunday 1 November 1925 apparently without ceremony. The last car from Castleford to Normanton was driven by local councillors in their respective areas, and then returned to depot. Six cars were taken back to the main system at Wakefield, but ten remained in store at Castleford and were sold there in November 1927. The generating plant at Castleford depot was retained, probably as standby for the lighting supply, until sold in 1930. £9,000 was set aside for road reinstatement, and the company's capital was written down by £178,601. The tramway launched with such enthusiasm in 1906 had lasted only for nineteen years.

On 24 July 1926 Sir Herbert Leon, chairman of the company since 1903, died at the age of 76 and was succeeded as chairman by his brother George Leon. Ben England, who had been local manager at Castleford, became assistant manager in 1925 at Wakefield, but left the company in 1929 to become general manager at St. Helens, moving to Southend in 1933, to Leicester in 1936 and then from 1939 at Nottingham, until his retirement in 1962; he died in December 1978. West Riding then appointed a commercial manager, Walter Luff, who from 1932 to 1954 established a fine reputation as general manager at Blackpool.

During the General Strike from 4 to 12 May 1926 no West Riding tramcars ran, but West Riding Automobile continued to operated school buses. In the following month, the company asked Wakefield city council to institute protective fares for bus journeys covering the same routes as the trams; where the tram fares were respectively 1½d. and 2d., the bus fares should be 2d. and 3d. The company became a shareholder in County Motors (Lepton) Ltd., which ran a Wakefield—Huddersfield bus service, and opposed (without success) an application for a Huddersfield Corporation—Y.W.D. joint bus service from Dewsbury to Huddersfield. Five trams were scrapped during 1927, reducing the fleet to 60 cars.

With the loss-making Castleford tramway cleared from the accounts, the remaining tram services produced a useful surplus, except possibly for the Rothwell branch. This may be the reason why in May 1927 the board decided to abandon the Rothwell—Leeds route, but they did not proceed with the idea. The rest of the system was to function as it was, pending developments. In December 1928 a further attempt was made to take over the Dewsbury & Ossett Tramways, and discussions took place with the National Electric Construction Company in 1929, but to no avail. In February 1928 the board considered buying an automatic point controller, and at about this time short-working cars were introduced to the Wakefield city council's Lupset housing estate, on the Horbury route.

The company was probably waiting to see the outcome of legislation before Parliament which was to change the structure of the industry. The four main line railways in 1928 promoted Bills to allow them to carry goods and passengers by road, and a Royal Commission on Transport was set up in 1929, whose recommendations took shape as the Road Traffic Act of 1930. This introduced a system of road service licences that survives today, and gave prior rights to all existing operators. Armed with their new powers, the main-line railway companies were buying an interest in the existing bus companies, and in January 1931 a conference was held in which the L.M.S. and L.N.E. Railways proposed an agreement for the joint working of West Riding's bus services. West Riding, however, preferred to remain independent.

In June 1931 West Riding notified the Ministry of Transport that it proposed to replace the Leeds—Sandal and Leeds—Rothwell trams with buses, and in September gave similar notice in respect of the Ossett—Wakefield—Agbrigg route. Applications for the necessary road service licences were heard by the Traffic Commissioners on 12 August 1931, and a decision was deferred. Meanwhile an agreement was concluded with Wakefield Corporation under which the city would take up the tramway and restore the road surface, though in many cases the new road surface was superimposed, leaving the tracks buried underneath; some are still there today. By this time, maintenance of the track had been reduced to a minimum, and a tram ride from Leeds to Wakefield was·becoming a rather unnerving experience.

For exactly 27 years, from 1 June 1905 to 31 May 1932, the West Riding company's trams ran through into the centre of Leeds, traversing the municipally owned tracks of the Hunslet route and terminating near the Corn Exchange. The upper view (courtesy R. Brook) shows No. 7 waiting at the top of Lower Briggate; the lower photograph by S. L. Smith shows English Electric car 35 of 1920 in Duncan Street, passing Leeds 298. Company cars showed "Wakefield" as destination when leaving Leeds, and changed it to "Sandal" before reaching Outwood.

In its submission to the Traffic Commissioners in 1931, the company gave a useful summary of its corporate and financial history, which is well worth quoting. The total expenditure on the tramways to 30 December 1930 had been £862,208, of which £179,114 was lost through the enforced abandonment of the Castleford lines in 1925. Although providing an extensive transport service since 1904, the company's financial results had been unsatisfactory. The interest on the debenture stock had been paid, but no dividend was paid on the preference shares until 1912; 3% was paid in 1912, 4% in 1914, and 6% since. Only three dividends of 5% each had been paid on the ordinary shares since 1905, although the ordinary shares formed £204,885 of the company's capital. Profits had been earned by three subsidiaries; the company held the whole of the shares in the West Riding Automobile Company Ltd. and in Newton & Ward Ltd. and a one-third interest in County Motors Ltd., but despite this the parent company was still unable to pay any dividend on its ordinary share capital. Although the company had been in operation for 27 years, the ordinary shareholders were still waiting for a return on their outlay. The company was the pioneer in providing transport in the area, and had provided transport in the spirit of a public utility undertaking, without adequate reward. The wage bill for 1930 was £138,000, with 1027 men and youths on the payroll, (giving an average wage of £134 7s. 6d. per annum, or 51s. 6d. per week). All employees were paid in accordance with standard trade union agreements and in accordance with Clause 93 of the Road Traffic Act 1930.

The company's application for licences to continue their 99 bus routes and to substitute motor buses on the remaining tram routes was granted in January 1932, and buses were ordered to replace the trams. The last day of operation of the Leeds—Sandal and Leeds—Rothwell tram routes was Tuesday 31 May 1932, when the last car was driven all the way from Leeds to Wakefield by the company's traffic manager, Mr. Albert Bennett, who as a tram driver in 1904 had driven the first car out of the depot for the start of service. The car arrived just before midnight at Belle

The Leeds—Wakefield—Sandal tramway in its last months of operation in 1932. West Riding 34, one of the eight new cars bought in 1920, stands in the Bull Ring at Wakefield, about to depart for Leeds. Buses took over on 1 June 1932.   (M. J. O'Connor

Isle, and a cheer went up as it entered the depot, the last of the old order of transport on the major portion of the company's routes. There were no civic notables present, and trams were to continue for a while on the Ossett to Agbrigg route. From next day, West Riding buses provided the service to Rothwell as well as to Wakefield. More new buses arrived in July, and the last cars to Ossett and Agbrigg ran on 25 July 1932. There was no formal ceremony.

At the extremities of the company's routes, Leeds trams still ran to the boundary at Thwaite Gate, Hunslet, a service that continued until 18 April 1959. Dewsbury and Ossett trams still ran to Ossett Market Place, and in the autumn of 1932 West Riding made yet another attempt to take over the Dewsbury—Ossett route, but the British Electric Traction group who had bought out the N.E.C. in 1931 replaced the D.&O. trams on 19 October 1933 with their own Yorkshire Woollen District buses.

The West Riding trams were replaced by distinctive double-deck centre entrance buses, which cut the journey time from Leeds to Wakefield and were well received by the travelling public. These buses, which charged the tram fares, accepted local passengers in Leeds and were not subject to protective minimum fares in Leeds, were in a light red livery, whereas the other West Riding buses on which higher fares were charged continued to be painted in green, an arrangement that continued until nationalisation in 1967; the last red bus was repainted green in 1968. At the company's annual general meeting in London in March 1934 the chairman, Mr. George Leon, said that the abandonment of the tramways had resulted in a capital loss of £182,306 in respect of cars, rails, cables and power plant, which would be written off as the income of the company permitted. It was a matter of

The last Yorkshire (West Riding) Electric Tramways Co. route to remain in operation was Agbrigg—Wakefield—Ossett, which closed on 25 July 1932. These photographs by Dr. Hugh Nicol show West Riding 30 and Dewsbury and Ossett 11 at their common terminus in Ossett Market Place, and West Riding 42 at Agbrigg terminus, using the automatic trolley reverser installed about 1913. The Dewsbury and Ossett trams continued until 19 October 1933.

(Dr. Hugh Nicol

congratulation that they had been able to change over from tramways to omnibuses without having to raise a penny of new capital. £27,000 was to be spent on a bus depot and offices at Belle Isle. The last year's operations had yielded a net income of £40,517, and he declared a dividend of 6% on the cumulative preference shares and 5% on the ordinary shares.

The buses were concentrated at the Belle Isle and Castleford depots, and in April 1933 the small depots at Ossett and Rothwell Haigh were offered for sale. Ossett depot is now used by the Bridges and Highways Department of the county council, with its tracks and buildings still intact, though a section of the three tracks inside the car shed has been covered by a new floor. Rothwell Haigh depot is now used by a motor engineering firm, and some of the tramway inspection pits are still in use, though the tracks in the yard have been covered. In both cases the tramway substation buildings are still intact, though used for other purposes, but Union Street substation in Wakefield has disappeared to make way for Wakefield bus station. The withdrawal of the trams coincided with the building of a new bridge across the river Calder, opened on 1 June 1933 alongside the Chantry bridge.

In readiness for a proposed change of name of the tramway company, the West Riding Automobile Company Limited of 1923 was placed in voluntary liquidation on 20 March 1935 and wound up on 30 June, its assets (now worth £180,000) being transferred to the Yorkshire (West Riding) Electric Tramways Company Limited, which changed its name to West Riding Automobile Company Limited on the same date. It is not the purpose of this book to chart the subsequent history of West Riding as a bus operator, but George Margrave continued for two decades as general manager, and steadfastly refused all take-over bids from the big groups and (in 1948) from the British Transport Commission. Instead, West Riding in 1950 bought out its former rival J. Bullock & Sons, and by 1963 was the largest independent bus operator in Britain, with 431 vehicles. It retained its independence until 30 October 1967, and then became a subsidiary of the state-owned Transport Holding Company. From 1970 the West Riding and Yorkshire Woollen District companies have had a joint management based at Belle Isle, Wakefield, bringing unified control of almost all the services in the area of this book. The present bus route 110 (Kettlethorpe—Leeds) which follows the main route of the tramway is still one of the mainstays of the company.

The buildings at the company's main depot at Belle Isle, Wakefield, are typical examples of electric tramway architecture of the early years of this century, built in red brick with clerestory roofs. The former generating station served as a bus paint shop until demolished in 1972, and behind the site are wooden piles in the river that formed part of the coal wharf where coal from the collieries was landed from the barges. Parts of the tram depot survive as a bus garage, still with their tram tracks, sett paving and even some tramway inspection pits. The tracks in the yard have been lifted or covered, but one tramway pole survives as a lighting standard.

At Wheldon Lane, Castleford, the easternmost shed of the present West Riding bus depot is the old tram shed, and still contains three tracks and a crossover. The depot faces the River Aire across the road and in times of flood the inspection pits have often become filled with water, the maintenance staff having to work in Wellington boots, as must have occurred in tram days. Miles of track are still buried beneath the present road surfaces throughout the area, and come to light when the tarmacadam surface has worn through (as at Rothwell in 1969) or when road repairs or pipe-laying are in progress. When this occurred some years ago in the Bull Ring, Mr. P. Dowd of Wakefield fetched a hacksaw, cut off a shim, and polished it for use as a paper weight.

Extracts from Board of Trade Returns, 1904 to 1913
Yorkshire West Riding (formerly Wakefield & District) Tramways

	Capital expenditure to date	Net surplus on year	Miles open	Number of cars	Passengers carried
1904	£46,425	£2,929	16.5	18	2,641,915
1905	£262,758	£18,088	16.5	55	5,003,637
1906	£438,838	£22,962	24.4	67	6,169,148
1907	£475,480	£30,542	24.4	67	8,627,647
1908	£493,586	£32,078	24.4	67	9,056,132
1909	£497,986	£29,200	24.6	67	8,817,229
1910	£502,486	£31,628	24.6	67	9,220,853
1911	£741,091	£34,355	24.6	67	9,640,027
1912	£750,084	£35,086	24.6	67	9,787,444
1913	£770,187	£40,920	24.6	67	10,900,263

Extracts from Ministry of Transport Returns, 1919 to 1932
Yorkshire (West Riding) Electric Tramways Co. Ltd.

	Capital expenditure to date	Net surplus on year	Miles open	Number of cars	Passengers carried
1919	£781,381	£66,684	24.6	67	15,769,241
1920	£808,966	£60,786	24.6	67	16,458,803
1921	£812,892	£52,398	24.6	75	17,599,657
1922	£812,892	£49,338	24.6	75	14,739,847
1923	£812,892	£64,189	24.6	75	14,686,690
1924	£826,337	£62,922	24.6	75	14,585,465
1925	£834,356	£50,234	24.6	75	15,772,417
1926	£842,002	£40,828	24.6	75	14,623,391
1927	£842,002	£30,357	16.9	65	12,400,951
1928	£663,401	£31,663	16.9	60	12,655,260
1929	£663,401	£45,881	16.9	60	13,845,147
1930	£663,401	£41,321	16.9	55	12,229,837
1931	£660,182	£47,533	16.9	55	11,700,493
1932	—	£12,499	—	—	4,309,180

Yorkshire (West Riding) Electric Tramways

Route Mileage, 1906 to 1925

	Miles
Wakefield—Sandal	2,112
Wakefield Bridge—Agbrigg ...	1.163
Wakefield—Thwaite Gate ...	6.895
Wakefield—Ossett	4.926
Rothwell Haigh—Rothwell ...	1.550
Depots and sidings	0.304
	16.950

	miles
Normanton—Castleford ...	3.851
Castleford—Pontefract	3.116
Other track in Castleford ...	0.492
	7.469

Total of both systems	24.419

A short extension at Normanton in 1909 brought the total to 24.6 miles.

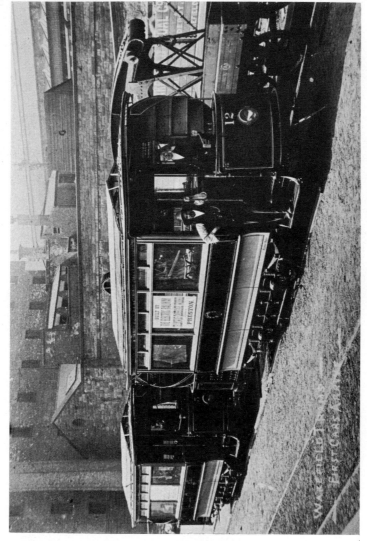

The arrival of the first Wakefield and District trams at Kirkgate station goods yard on 25 June 1904.

(Courtesy West Riding Automobile Co. Ltd.

168

CHAPTER NINE

WEST RIDING ROLLING STOCK

Compared with that of the Yorkshire Woollen District tramways, the rolling stock history of the West Riding tramways is relatively uncomplicated. The lines were constructed by Dick, Kerr & Co. Ltd. under comprehensive contracts that included the provision of rolling stock, which was therefore supplied from the same group's Preston factories and followed to a considerable extent their standard designs. The initial orders for cars (55 for delivery in 1904, 12 more in 1906) proved sufficient for many years, and many lasted to the end of the tramways in 1932. The changes that were made to them were limited to the provision of top covers and, in some cases, more powerful motors.

Nos. 1-30   Double deck open top four wheel cars with three windows per side, built 1904. Bodies built by The Electric Railway and Tramway Carriage Works Ltd., Preston.
Dimensions: 16 ft. 0 in. long over corner pillars, length over fenders 27 ft. 6 in., width 7 ft. 0 in., interior height 6 ft. 9 in., height to trolley plank 9 ft. 10 in., weight 8 tons 5 cwt.
Seating for 22 passengers inside and 34 outside, total 56.
Electrical equipment supplied by Dick, Kerr & Co. Ltd., Preston. Two DK25A motors of 25 horse power each. Two Dick Kerr DB1 Form C controllers.
Truck: Brill 21E of 6 ft. 0 in. wheelbase.
Braking: Hand wheel brake, rheostatic brake.

On 16 October 1903 the Wakefield and District Light Railway Co. Ltd. placed an order with Dick, Kerr & Co. Ltd. for 55 of their standard three window open top cars, of which thirty were required by mid-1904 and the other 25 were to follow later. In the event, building the lines took longer than anticipated and changes were made to the second batch before delivery. The first 18 cars spent some weeks in store before operation commenced in August 1904, and photographs exist of them in the company's main depot, still bearing the window bills carried during the journey from the builder's works at Preston. They had come by rail to Wakefield Kirkgate station, where a temporary track was laid from the station goods yard to meet the permanent track in Kirkgate, from which point they were moved on their own wheels to Belle Isle depot for fitting out. The arrival of the first cars at Kirkgate station on 25 June was photographed.

Nos. 1-30 were examples of the standard Dick, Kerr open top tramcar built in large numbers since 1900, except that they had 180 degree reversed stairs instead of the 90 degree type which was more usual at the time. They had longitudinal seats inside and were delivered with loose carpet seat covers and with curtains to the windows, which were soon removed. There were three lighting circuits of five lamps each, with six lamps in the saloon and two oyster lights on the top deck. In addition, each car carried for the first two or more years an oil lamp on the nearside bulkhead, below the lantern panel. The platforms had offside grilles in wrought iron scrollwork, and extending gates. The original order specified Miller's 30-inch chilled iron wheels, but this was changed to 32 in. steel tyred wheels by John Baker & Co. (Rotherham) Ltd. Illuminated destination indicator boxes were carried on stanchions above the upper deck end railings, and the lifeguards were of the Hudson & Bowring type.

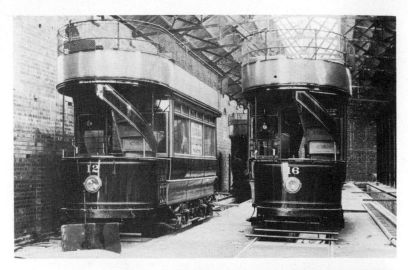

Fitting out the first batch of cars in Belle Isle depot, Wakefield, in July 1904. The work included the fitting of upper deck seats, panels and handrails, and mounting the trolley standards and destination indicators. (L. Holt

Between 1911 and 1914, open top cars 1-30 were given three window top covers. Some of these cars were lost in the Castleford depot fire of 5 March 1917, but several survived until the end of tramway operation in 1932. This view shows No. 5 in Kirkgate, Wakefield in the last year of operation. (M. J. O'Connor

All 30 cars remained open topped until 1911, and all had been given balcony top covers by 1914, when the half-yearly meeting in February was told that all cars were now top-covered. In the absence of any known order placed with outside firms, it seems likely that the covers were made in the company's own workshop at Belle Isle, Wakefield. The top covers had three windows per side, surmounted by hinged ventilators, and matched the lower saloons. The destination boxes were moved down to occupy the space between the upper and lower balcony rails. The capital outlay on top covers for 36 cars was £3,769 14s. 2d., just under £105 per cover. Shortly after this was done, all cars in the fleet were fitted with geared adjustable handbrakes.

From 1906 onwards, some of these cars were used on the detached Castleford section. Originally six were transferred, thought to have been 25 to 30, but two more (23 and 24) went later. Several (including No. 28) were among the 16 cars lost in the Castleford depot fire of 5 March 1917, and were replaced by others transferred from Wakefield, including Nos. 11, 13, 17 and 21. The cars sold at Castleford in 1927 would have been partly of this type, though at least five (13, 17, 26, 27 and 30) returned to Wakefield and survived until the main system closed in 1932. A note about motor changes appears later.

Car 40 of series 31-55, as newly delivered in 1905, standing at Sandal terminus.   (L. Holt

Nos. 31-55 Double deck top covered cars with open balconies and with four windows per side on each deck, built 1905. Bodies built by the Electric Railway and Tramway Carriage Works Ltd., Preston, with half-turn staircases as Nos. 1-30, and with framed drop windows in the upper saloon. Oil lamps were not provided on this batch.
Dimensions: 16 ft. 0 in. long over corner pillars, length over fenders 27 ft. 6 in., width 7 ft 1 in., interior height 6 ft. 9 in., height in upper saloon 6 ft. 0 in., height to trolley plank 16 ft. 2 in.
Seating for 22 passengers inside and 34 outside, total 56.
Electrical equipment supplied by Dick, Kerr & Co. Ltd., Preston. Two DK25A motors of 25 horse power each. Two Dick Kerr DB1 Form C controllers.
Trucks: Brill 21E of 6 ft. 0 in. wheelbase.
Braking: Hand wheel brake, rheostatic brake.

These cars were the balance of the original order for 55, but the specification was changed in 1904 to include top covers, the lower saloons being provided with four windows instead of three to carry the extra weight of the top covers. Other changes were the use of bamboo poles, Tidswell lifeguards, and dwarf trolley bases by S. Dixon and Son Ltd., Leeds, in place of Dick, Kerr trolley masts. The cars were delivered during the first six months of 1905.

Few changes were made to these cars during their lives, except for some motor and truck changes, described later. Six cars, 31 to 36, were transferred to the Castleford tramways when these lines opened in 1906, and two more (37 and 38) soon followed. At least four of them (31, 34, 35, 37) were destroyed in the Castleford depot fire of 5 March 1917. At least one more of the type (No. 45) was

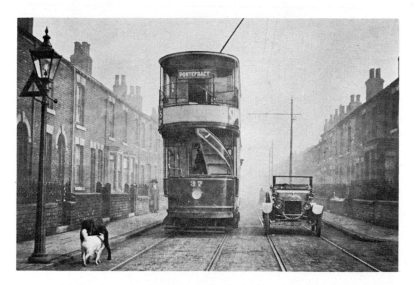

Eight of the covered-top reversed-stair cars, Nos. 31 to 38, were transferred in 1906 to Castleford depot to work the Normanton—Castleford—Pontefract tramway. Some of them, including No. 37 seen above in Oxford Street, Castleford, were destroyed in the Castleford depot fire of 5 March 1917 and were replaced in 1920 by new cars built by English Electric at Preston. The new No. 37 of 1920 is shown below in Wakefield.

(West Riding Automobile Co. Ltd. and M. J. O'Connor

The 31-55 class cars remained structurally unaltered throughout their lives, except for a few whose trucks were replaced by new trucks of 7 ft. 6 in. wheelbase. One of these cars was No. 44, seen here at Sowood Lane depot, Ossett. (Dr. Hugh Nicol

among the eight cars sent from Wakefield to replace them. When the Castleford lines closed in 1925 some of the survivors, including No. 32, were sent back to Wakefield, but others may have been in the Castleford sale of 1927. Of those which had remained at Wakefield, Nos. 44 and 53 (and possibly others) were later remounted on Brill type trucks of 7 ft. 6 in. wheelbase.

Nos. 56-61 Double deck top covered cars with open balconies and with four windows per side on each deck, built 1906.
Bodies built by the United Electric Car Company Ltd., Preston.
Dimensions and seating as for cars 31-55.
Equipment, trucks and brakes as for cars 31-55.

On 27 March 1906 the company placed an order with the Dick, Kerr group for twelve cars (six open top, six with top covers) for the Pontefract and Castleford tramways, to be delivered by June 1. In fact these new cars were used on the main system, and older vehicles were transferred to Castleford. They were identical with Nos. 31-55 and had the same arrangement of four framed top deck windows without toplights, which could be adjusted in pairs by means of wheels at each end, operated by the conductor. These cars remained on the main Wakefield system throughout their lives and were unaltered apart from motor changes described later.

Nos. 62-67 Double deck open top four wheel cars with three windows per side, built 1906. Bodies built by the United Electric Car Co. Ltd., Preston.
Dimensions and seating as for cars 1-30.
Electrical equipment supplied by Dick, Kerr & Co. Ltd. Two DK25A motors of 25 horse power each. Two Dick Kerr DB1 Form C controllers. Trucks and brakes as for cars 1-30.

The purchase of open top cars at a date when the company had already adopted covered tops is unusual, but it may be that the intended development of Lofthouse Park as a pleasure resort would be assisted by the availability of open top cars on fine days. It is also possible that the open top decks were smoking accommodation, since a photograph exists of a West Riding top covered car with notices prohibiting smoking in the upper saloon.

174

In 1912-13 all six cars were fitted with matching three-window top covers as described under cars 1-30, their overall height being then slightly greater than that of cars 56-61. They remained on the Wakefield system and were not altered save for the probable fitting of new motors.

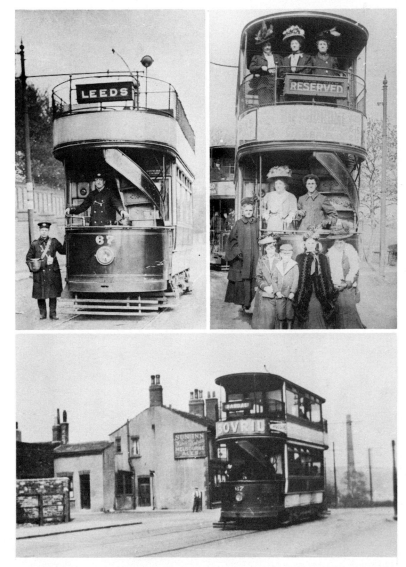

The 1906 delivery comprised six open top cars (62 to 67) resembling original cars 1-30, and six four-window covered top cars (56 to 61) identical with Nos. 31-55, of which No. 60 is seen here on a private hire. All twelve cars remained on the Wakefield system, and in 1913 the open vehicles were given three-window top covers, as on No. 67 seen here at the Sun Inn, near Lofthouse. (R. Brook, C. Wood, A. W. Brotchie

In 1919 the company ordered eight new cars to replace those lost in the depot fire at Castleford. These new cars were to have 40 h.p. motors and would thus be faster than the existing fleet. This extra turn of speed could be put to good use on the Leeds—Sandal through service, but would require the other cars on the route to be capable of similar performance. During 1919 an order was therefore placed with British Thomson-Houston for 20 pairs of GE200K 40 h.p. motors, and these were fitted to sufficient of the Wakefield-based cars to enable the entire Leeds—Sandal service to be worked by cars with 40 h.p. motors. No record exists of the car numbers, and the cars were probably selected according to when they were due for overhaul, without forming a continuous series.

At a Tramways and Light Railways Association conference in August 1919, Harry England criticised manufacturers of tramcar motors for fitting gear-cases that gave insufficient ground clearance to prevent damage. This may explain his next purchase, of 20 pairs of the new lightweight box-frame BTH 265C 35 h.p. motors in 1924, which appear to have been fitted to the surviving 1904 cars used on the Wakefield lines. At the same time, two cars were fitted with the new Metropolitan-Vickers MV 104 motors. This left only 29 cars fitted with the original DK25A motors (the surplus DK25A motors having been offered for sale) and some of these were eliminated by the Castleford closure in 1925. By 1926 only nine or ten cars still had 25 h.p. motors. Other equipment purchased over the years included two 3C motors and DB1 Form C controllers in 1908, a 21E truck in 1913, two DB1 Form K3 controllers in 1916, two DK84 32 h.p. motors in 1923 and two BTH B510 controllers in 1926. The DK84 motors were on trial, and were later returned to their makers.

A manufacturer's advertisement for the lightweight BTH 265 tramcar motor of which 20 pairs were bought by the West Riding tramways in 1924 with the aid of a government unemployment grant. After tramway operation ceased in 1932 these motors were resold to Blackpool Corporation.   (from *The Tramway and Railway World*

West Riding 74, one of the eight cars purchased in 1919 from Leeds City Tramways photographed in the Bull Ring, Wakefield, in 1932. They had been built as open top cars in 1899 and were fitted with short top covers by Leeds in 1913. (M. J. O'Connor

Nos. 68-75 Double deck top covered cars with short canopies, hired in 1917 and purchased in 1919 from Leeds City Tramways.
Bodies built in 1899 by the Brush Electrical Engineering Co. Ltd., Loughborough with open top decks. Top covers fitted by Leeds in 1913.
Dimensions: 16 ft. 0 in. long over corner pillars, length over fenders 28 ft. 0 in., width 7 ft. 0 in., interior height 6 ft. 5 in.
Seating for 24 passengers inside and 32 outside, total 56.
Electrical equipment supplied by the British Thomson-Houston Co. Ltd. Two GE58 motors of 37½ horsepower, two GE K10 controllers.
Truck as built: Peckham Cantilever No. 8 of 6 ft. 0 in. wheelbase.
Braking: Hand wheel brake, rheostatic brake.

Immediately after the Castleford depot fire of 5 March 1917, the West Riding company hired eight cars from Leeds City Tramways, their Leeds numbers being 133, 138, 147, 148, 163, 170, 177 and 180. They were part of a batch of 50 cars (133 to 182) built in 1899 and top-covered by Leeds in 1913, and were known in Leeds as Bathing Vans. The lower saloons had four tudor-arch windows, the upper saloons were shorter but had short glazed wings at the ends, creating a small balcony with a seat for three persons, plus a single seat. In July 1919 the eight cars were purchased by the company for £800 each, and were numbered into the West Riding fleet as 68-75, not necessarily consecutively.

During the period of hire, other Leeds cars may have been involved. One correspondent, while confirming the hire of 133, states that another Leeds car hired by West Riding was 45, a 1902 Brush car. However, the eight cars eventually bought by West Riding were 1899 type cars on Peckham cantilever trucks, and photographs show that all except No. 75 were later remounted on 6 ft. wheelbase Brill 21E trucks, which the *Wakefield Express* said came from cars destroyed in the Castleford fire. One of the eight cars may however have been retrucked and remotored at Leeds prior to being sold, since Garcke's Manual for 1924 credits West Riding with seven sets of GE58 motors and one set of DK35A type, which are otherwise unexplained. Cars 68-75 were withdrawn gradually from 1925 onwards, the West Riding fleet declining over these years from 75 cars to 57 cars in 1930, but some of the ex-Leeds cars (including 70 and 74) survived to the end in 1932. For many years these cars had been confined to the Ossett—Agbrigg route, and were distinguished by their drooping platforms.

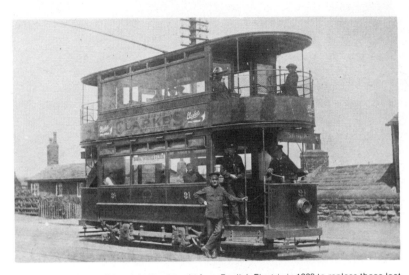

West Riding 31, one of the eight cars bought from English Electric in 1920 to replace those lost in the fire at Castleford. These cars entered service in the all-green livery used from 1916 to 1924, and differed from the older cars by having direct spiral stairs, air scoops on the cant rail, and a destination box (incorporating a rear light) beneath the driver's canopy. Note the paper destination sheet pasted to the centre lower deck window.   (Courtesy R. Brook

Eight cars
(see text)

Double deck top covered cars with open balconies and with three windows per side on each deck, built in 1920.

Bodies built by the English Electric Company Ltd., Preston.

Dimensions: 16 ft. 0 in. long over corner pillars, length over fenders 28 ft 0 in., width 7 ft. 1 in., height to trolley plank 16 ft. 0 in.

Seating for 22 passengers inside and 34 outside, total 56.

Electrical equipment supplied by the English Electric Company Ltd., Preston. Two DK 20 motors of 40 horsepower, two DB1 Form K4 controllers.

Trucks: Preston Standard of 7 ft. 6 in. wheelbase.

Braking: Peacock geared hand wheel brake, rheostatic brake.

These cars were ordered from the English Electric Company in May, 1919 to replace those lost in the Castleford depot fire. The cost was presumably borne in part by insurance, and the cars took the fleet numbers of those they replaced. All eight would therefore have been in the number range 23 to 38, but only five have been confirmed from photographs, Nos. 28, 31, 34, 35 and 37. By eliminating older cars known to have survived the fire, the possible fleet numbers for the other three new cars become 23, 24, 25, 29, 33, 36 or 38, but firm evidence is lacking.

These new cars with their 40 h.p. motors were not sent to Castleford. Instead, they were placed on the main Leeds—Sandal route, on which they remained. They could be identified at once by having direct half-turn stairs instead of the reversed stairs fitted to the older West Riding cars, and by having their destination box (which incorporated a rear light) slung from the driver's canopy instead of mounted upstairs. Ventilation was by hinged toplights above each side window, and by four air scoops along each cant rail. The cars had Brecknell, Munro and Rogers dwarf trolley bases.

Water Car Combined water and scraper car, built by the Electric Railway and Tramway Carriage Works Ltd., Preston, in 1904.
Electrical equipment as for passenger cars 1-30.
Truck: Brill 21E of 6 ft. 0 in. wheelbase.
Braking: Hand wheel brake, rheostatic brake.

This vehicle, which had no fleet number, was ordered from Dick, Kerr on 28 April 1904 and delivered later that year. It contained a cylindrical water tank, surmounted by a roof carried on side stanchions. Based originally at Wakefield, it was transferred to Castleford during 1905 and used for pre-opening test runs there. According to a 1906 article, it was also used at Castleford as a snow plough. It was involved in the 1917 Castleford fire, but both this car and a fire-damaged passenger car were salvaged and later rebuilt as permanent way cars, one for each system. As such, they appear in the fleet totals in Garcke's Manual, with DK25A motors. The company also owned some snowplough attachments to be fitted to passenger trams.

Other work equipment on the West Riding tramways included four salt trailers, rebuilt in 1908 from four-wheel steam trailers of the Dewsbury, Batley & Birstal line, a Lancashire Steam Wagon of 1907 which was taken out of use in 1926 and sold in 1933, a steam road roller (also sold in 1933), and an axle-carrying bogie bought in May, 1921. There was also an Orwell battery-electric tower wagon supplied by Ransomes, Sims and Jefferies on a 2½-ton chassis, which was illustrated in *Motor Traction* for 6 December 1920. This joined a fleet of horse-drawn tower wagons, one to each depot, which had been built by a Mr. Heathman. There was also a horse drawn dray which used to make a daily journey between Castleford depot and Belle Isle depot carrying cash and ticket boxes, but the use of horses ceased in 1923 when further motor vehicles were purchased.

The works car of the Yorkshire (West Riding) Electric Tramways proceeding up Kirkgate, Wakefield. This car did not carry a number. (Courtesy R. B. Parr

Liveries

The original livery of the Wakefield and District trams was crimson lake and cream, the cream being described in the technical press as light lemon. The crimson lake was used for the dashes, waist panels and stairs, with gold leaf lining and corner transfers. Other parts of the car were painted cream, with lining in dark tan and an orange line one-tenth of an inch wide further picked out with dark chocolate. The fleet number placed above the dash lamp was in gold leaf, blocked and shaded, and in the centre of the waist panel were the initials of the "W.&D. Lt. Ry. Co." on a garter. This livery and lettering was applied to the first 67 cars as new, and continued until the first war, with a change of initials on the garter to suit the new title.

During the first war, shortage of paint brought a change to a livery of two shades of green—dark green for the waist panel, dashes and stairs and lighter green elsewhere. The dark green was double-lined-out, but without corner transfers, and the garter in the centre of the waist panel now bore the full title of Yorkshire (West Riding) Electric Tramways Co. Ltd. As the war continued, some cars were painted battleship grey, one at least appeared in all-over brown, another in yellow and a third in white. On the Normanton system at least two different shades of brown were in use.

From 1924 onwards, the West Riding cars were finished in a new livery devised by Mr. Robert England, using a brighter green for the dashes, stairs and waist panels (double lined out) and cream lined in black for the other areas. The fleet number appeared above the headlamp and twice on each waist panel, blocked and shaded. The most striking feature was the badge, a large White Rose of Yorkshire between the words "West" and "Riding" in large letters (shaded and underlined) tapering inwards towards the rose, which had ribbons above and below with the words "Tramways" above and "Omnibuses" below. In this livery, the enamel plate advertisements were confined to the balcony end panels. At least two cars, 11 and 13, received this livery while on the Castleford section.

West Riding No. 9 at Agbrigg terminus in the post-1924 green and white livery with the White Rose of Yorkshire emblem on the side panels. (Dr. Hugh Nicol)

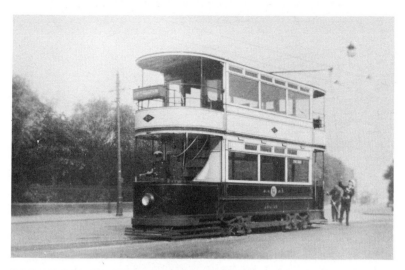

Only two Yorkshire (West Riding) trams were sold for further service elsewhere. Two of the 1920 English Electric cars were sold to South Shields Corporation Tramways, who retrucked them and ran them until 1938. South Shields 20 is seen here at Pier Head in 1933.

(M. J. O'Connor

Disposals

The trams in stock at closure in 1932 were offered for sale, the general manager being instructed to sell at the best price obtainable over £500. This figure proved far too optimistic. The first sale took place in October 1932, when two of the English Electric car bodies were sold to South Shields Corporation for £55 each. They were mounted by South Shields on ex-Lanarkshire Hurst Nelson trucks and became South Shields 18 and 20. A further sale was reported in January 1933, the purchaser not being named, and a year later the remaining BTH 265C motors were sold to Blackpool Corporation, who used them to re-equip their open toastrack trams Nos. 80, 82, 86-89, 91 and 92.

BIBLIOGRAPHY

a) **Local newspapers:**
"The Dewsbury Reporter" 1870 to 1933 (also "The Dewsbury District News" from 1870 until combined with the Reporter).
"The Batley News" 1870 to 1933.
"The Spenborough Guardian" 1881 to 1933.
"The Ossett Observer" 1907 to 1932.
"The Wakefield Express" 1879 to 1932.
"The Pontefract & Castleford Express" 1906 to 1925.

b) **Technical and transport journals:**
"Modern Tramway" (especially May, 1946).
"The Tramway Review" (various issues).
"Tramway and Railway World" 1901 to 1933.
"The Light Railway and Tramway Journal" (especially March 1903, November 1906 and December 1908).
"The Electrician" 1901 to 1908.
"The Electrical Review" 1901 to 1908.
"The B.E.T. Gazette" 1900 to 1907 (produced for private circulation).
"Passenger Transport" 1963. (Y.W.D. jubilee article).
"Motor Transport" 6 December 1920.

c) **Printed books**
"Tramways, their Construction and Working" by D. Kinnear Clark (1st edition, 1878; 2nd edition, 1894).
"Great British Tramway Networks" by W. H. Bett and J. C. Gillham (4th edition, 1962).
"Manual of Electrical Undertakings" (Garcke; various editions).
"The Tramways of Huddersfield" by Roy Brook (1959).
"History of the Steam Tram" by Dr. H. A. Whitcombe (1954).
"Tramways in West Yorkshire" by H. Brearley (1960).
"The Brush Electrical Engineering Co. and its Tramcars" by J. H. Price (1976).
"The British Electric Car Company Limited" by J. H. Price (1978).

d) **Commemmorative publications**
"Yorkshire Woollen District Transport Company Limited Diamond Jubilee" (1963).
"Yorkshire Woollen District—A Short History of the Company" (1978).
"A Pictorial Survey of the West Riding Automobile Company Limited and its predecessor companies" (1979).

e) **Official publications**
Board of Trade Tramway Orders and Light Railway Orders.
Board of Trade (later Ministry of Transport) Returns on Tramways and Light Railways.
Board of Trade (Railway Department) accident reports.
Company files transferred from the Companies Registry to the Public Record Office.
Minutes of company meetings of the Yorkshire (Woollen District) Electric Tramways, the Wakefield and District Light Railway Co. Ltd., the Yorkshire (West Riding) Electric Tramways Co. Ltd., and the West Riding Automobile Co. Ltd.
Merryweather's Tramway Engine Catalogue 1882.

f) **Local authority minutes**
Minutes of the meetings of the Councils and Committees of Batley Town Council, Castleford Urban District Council, Dewsbury Town Council, Hartshead Parish Council, Heckmondwike Urban District Council, Leeds City Council, Mirfield Urban District Council, Ossett Town Council, Pontefract Town Council, Ravensthorpe Urban District Council, Soothill Nether Urban District Council, Spenborough Town Council, and Wakefield City Council.

Appendix I

Tickets and Fares

Some years ago, the late Mr. W. H. Bett kindly supplied the present author with a complete list of the 69 different tickets in his collection from the tramways described in this book. The notes which follow are based on this and other sources, but since the specimens used are mostly from the 1920s, it does not necessarily apply to earlier periods. The tickets illustrated have been kindly provided by Mr. H. B. Priestley.

Dewsbury, Batley and Birstal Tramway Co. Ltd.

No tickets bearing this title were known to Mr. Bett. Fare collection was by Kaye's Fare Box, described on page 15, and these may have continued in use after the B.E.T. take-over in 1902. The line appears to have been divided into three penny stages meeting at Hick Lane and Birstall Smithies. The B.E.T. introduced red penny celluloid tokens embossed with the D.B.&B. company title and the magnet and wheel device, of the design kindly copied by Mr. G. E. Baddeley for the cover of this book. It is possible that Yorkshire (Woollen District) tickets may have come into use on the steam tramway prior to electrification. Overlapping stages such as Batley Carr—Branch Road were introduced by the B.E.T., but this may not have occurred until the electrification.

Yorkshire (Woollen District) Electric Tramways Ltd.

Fares on this company's system were always somewhat higher than on the large municipal tramways, perhaps because the local authorities made high charges for the supply of electricity (and then grumbled at the resulting fare levels!). Tickets are known in halfpenny steps from 1d. up to 6d., those from the 1920s being printed in every case by the Bell Punch Co.

The first Y.W.D. tickets were full geographical and were printed by the Glasgow Numerical Printing Co. This is known from the 1d. white ticket reproduced in facsimile by Bell Punch for the Diamond Jubilee celebrations of 1963, with stages Dewsbury Market Place—Thornhill Station and Thornhill Station—Combs Pit (approximately one penny per mile, at 1903 values). One penny was the minimum adult fare, but there was an equivalent halfpenny workman fare, as indicated on page 58.

In the summer of 1910 the various B.E.T. tramways (including Y.W.D.) introduced the "Fair Fare" system, with multiple overlapping stages, some values involving the use of farthings. No tickets with odd farthing values are known in the case of Y.W.D., but Mr. Bett's collection included a 5d. "Fair Fare" ticket with 28 numerical stages. This may have been the point in time at which Y.W.D. changed from geographical to numerical stages on its adult tickets, indeed the Fair Fare system could hardly have been worked in any other way on a lengthy system such as this. To the people of the Woollen District, fair fares were merely a euphemism for an increase; their reaction is recorded on page 59.

Two Yorkshire (Woollen District) tickets of November 1928, 4d. olive and 6d. blue, compared with a yellow bus exchange with red overprint. (Courtesy H. B. Priestley, M.A.)

The subsequent simplification of the fare system is shown by the fact that Y.W.D. tickets of the 1920s bear stage numbers 1-13 or occasionally 1-16; a few high values are known with stages 1-30 or 1-32 perhaps printed from the bus ticket plate with "bus" altered to "car". Colours in use for adult tickets on the trams between 1924 and 1928 were 1d. white (with red fare overprint), 1½d. blue, 2d. pink, 2½d. buff, 2½d. yellow, 3d. buff (with red fare overprint), 3d. white (with blue fare overprint), 3½d. orange, 4d. olive, 4½d. purple, 5d. white (with red overprint), 5½d. pale yellow and 6d. blue. All are numerical Bell Punch tickets 2½ in. in length.

The workmen and child tickets appear to have continued in full geographical form until 1926. Different colours applied in the case of certain workmen's tickets, examples being 1d. lilac, 1½d. salmon, 2d. pink, 2½d. yellow, 3d. orange and 3½d. green. The last-named was the highest workmen value and covered the journeys Dewsbury—Birkenshaw and Dewsbury—Moorend; the 1½d. workmen ticket reflected the fact that stages on the former steam tramway were longer than those on the Spen Valley lines, for it took a workman from Dewsbury to Carlinghow on the Bradford Road route but only to Thorncliffe Road on the Halifax Road route. There may even have been an element of charging more for the routes with steep gradients. One penny would take a child from Dewsbury to Heckmondwike, Thornhill, Birstall or Shepley Bridge, with a further penny to the limits of the system at Hightown, Moorend or Birkenshaw. The final sets of tickets were of numerical type with overprints "Child" or "W" (for Workman).

The Yorkshire (Woollen District) Transport Act 1931 sanctioned the running of buses on the tram routes at fares not exceeding 1½d. per mile or fraction thereof, and return fares at 1d. per mile for workmen. The Corporations of Dewsbury and Batley agreed under the terms of the Bill not to seek to operate their own transport undertakings and the Company was bound to pay to each authority a share of the revenue taken on tram-replacement bus services, based on the revenue collected less the average cost of operating the whole undertaking with an allowance of 3½d. per mile for depreciation and interest on capital. The local authorities share of the net

Ticket advertisements of 1925-8 from (left to right) Yorkshire (Woollen District), Dewsbury & Ossett, and Yorkshire (West Riding) trams. Ruddlesdens' were tram painters to the Dewsbury & Ossett line.
(Courtesy H. B. Priestley, M.A.)

184

profits was six tenths to 1 July 1953, eleven twentieths to 1 July 1973 and one half thereafter. In 1978 the company sought release from these obligations on the grounds that the local authorities were now in the area of a P.T.E. with whom it has concluded an operating agreement. At the time of writing this is not resolved, but is still under consideration.

All Y.W.D. tickets from the tramway period bore a commercial advertisement on the reverse side, some for local traders, others for the larger stores in Bradford and Huddersfield. There were also red penny tokens similar to the D.B.&B. specimen on the dust-jacket but bearing the Y.W.D. title. These were mainly issued to children travelling to and from school, particularly the Grammar Schools.

Dewsbury, Ossett & Soothill Nether Tramways

Despite the fact that Dewsbury absorbed Soothill Nether in 1910, the full title remained in use on this undertaking's tickets until abandonment in 1933. The simple route pattern of one main line and a short branch led to the retention of geographical tickets, and only five ticket forms were required. In 1930, these were 2d. adult blue (Dewsbury—Ossett), 1½d. magenta (Ossett—Chickenley Heath Station, Dewsbury—Chickenley Heath Station), 1d. white for intermediate stages and the Earlsheaton branch, ½d. half fare white with two red diagonal stripes superimposed on the text of the 1d. adult value, and 1d. blue half fare with red stripes on the text of the 2d. ticket. The half-fare tickets show by their conditions that they were used for both workmen and children, during certain prescribed hours.

At an earlier period, probably from 1918 to about 1922, fares were higher and bore different stages. Dewsbury—Ossett was then 3d. (blue), the 2d. ticket was pink and covered Ossett (Mkt. Place); Trinity Ch. (Ryecroft Street)—Junc. of Wakefield Road and High Road; Flying Horse Inn—Dewsbury (Mkt. Place). The 1d. half-fare ticket was pink, again with red overprint. Two different colours were also used (perhaps at different periods) for the D.&O. penny token (yellow, and dark red).

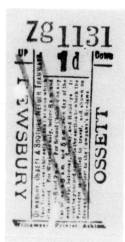

Whereas the two larger tramway companies adopted numerical-stage tickets in the 1920s, the Dewsbury & Ossett always used tickets with geographical stages (and the undertaking's original title). These D.&O. tickets dating from April 1925 are the adult 1d. (white), the adult 2d. all-the-way (blue), and a blue half-fare all-the-way ticket with red overprint for issue to a child or workman. (Courtesy H. B. Priestley, M.A.)

Yorkshire (West Riding) Electric Tramways

Mr. Bett's collection included 25 different tickets of this undertaking, all with the West Riding title rather than that of its predecessor, the Wakefield & District Light Railway. All the tickets were supplied by the Bell Punch Co., and varied little down the years apart from a once-for-all change from geographical to numerical stages in the early 1920s.

The original fares gave just under 1½ miles for one penny, Normanton to Pontefract (8 miles) being charged 6d. The same sum was charged for Wakefield to Leeds (10 miles), this being a special fare explained by railway competition and the generous municipal fare-scale in Leeds of two miles for one penny. All Y.W.R. passengers were charged half-fare before 7.30 a.m., and bona fide workmen travelling on the upper deck could travel at half fare between 5 p.m. and 6 p.m.

In April 1918 ½d. was added to most fares and shorter 1d. stages introduced, some ticket values being produced by surcharging existing ticket stocks by rubber stamp. From September 1919 all fares were fixed at 50% above prewar rates (workmen, 100%). Thwaite Gate—Rothwell became 3d. instead of 2d., this West Riding ticket being issued on Leeds cars operating the through service. In his report for 1919, the chairman (Sir Herbert Leon) considered the new fares quite reasonable and said that "For 1d. a workman in pre-war days could travel 2.495 miles (practically 2½ miles). The Order authorises us to double that fare so that the distance now travelled by a workman for 1d. is approximately a mile and a quarter. Again I say this must be cheap, because a mile and a quarter's walk would do more than 1d. worth of damage to his boots". However, the onset of unrestricted bus competition in parts of the company's area led to selective fare reductions in 1922 and 1927, and to the introduction of weekly tickets in 1923.

In the days of full geographical tickets, the long routes of the Yorkshire (West Riding) Tramways required the use of separate ticket forms for each route. On two of these (Sandal—Wakefield—Thwaite Gate, and Normanton—Pontefract) the stages occupied all the front and about half the reverse, leaving room for a small advertisement, but the other two forms (Agbrigg—Ossett, and Thwaite Gate—Rothwell) managed to accommodate all the stages on the front. Colours were 1d. white, 1½d. blue, 2d. green, 2½d. buff, 3d. orange, 3½d. salmon, 4d. yellow, 4½d. brown, 5d. white, 6d. mauve, 7d. lilac, 8d. apple green, 9d. grey and 11d. white. (No 10d. tickets seen, but they doubtless existed).

There then followed a change to universal numerical stage tickets with red or green fare overprint, always with 28 stages (1-14 left, 28-15 right). Colours remained unchanged, and the reverse of all tickets was let to advertisers. There was a progression of overprint styles, reflecting Bell Punch's whims more than anything.

The arrangements for through running into Leeds are explained on page 132. Through bookings between Leeds and the West Riding system were dealt with by issuing a Y.W.R. and a Corporation ticket together, and at one time there were special L.C.T. tickets for this purpose with conditions explaining that they were Y.W.R. marriage tickets. The through Leeds return and exchange ticket were always geographical, specimens of the return being somewhat rare since this ticket was always surrendered on the homeward journey. The return (at least in later years) was green with a red R, the exchange was originally salmon with a red X, and later deep pink with a green X. The original 1s. fare was still the same twenty years later, though the issue may have been suspended from 1918 to 1923. Almost exactly similar issues headed W.R. Auto (but priced at 1s. 3d.) were issued on the replacing buses, which bore a red livery signifying tram fare-scales instead of the company's usual green livery, as explained on page 165. No specimens are known of the 6d. return to Lofthouse Park.

186

Tickets of the Yorkshire (West Riding) tramways, 1925-8. 1d. white, 2½d. buff, 3d. orange (with green overprint instead of red), 5d. white, and the deep pink ticket issued in exchange for a Wakefield—Leeds 1s. return. (Courtesy H. B. Priestley, M.A.)

Proposed Tramway Extensions in Dewsbury

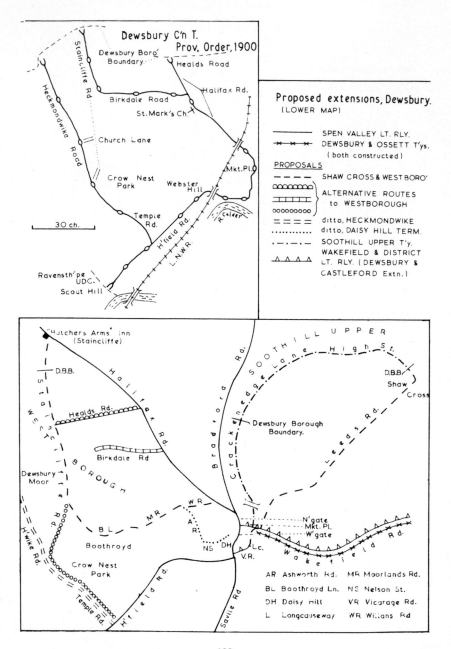

Appendix 3

Legislation

Dewsbury, Batley and Birstal Tramways Company Ltd.
The Tramways Orders Confirmation Act, 1873 (c. cxcvii)
The Tramways Orders Confirmation Act, 1879 (c. cxciii)
The Dewsbury, Batley and Birstal Tramways Act, 1903 (c. clxxxiv)

Spen Valley, Dewsbury and District Tramways Company Ltd.
The Tramways Orders Confirmation (No. 3) Act, 1883 (c. cxxxiii)

Batley Corporation Tramways
The Tramways Orders Confirmation (No. 3) Act, 1900 (c. cc)

United Kingdom Tramways, Light Railway and Electrical Syndicate Ltd.
The Tramways Orders Confirmation (No. 4) Act, 1901 (c. clxxxiii)

Wakefield and District Light Railway Company
The Wakefield and District Light Railway Order, 1901
The Wakefield and District Light Railways (Dewsbury and Castleford Extensions) Order, 1901
The Wakefield and District Light Railways (Extensions) Order, 1902
The West Riding Tramways Act, 1904 (c. xxiv)
The West Riding Tramways Act, 1907 (c. iii)

Yorkshire (Woollen District) Electric Tramways Ltd.
The Spen Valley Light Railway Order, 1901
The Spen Valley Light Railway (Extensions) Order, 1901
The Spen Valley and Morley Light Railways (Extensions) Order, 1902
The Spen Valley Light Railways (Amendment) Order, 1920
The Yorkshire (Woollen District) Transport Act, 1931 (c. lxii) (abandonment)

West Riding Tramways and Electricity Supply Company Ltd.
The Tramways Orders Confirmation (No. 2) Act, 1902 (c. cciii)

Soothill Nether Urban District Council Tramways
The Soothill Nether Urban District Tramways Act, 1904 (c. cv)

Dewsbury Corporation Tramways/Ossett Corporation Tramways
The Tramways Orders Confirmation (no. 2) Act, 1904 (c. clxxxi)
The Tramways Orders Confirmation Act, 1906 (c. cxxxiv)
The Dewsbury and Ossett Transport Act, 1933 (c. xxvi) (abandonment)

Dewsbury Corporation Tramways
The Tramways Orders Confirmation Act, 1911 (c. clxxi)
The Tramways Orders Confirmation Act, 1912 (c. cxliv)
The Dewsbury Corporation Act, 1915 (c. lxxiv)

Each confirmed tramway order listed above was preceded by a provisional order issued generally in the same year.

Addenda

In September 1979 the West Riding Automobile Co. Ltd. celebrated its 75th anniversary with the issue of a 48-page commemmorative book, principally in the form of a pictorial survey. This contains some useful quotations from past annual reports, and gives additional statistics such as car mileage, revenue and operating expenses (West Riding's operating expenses for 1906 were only 3.768 pence, the lowest in Britain), labour turnover and conditions, etc. The book also contains many interesting photographs of West Riding buses. This book complements rather than duplicates the present work, and is commended to readers.

Other points which have come to light since the main text of this book was printed include the following.

Chapter 2

Since pages 46-48 were written, some further information has been traced concerning the track in Halifax Road, Staincliffe. As described in the main text, the Yorkshire (Woollen District) company and Batley Corporation each laid and owned one track, the company owning the track towards Heckmondwike and the Corporation that towards Dewsbury. The two tracks (one a light railway, the other a tramway) formed a double line and were intended to be shared by both undertakings. The company's track was completed first, by April 1903, and a facing crossover was laid near Common Road, so that the single track could be used to transfer cars between the two parts of the Y.W.D. system. Public service did not begin until both tracks were ready, three months later.

Beyond Thorncliffe Road to the Dewsbury boundary in Halifax Road, the two tracks were similarly in the area of Batley Corporation and that body had sought powers to build and own them. The Light Railway Commissioners rejected this, saying that "having regard to the gradient along the portion of Halifax Road which is within the borough of Batley, it would be dangerous to the public to have any dual control of such portion of the line or to have cars belonging to different authorities using such portion of the line". The result was that Yorkshire (Woollen District) were allowed to build and own this piece of track themselves.

In Dewsbury, it should be explained that the Y.W.D. tracks owned by Dewsbury Corporation were those within the pre-1910 borough boundary. The outer portions of the Ravensthorpe and Thornhill routes were outside the Dewsbury boundary at the time they were built, and although Dewsbury was enlarged in 1910 to include these districts, ownership of these portions of track remained with the company.

Chapter 8

The creation in 1924 of an off-street tram terminus at the Sandal terminus is mentioned on page 159. The purchase also included a plot of land for a house for the chief inspector, and this house (now a private residence) is in the same style as the present head office traffic department building at Belle Isle, which was built at the same period as a house for the Rolling Stock Engineer.

A Postscript
by J. Breeze Bentley, Guiseley, near Leeds

Mr. Pickles' book brings back many nostalgic memories, and I look forward to publication. My interest in these tramways dates back to 1917 when (as a young boy) my father took me for a ride on the 35 mile circuit Bradford, Birkenshaw, Dewsbury, Ossett, Wakefield, Leeds, Bradford.

We boarded the car for Birkenshaw at the back of Bradford Town Hall, and it took us up the steeply graded Wakefield Road to Dudley Hill, then past Tong Cemetery and on a single and loop section through Birkenshaw village to the Halfway House Inn. At the other side of Whitehall Road, two brown and cream Yorkshire Woollen District cars were waiting, one for Batley Market Place via Heckmondwike, the other for Dewsbury. The cars ran together for a short half mile, then our car for Dewsbury turned left and after Birstall Smithies entered an increasingly industrialised zone. At Dewsbury, the car stopped in Northgate, just before the junction with Halifax Road.

We walked through Dewsbury Market Place to the foot of Wakefield Road, where stood two neat maroon and cream cars of the Dewsbury, Ossett and Soothill Nether Tramways, one bound for Earlsheaton, the other for Ossett. We took this car up the steep Wakefield Road and on to Ossett Market Place, where we changed to a Yorkshire (West Riding) car which ran along the very narrow Station Road, through Horbury and along a rural section to Wakefield, where we alighted at the little Bull Ring, the hub of the Wakefield system.

Here we transferred to a car that had come from Sandal and was going to Leeds. This section was exhilarating—eight miles along an undulating country road through a succession of mining villages. A rapid descent of Bell hill brought us to Thwaite Gate, where the car entered Leeds territory. The next two miles lay in a busy industrial area, and at the top of Lower Briggate the car turned right into Duncan Street, then swung left into New Market Street and right again into Kirkgate, to pull up outside the Markets.

A few yards' walk took us to Corn Exchange turning circle, used by the cars to Bradford, Rodley and Pudsey. I listened for the distinctive sound of a dual-gauge through car as it approached along Duncan Street. It proved to be a "chocolate and mustard" car belonging to Leeds Corporation, with the Through Car notice below the top deck windows. Leaving the city along Wellington Street, it exhibited the tail-wagging motion typical of Leeds dual-gauge cars. There was open country after Armley Jail, and at Bramley Depot the driver turned his key in the time clock. At Stanningley we slowed right down to traverse the 12-foot length of taper track, where the gauge narrowed from 4 ft. 8½ in. to 4 ft., and entered Bradford territory. Further along, we saw the trackless route at Laisterdyke, and at the foot of Leeds Road our journey ended. The through car disgorged its passengers, then shunted to the back of the Town Hall for its seven-minute layover before returning to Leeds.

In later years, from about 1926 to 1932, I made the trip several times, alternately clockwise and anti-clockwise to take advantage of the cheap return ticket issued between Wakefield and Leeds—which was never queried when offered to the conductor twelve months after issue. The Y.W.D. fare always seemed to be the most expensive (5½d.) though, on one occasion, catching a car in Dewsbury in the "evening workman" period soon after 5 p.m., I was issued with a 3d. workman. To get from Dewsbury to Birkenshaw for 3d. instead of 5½d. was much appreciated by a schoolboy in his late teens! Of the company sections, the Dewsbury & Ossett was the cheapest (3 miles for 2d.), but this could not compete with the 5½ miles for 2d. between Corn Exchange and Stanningley, introduced when W. Chamberlain was manager at Leeds.

191

THE END OF THE LINE
Y.W.D. 20 at Thornhill
terminus.
(Courtesy Mrs E. M. Hepworth

192

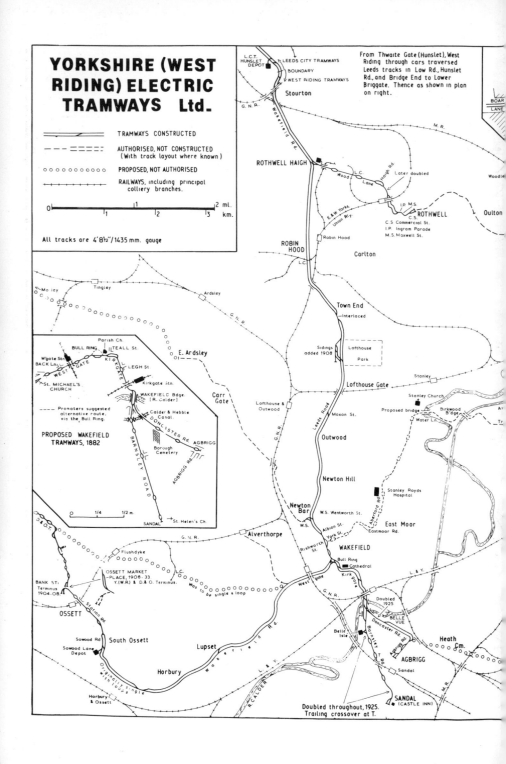

YORKSHIRE (WEST RIDING) ELECTRIC TRAMWAYS Ltd.

From Thwaite Gate (Hunslet), West Riding through cars traversed Leeds tracks in Low Rd., Hunslet Rd., and Bridge End to Lower Briggate. Thence as shown in plan on right.

	TRAMWAYS CONSTRUCTED
	AUTHORISED, NOT CONSTRUCTED (With track layout where known)
o o o o o o o o o o o	PROPOSED, NOT AUTHORISED
	RAILWAYS, including principal colliery branches.

0 _____ 1 _____ 2 ml.
0 ___ 1 ___ 2 ___ 3 km.

All tracks are 4'8½"/1435 mm. gauge

PROPOSED WAKEFIELD TRAMWAYS, 1882

Promoters suggested alternative route, via the Bull Ring.

BULL RING   TEALL St.
Parish Ch.
W'gate Stn   WEST GATE   KIRKGATE   LEGH St.
BACK Lne.
St. MICHAEL'S CHURCH
Kirkgate Stn.
WAKEFIELD Bdge. [R. Calder]
Calder & Hebble Canal.
DONCASTER Rd.   AGBRIGG
Borough Cemetery
BARNSLEY ROAD
AGBRIGG Rd.
SANDAL   St. Helen's Ch.

1/4   1/2 m.

L.C.T. HUNSLET DEPOT
LEEDS CITY TRAMWAYS
BOUNDARY
WEST RIDING TRAMWAYS
Stourton
G.N.R.
Wakefield Rd.
BOAR LANE
M.R.

ROTHWELL HAIGH
Wood Lane
Haigh Rd.
L.C.
Later doubled
Woodle
E. & W. Yorks Union Rly.
I.P. M.S.
ROTHWELL   Oulton
C.S.
C.S. Commercial St.
I.P. Ingram Parade
M.S. Maxwell St.

Robin Hood
ROBIN HOOD
Carlton
L.C.

Moley   Tingley
Ardsley
G.N.R.
Town End
Interlaced
Sidings added 1908
Lofthouse Park
Stanley
Lofthouse Gate
Stanley Church
E. Ardsley
Carr Gate
Lofthouse & Outwood
Leeds Road
Moxon St.
G.N.R.
Proposed bridge
Birkwood B'dge
Water Ln.
Outwood
Newton Hill
Stanley Royds Hospital
Newton Bar
W.S. Wentworth St.
Aberford Rd.
East Moor
Eastmoor Rd.
W.S.
Albion St.
York St.
Alverthorpe
Rishworth St.
WAKEFIELD
Bull Ring
Cathedral
Westgate
Kirkgate
G.N.R.
Doubled 1925
BELLE VUE
Doncaster Rd.
Belle Isle
Barnsley Rd.
Heath Cm.
Sandal
AGBRIGG
SANDAL (CASTLE INN)

D. & O.T.
BANK St. Terminus 1904-08.
Flushdyke
OSSETT MARKET PLACE, 1908-33 Y.(W.R.) & D.& O. Terminus.
L.C.
Was to be single & loop
Station Rd.
OSSETT
Sowood Rd.   South Ossett
Sowood Lane Depot
Lupset
Horbury
Horbury & Ossett
Originally single with loops
Wakefield Rd.
L. & Y.
R. CALDER
M.R.

Doubled throughout, 1925.
Trailing crossover at T.